There are historic situations in which refusal to defend the inheritance of a civilization, however imperfect, against tyranny and aggression may result in consequences even worse than war.

Reinhold Niebuhr

BITTER RAINBOWS

Pederasts, Politics, and Hate Speech

MARISA MARTIN

BITTER RAINBOWS:
Pederasts, Politics, and Hate-Speech

eBook edition 2017

Published by Rosalva Books LLC. Vancouver, Washington

 This book is intended as social and political commentary, with an educational purpose.

For information and permissions, contact:
Rosalva Books LLC
PO Box 2502
Vancouver, WA 98668

RosalvaBooks@gmail.com ISBN 978-0-9989964-0-0

DEDICATION

This book is dedicated to my great gifts from God, my sons. And by extension, to all of our children. May they keep that joyous place of innocence, which is their natural birthright, and may no one take it from them by force or deceit.

MY CAUSE

Satirist Johnathan Swift mocked the wickedness of his time, including corruption of Parliament and Kings - or what we now call 'politics.' Hoping to keep his head, he used fiction to make his points; and did it spectacularly well. This book uses the one of his best tools – aggravation. "The chief end I propose to myself in all my labors is to vex the world, rather than divert it" Swift wrote in 1725. Questioning cultural absolutes on homosexuality is our newest form of blasphemy, and "vexing" in much of the Western world. But it will do the sleeping giant good to shake off his tiny, socially-imposed chains, role over, and take a good look at what has been tormenting him.

AND AN APPEAL TO THE OFFENDED

This book addresses gay militancy and hatred, and its campaign of terror against conservative, religious, and traditional peoples. It was never intended to target homosexuals merely because of their sexual choice or lifestyle. Accusations in these pages are equally directed at the far-left, who cynically use the gay community as a battering ram against their neighbors. For all others, please look beyond what appears to be an attack on your right to choose. Consider the end-game of a worldwide campaign of malice and spite, played out with proxy armies. It won't be pretty. There is still time to change course.

Chapters

Chapters

1

BUGGERY & THUGGERY

This book addresses gay militancy and hatred, and is not meant to target homosexuals as individuals. If you are gay and not a 'hater' the following doesn't apply to you, and isn't intended to offend you. Perhaps you may be offended for what is being done in your name, and find the motivation to help end it.

On his tenth birthday Alex* wanted to die more than anything else in the world. Watching his favorite films, he imagined himself as the wounded hero. "Boy defies a hail of bullets while shielding a group of blind orphans!" "Doctor intentionally infects himself with Ebola to find a cure!" Any plot was better than the secrets licking at his insides – as long as they weren't about families. He didn't like thinking about them.

Daddy discovered his budding gayness when Alex was three, and mom fled in panic. His sentence as an unwilling participant in homosexual life began that day. Decades later it ended, as Alex dealt with the reality of his father's neglect, absence of natural affection, and a parade of live-in child molesters. While the boy's childhood was wretched, he had not yet begun to feel the depths of human contempt. That came after he began to speak up, at the age of 28.

Releasing memoirs about his childhood set Alex in the gunsights of organized revenge. Death threats are now routine, and harassment from the gay community has lost him several jobs. "I really cared for many people I grew up with. It's hard to believe they see me as a betrayer!" Alex forgave his father, his mother, and the men who used him. Still, not one of his attackers spent a moment in jail for raping a child. At 46, Alex has been a victim of the homosexual community his entire life.

Brave souls coming to his defense are abused as well, and accused of being "haters." But when did publishing an honest autobiography become an act of aggression? And why are millions of us mocked for beliefs we had years before a cadre of self-anointed "hate specialists" were even born?

First, we must uncover who is responsible for all this anathema and loathing – and why.

*(*Alex is based on interviews with a real person, with details altered to protect from further retaliation.)*

MAKING HATE FASHIONABLE

Hate is the crack cocaine of our time. It's easy to swallow, because it's been packaged in attractive, little "anti-hate" wrappers. Between feigned compassion and gushing celebrities, few realize that the "anti-hate speech" movement is still a campaign of *hate.* But in this version, perpetrators claim to be victims, and our common understanding of what constitutes "hate," is radically altered for political purposes.

How did this ugly dystopia come to be? Originally, anti-hate speech laws were intended to be a rescue from neo-Nazis and other nasty stuff. Somewhere, the potential for shutting down free expression through accusations of "hate" became glaringly obvious (to the kind of people who would want to do that sort of thing). Homosexual militants were one of the first to see its beckoning possibilities, and took to it energetically.

Gay zealots hijacked anti-hate-speech legislation for their personal pleasure, and to punish perceived opposition. This charge isn't aimed at the entire gay community, only at those snorting for conservative blood. They know who they are, and many of us are beginning to find out. These are the people who are attempting to ruin Alex's life.

A SHORT AND SPOTTY HISTORY OF MODERN HOMOSEXUALITY

Poetically referred to as "the love that dare not say its name" in 19th century England, sodomy may have been technically illegal, but tolerated if it wasn't too obvious. Rather like how conservatives are treated now.

History doesn't record the huddled masses of gay men living short, wretched lives under bridges and begging for bread. That's because there weren't any – nor were they tortured until they agreed to shovel coal or do other manly things. Instead, it was an open secret that some (in the arts especially) were "a little queer" in their affections. Devoted, lifelong female roommates were seen as lonely spinsters with tragic pasts, and almost never questioned. Homosexuals have coexisted with Western "Christendom" for a very long time.

A drag Queen Victoria wouldn't have gone down well at all in 1870, though. Those old social taboos were useful: they spared Victorians from the sexually demented celebrities we are stuck with now. Oscar Wilde's infamous trial for "gross indecency" in 1895 was an example of how much Victorians detested hearing lurid details of *anyone's* sex life. At least in public. Wilde's troubles are legendary, and about as well known as the national anthem. But he caused most of them himself. Oscar sued the Marquess of Queensberry for slander, after the nobleman called him a "posing Sodomite." Yet, his trial proved that married Wilde was romancing the Marquess' son – while also taking advantage of various lower-class boys.

Oscar went to prison more for his flamboyant sexual expression (posing) than being gay. Arrests for sodomy were rare, but the Marquess had already lost one son to suicide after a gay liaison. Oscar publicly aggravated him, although he understood Victorian prohibitions against public displays of sexuality. "I am here for having tried to put your father in prison" he admitted to lover Alfred Douglas. He was no saint.

Gays claim to be victims of grievous victimization, and our anti-hate crime laws are based on their assertions. But they weren't the only victims of stringent moral codes of the past. Laws against mixed-race sex and marriage were common, and persisted until 1990 in South Africa. Heterosexual adultery was a criminal offense in most of the world, and can still net a death sentence in some places. Porn producers were imprisoned, and prostitutes and pimps still are. Virtually no anti-hate legislation has been drafted for any of them. In spite of the fact that adulterers *far* outnumber homosexuals, there is, shockingly, no National Adultery Month. What's the deal?

THINK OF THE HORSES

If society didn't applaud gay liaisons, neither did they particularly persecute them. Women fared much worse. Only females were arrested for sex-trade in Britain, while male prostitutes were ignored. Sodomy, rapes, and "buggery" were all capital crimes in early Plymouth Colony, (US) but rarely prosecuted. "Adultery" was added to the list of serious offenses as well.

Modern law didn't target consenting gay adults until the 1950s and even those prosecutions were sporadic and rare. By 2003, all US states had dropped or revised sodomy statutes involving adults only. Yet the narrative of callous injustice at the hands of State and Church has been kept on life-support – along with histrionics and gnashing of teeth. Abuse of homosexuals is almost entirely fictional.

Truth is, no one was much interested in what gay boys and girls were doing, as long as they weren't forced to participate or hear about it. They just aren't that interesting to the average person. As far back as 1910 actress and woman about town, Beatrice Stella Tanner, is recording as saying this in response to a gay scandal; "My dear, I don't care what they do, so long as they don't do it in the street and frighten the horses."

The Golden Gates creaked open in the 1990s. Three decades earlier, civil rights legislation of 1964 had made crimes committed for racial, religious, or ethnic reasons, all federally prosecutable. This was the armature on which all future, US hate-crime law is fastened. Gay strategists saw the potential in anti-hate legislation early in the game. By 1994 "protected classes" expanded to include gender. Strangely, protection for women was nixed by the Supreme Court in 2000. That didn't leave much "gender" for crimes to be based on, but dozens have since been invented.

Gay leaders realized early in the game that to be a protected class, there had to be some justification. Failing much reason to cry victim, they decided to co-opt the African-American civil-rights movement. It worked well for them – so why not? Martin Luther King Junior was aware of this hijack, and lost core team members when he refused to claim homosexuality as equivalent to race in his civil-rights struggle. When this circus began there were few openly gay African Americans, and the KKK were shamefully uninterested in homosexuals. What to do?

First, they would create a history of victimization, and dramatize it— for which they are gifted. The gay community found willing partners in colleges, journalists, and in the arts. Pressing their shoulders to the plow, they earnestly replanted the fields of history for a harvest of lies and half-truths. This move was a massive middle finger salute to the rest of us, who stand to gain nothing by social revisionism in favor of Marxism and homosexuality.

GAY IS GOOD, SAYS SMITHSONIAN

Pioneer militant, Franklin Kameny, pushed gay activists for "aggressive direct" action in the 1960s. Riding the crest of the civil-rights movements, they designed parallel campaigns to Rev. King. Yet homosexuals had no background of slavery, and could vote. Club 21 didn't seat gays near the kitchen, and Macy's had no "faggot" water fountains. Andy Warhol, in his flaming counter-sexuality, was celebrated and feted in high society. No group had less in common with African Americans.

Kameny also conjured up the vapid phrase, "Gay is good." In 1966, most people could recognize sheer hucksterism – but not many now. Proof is the slogan's inclusion in a 2007 Smithsonian exhibit, as one of our "Treasures of American History."[1] Yep. "Gay is good" is a *treasure* – the poetry, the profundity! It leaves one speechless. Our premier history museum is shilling for Kameny years after his death, as they provide LGBTQs with disproportionate numbers of free exhibits. Will they dig up his body next as a sacred relic?

By the late 1960s, a parallel movement in the arts accompanied Kameny's "Gay is Good" stratagem. Witty gay writer and public figure, Gore Vidal, openly pushed the joys of sodomy in his essays and novels. Vidal never claimed to be a victim, but used it as a springboard. At least in that he was honest, unlike contemporary gay propagandists. Gore was spectacularly wealthy and successful, and was allowed to speak into American life on thousands of platforms. Equally witty conservative writer, William F. Buckley, (they detested each other) depicted Gore as an evangelist for bisexuality. During their contentious televised debates in 1968 he said of Gore: "The addict is to be pitied and even respected, not the pusher."[2] Buckley asked America to make distinctions between victims and opportunists. We failed.

STONEWALLED...

Contemporary gay rights campaigns didn't begin at lecture halls or Churches, like emancipation did. Birthed in drunken riots, its most renown moment was violence after a raid on the Stonewall Inn (bar) in New York City. In an effort to ennoble the birth of gay thuggery, it's been primped up in history books. Sordid aspects of the place gave police perfectly good reasons to visit quite often.

Stonewall was owned by the Genovese mafia family. "Fat Tony" was the perfect host for such ventures, ignoring illegal drugs, various forms of filth, and an active sex trade. Patrons blamed a lack of running water for an epidemic of hepatitis in 1969. There was no rear exit, as well as other fire and safety-code violations. Stonewall would have closed down long before, if not for Fat Tony's helpful donations to the Sixth Police Precinct of about $1,200 a month.[3] A goodly amount back then. While gay historians make silly claims such as it was "illegal" to serve gay people alcohol or for gays to dance together, they are untrue. Stonewall served watered-down alcohol, according to even the most gay-centric sources – and did it without a liquor license.

Beyond Stonewall's lack of basic hygiene, police tended to raid gay dives more than straight ones for "indecent conduct" – of which they found plenty. This wasn't hand-holding. On June 28, 1969, a mob of 600 attacked police in a pique, after their soirées and hair were messed up again. Rioting spread to other parts of Greenwich Village, with enraged gays and drag queens looting, tossing bricks, and other heroic acts. Until things settled down, cops closed the place.

Today, the Stonewall Inn is a US National Historic Register building, while Lincoln's log cabin is only a state site.

TEACHER'S PET PREDILECTION

Early on, academia enthusiastically rolled up their sleeves to help make homosexuality respectable. In 1997, AIDS activist, Larry Kramer, offered Yale (his alma mater) $4 million to endow a permanent, tenured professorship in gay studies. Now, $4 million wasn't even close to what it costs to do something of the sort, even then. But they jumped on it, and dozens of colleges followed suit. The entire concept took hold through intimidation, wheedling, and every means but academic. But if the mountain won't come to Mohammed, just write a column in the *Huffington Post* or *New York Times* claiming it did. You would be surprised who believes it.

Not unexpectedly, the Obama administration was *very* generous to homosexuals in these endeavors. His administration was a fount of helpful legislation, using a tragic death for traction. The Trojan horse "Matthew Shepard and James Byrd, Jr. Hate Crimes Prevention Act" of 2009, quickly picked up speed. For the first time in American history, concerns about "gender identity" became a federal obsession. It's now a hobby for our courts. Fascination over the sex lives of complete strangers was relegated to voyeurism or a bad childhood, in the dark pre-Obama days.

Legally, "gender" goes far beyond the boring, old "male" or "female", so about 97 % of us are not up for any federal goodies. If you're not having sex outside Kinsey's box, the DOJ isn't about to sit up nights fretting over your piddling civil rights. But they are *very* concerned about wedding photography. Less than 4%* of people self-identify as gay, bisexual, or trans anything. Being a teensy minority helps with the victim pitch, because many are easily confused over quantity and quality. How can you be both an oppressed minority, and the norm; which is the case the gay lobby makes? Moreover, homosexuals are generally some of the most prosperous in any community, and are always among the better educated.[4]

Radical elements claim homosexuality is natural, and heterosexuality is perverse. If no one confronts them, it's likely your children or grandchildren will grow up believing this. Our current plague of puzzled sexual torpor is nothing new, but it's unusually deep and unsettling. The entire nation is being forced to hold these types of irreconcilable facts, which contradict each other, nature, and both halves of our brains. But this isn't much of a problem, because logic is now soundly discouraged as well.

**Estimates of homosexual population have historically been 1.6% to 4% at highest. Recent CDC surveys found only 2.6% self-identity as gay or bi-sexual. Adding 'transgender' or 'gender undecided' racks up to 3.8% in 2016. Yet, most college-age Americans are under the impression gays make up approximately 25% (one-quarter) of the population!*[5]

2

BEING GAY IS ABOUT SEX. ONLY.

Make no mistake, the gay rights movement and all its legal paraphernalia has little to do with love. It is about power and sex, sometimes simultaneously. That's all theoretical "anti-gay hate crimes" are about. Not lynchings, nor emotional cruelty, nor happy little families yearning to breathe free.

There isn't anything else, but they can't just come out and say it. Then, there would be no means for the rest of us to accept our inferior status via hate-crime laws. No terror of catching "homophobia." It would strip away cherished delusions and outright lies. People who preach gay mythology would lose jobs, and myths are absolutely necessary to ram a great, unctuous lie against a nation. It's a form of cultural rape. You may be numb to it, you may be a perpetrator, or may have just given in and joined the gang. It's still rape.

There is a reason the term for gays is homo-*sexual,* as it clearly pertains to sex acts. A man who enjoys the company of other men may dearly love them – but if he is not *sexually* involved he not a homo*sexual.* Homosexuality concerns SEX, and is an erotic deviation from the norm by definition. Gayness is an anomaly, trait, perversion, predilection, or choice. We have our opinions, but the central feature here is *sex:* women with women, men with men, or some variation thereof. It is so defined by the sages who decided to make laws enshrining the practice. Gay men (or women) are not homo*florists,* or homo*arsonists,* or homo*economists.*

CARNALIS COPULA CONTRA NATURAM

Forcing people to use the term "gay" is a completely Orwellian tactic. Overtones of lithesome frolic detracts from the sex, which is their only significant difference from Amish honeymooners. Coy activists claim the term "homosexuality" was invented by 19th psychiatrists, and chalk it up to excessive Edwardian priggery. But that word was medical and mild, compared to centuries gone before. It was all "sodomites", "Gomorrheans", "shitten pricks" and "buggerers" back then – in many languages, and far beyond Europe.

For example, in 1797, a "Madge Cove" was either a gay man or a place to meet them – using the female name as a clue. Social scientists in the 19th century used the term "contrarysexual." Until quite recently, gay sex acts were referred to as "unnatural intercourse", and legally grouped with bestiality. Its Latin handle was "carnalis copula contra naturam, & hoc vel per confusionem specierum." All terms related to homosexuals in Western literature were pejorative, and referred solely to the sex act itself, not a separate culture. Being "gay" is a new Western concept, born for identity politics.

Over a 20-year rehabilitation forced on Americans concerning the Joys of Gayness, the actual act is generally ignored, or not allowed to be spoken. It's as if it were something too hallowed to be uttered by straight lips. But how can something (in this case anti-gay hate crimes) be promoted and yet not closely examined? Is it because many would find gay sex acts repulsive and unworthy of special legislation, under scrutiny? The truth is, heterosexuals have absolutely nothing to gain by promoting homosexual culture and rights in preference to their own. Many will lose a great deal.

Since America is now a giant, gay sex rally, it's way past time we had a frank discussion about it. Hate-speech and hate-crime legislation pivot around perceived anti-gay bias more than anything else. Shouldn't someone describe exactly what America's lawmakers are promoting, enabling, funding, and demanding that we must honor – and by force of law? Here's the peep show.

ADULTS ONLY PLEASE

Male gay sex often involves excrement. Unavoidable with anal sex, it's just part of the *Joy of Shit*. By nature unsanitary, anal sex can easily cause injuries and spread disease – particularly when large objects or body parts are shoved up a rectum (such as fists, bottles and baseball bats).

Related to fixations on feces, some partners move their members from anus to a partner's mouth. Anilingus, a more refined version, is often used by lesbians, for just a snack. Coprophagiacs will eat it, or force it on others. And if they still have a lust for the stuff, scatophiliacs have 101 things to do with excrement. Gay Bathhouse patrons may enjoy these delights with up to 30 or more strangers in an evening – or did, before the majority of them were closed down by health departments.

Fans of bodily waste may find urine just as sexy. "Golden Showers" is a common homosexual act of urinating on your beloved, for foreplay, or humiliation – or whatever. "Golden Baths" occur when a male urinates into the colon of his partner. San Francisco hosted gay bars in the 1970s with "piss tubs" – bathtubs for men to publicly urinate on each other. Some just like the taste, or practitioners of "urophagia." Lesbians use this in their own inimitable way. The delights of fluid waste are so wildly popular in gay communities that they call it "Water Sports." Continue this projection and it could eventually become an Olympic Sport. Why not? Anything gay is "good," and who is to stop it?

Three decades ago, it was unthinkable that two women would marry. These and the facts above are illegal to mention in some places (unless you are teaching kids in California). Their legislature *obligates* them to instruct K-12 graders in the wonders of the gay lifestyle. Five years-old, and sexual conditioning begins. Previously this was called "corrupting a minor," before our enlightened days of anti-hate speech laws, with their educational garrotes and handcuffs.

CHANNELING KIDDIE PORN

Until recently, anyone speaking to unrelated five-year-olds about sex was considered a lecherous, filthy old man (or woman). Indeed they are. Public school instructors are now forced to channel these predators, because of a powerful gay lobby. Isn't this unadulterated *hate* for every child it touches, and gross disrespect for their parents? No one asks the poor, test-rat kids if they really want to hear what two or more "daddies" do in bed – but if it makes politicians and adult homosexuals happy, why should 75 million children matter?

I remember a time of relative innocence, when children were more than tiny foot-soldiers in adult culture wars. Astoundingly, I had no real concept of homosexuality until I was 13, and even then, I was gobsmacked by the idea. Gay activists insist their lives are so natural that such a thing isn't even possible. I assure them it was perfectly normal, four or five decades ago, to live blissfully unaware of "Golden Showers" and confusion over your sexual identify. Homosexuality didn't register a blip with anyone I knew, and had *nothing* in common with the majority of people on earth. It doesn't now. Forcing this information on innocents is nothing short of evil. *Hate* is a weakly anemic term for conscripting children to dwell on your personal fetish.

While straights indulge in some of these sex acts, it's a small percent, and they have options most prefer. Homosexuals, on the other hand, glorify their preferred forms of getting off. They go into great detail in high school condom-demos and other inappropriate places. Sex is almost the sole theme in gay literature, gay arts, and gay scholarship. Search the internet. Type in "trannys" and first up may be "Spicy Tranny" featuring "Ladyboy Tubes and Big Cock", or worse. Sex is a consuming obsession, which defines the gay community far more than the straight – who seem to have other interests in life.

Compulsive gay activists neurotically drone on about their sex life to any audience, of any orientation, in any place and time. You don't need to be a *willing* audience. Variously called "LGBTQ sex education" or "diversity training" or sundry euphemisms, it's all about forcing *you* to understand *them.* Your opinion doesn't matter. Only the most aggressive exhibitionists and sociopaths have this irritating trait – yet there seem to be so many lately.

A bizarre 2015 Facebook post by a little boy (who looked at most nine), claimed he was sad because he was "a homosexual." That's a long, loaded word for a kid. Entirely by coincidence, then presidential candidate Hillary Clinton and lesbian entertainer Ellen DeGeneres simultaneously found this post.[6] Both responded with great sympathy over the fearful possibility that someone may not like him, someday. How can a child this age believe he is "gay" unless someone much older told him all about it? A caring adult would be concerned over what made this boy so prematurely sexual and depressed. But not DeGeneres or Clinton, who used him as a personal shout-out platform for gay fans. They probably had the privilege of a carefree childhood, but if they didn't, they are even more culpable.

And parents – who wouldn't be uncomfortable over strangers talking dirty to their children? If they could still muster those outlawed feelings of nurture and protection, parents could conceivably be angry – even infuriated at the aggression. But that could possibly hurt a militant adult's sensibilities, and nothing is more critical than avoiding that. Certainly not the well-being of a child. Lack of protection may explain why many of our children are depressed, confused, angry, murderous, or suicidal.

Homosexuals, never wasting a tragedy they helped create, blame this on traditional morality. The Bible made them do it. Which is hilarious, because conservatives have had almost no effect on education, mass media, or culture for years.

HAPPY, SHINY GAYNESS – ON DEMAND

Apparently, few things are more direly needed than promoting homosexuality in a time of violence and terrorism. We must all lend a hand, something like WWII-era Victory Gardens. But this time, free thought, religion, and personal values are the weeds to be eradicated. We are absolutely *not* free to express our thoughts on homosexuality.

The straight majority are free to gush over the grandfather of eight who just "discovered" he is gay, leaving his wife for "Morty" and lucrative appearances on *The View*. We are at perfect liberty to encourage maiming, mutilation and lopping of body parts, but only for sex-changes. Those must always be acknowledged as a Good Thing and Attractive and Better. We must not show horror at the lurking, 6′ 4″, basso-profondo creature known as "Lola", even if it's blocking the door of the girl's room. We are free to pretend this is a natural occurrence in some universe.

Christian activist Bill Whatcott is finding how far freedom of speech extends in Ontario – only as far as gay autocrats decree.

Whatcott and a few friends attended Toronto's 2016 Pride Parade, passing fliers warning of health risks for homosexuals. They were costumed in green, Dr. Seuss-like bodysuits, which purportedly "traumatized" the almost nude assembly. Whatcott's existence on a public street in proximity of Canada's national pets, led to a $104 million lawsuit against the trio.[7] This wasn't dropped as frivolous harassment, but was joined by former Deputy Premier George Smitherman, who whined of "conspiracy to cause mental harm and distress" on part of more than a *million* Pride participants. They probably stood out, because they were the only ones fully clothed, and most participants were, uh, busy doing other things.

Gay spokesmen 30 years ago swore they only wanted to love each other and be left alone. Their slogan was "stay out of our bedrooms." Fine. But for those refusing coexistence with the rest of us, please have the decency to reciprocate. If you find our quaint creeds and lifestyle intolerable, and have no respect, then stay out of our businesses, our homes and our children's curriculum. You have freedom to create your own, where your glorious lifestyle is celebrated with the pomp and circumstance you feel you so richly deserve.

Facts are, homosexuality doesn't appeal to most people or they would be doing it. Gay sex hasn't benefited its host communities either – not *in itself*. Yet, many who contributed to the world happen to be gay. These gifted people are celebrated as artists, writers, performers, scientists, and in many other fields. But none of them received a Nobel Prize for their tight ass – a common gay laudation. It's one thing to be proud of sexual escapades, and for some it may be their highest achievement in life. But celebrating homosexuals merely because of what gives them orgasms, is truly queer.

3

GAYTHEISTS vs. CHRISTIANS

Most religions prohibit homosexuality as a way of life. Too bad for religion, it will just have to go. Bibles of Jews and Christians clearly state that God created humanity "male and female," and Islam makes sexual difference a central tenet. Gender-flex adherents declared war on many faiths in their efforts to deny the obvious. Because a vast majority of Americans are Christian by any poll, this pits a tiny camp of strident homosexuals against the dominant faith of the land. Make that many lands. Outposts of the kingdom of "Christendom" are all under siege, and no one is allowed to live in peace at this point.

Traditional concepts of family and Christian morality are perceived as an enemy, but not because of violence to gays. Physical attacks are remarkably rare in the US and Europe. Church choirs don't roam streets looking to castrate some vulnerable gay guy, but that's the scenario homosexual activists create in their hate-scripts. Yes, there are minor bastions of true hate, such as all 40 members of the Westboro "Church". But using them as a ploy to attack Christianity is the equivalent of claiming Wayne Gacy is a stereotypical homosexual. Christians don't stoop that low.

For decades, gays have been quietly tolerated, ignored, or at the most, snickered at. But they weren't celebrated in any positive way. This is unbearable for people with delusions of grandeur. What do homosexuals find so unbearable about Christanity then?

It's in the book – obvious prohibitions against the lifestyle. These were written thousands of years ago, and are sacred to billions across the globe. Gaytheists are infuriated over the stubborn recalcitrance of conservative Christians to submit to their demands and surrender their souls. The Church's irritating non-compliance with their new cultural norms drives them mad. Or something else did. Or will.

An option is to ignore God and his people, but it's too much fun to jerk them around. Agitated LGBTQ thugs have no intention of "co-existing" with creeds that don't further their agenda. This is patently obvious, as they choose to live as hostile outposts, belittling their neighbors.

People in conquered gay territories of the West have suffered under that malice for quite some time. In 2004, a gay Spanish group sued Cardinal Antonio Maria Rouco Varela for claiming, *in his own church,* that society is best served by "the fecund love of the Christian family." Canada is also doing a bang-up job of using the state to troll and punish thought-criminals. Priests and pastors there have been stripped of human rights, and some are serving time for their faith. In the 21st century, Christians are designated The Unchosen People by LGBT leaders.

HAIL SAINTS MILK AND HAY!

California has made homosexuality a state religion, but they just won't come out and say so. "What? You dare defy Caesar (gay marriage) with your stubborn beliefs and ancient books? We have no other Gods before us!" Hail Saints Milk and Hay, whom we invoke daily in our Statehouse in Sacramental!"

The Golden Gay State demands tithes via mandatory taxes for homosexual expansionism. Devotional school materials extol the exploits of mighty gay heroes and their wondrous deeds. Its catechism must be maintained, and any evidence contrary is fuel for LGBT Inquisitors. Lack of "gay friendliness" is proof of impiety in California. Offenders are suspect, shunned, fined, or driven from the camp (their jobs). Look it up if you can't believe it.

Archbishop of San Francisco, Salvatore Joseph Cordileone, is aware that he faces the equivalent of a counter-religion. Cordileone is specifically despised for predicting (correctly) that redefining marriage will harm society and endanger religious LGBT forces immediately proved him spot on, swarn streets and launching nasty slander campaigns at the Ar on-op. Gay malice against the Church may be more evident in San Francisco than anywhere on earth, because the state so enthusiastically supports it there. In a show of force, lawmakers stood against the Catholic Church (which was there long before the nation existed). Even mildly pro-family statements can leave streets writhing in rage and sexual anarchy. Gay hate at its finest.

Berliners were treated to a 2015 hate orgy written by homosexual playwright Falk Richter, where the audience was directed to kill five *real conservatives.* Richter targets pro-family activists in "Fear", depicting them as zombies requiring a head shot or eye gouge. So inspired were some of his unhinged peers that cars, and a business of two women, were burnt to the ground. Part of his script read: "The zombie dies only when you shoot directly into his brain…. The zombie seeks world domination. The zombie is directed against the survival of humanity."[8] Amazing. The conservative is "against the survival of mankind" while these barren boy-lovers and ass-riding cowboys will save "humanity" from them. Nazis couldn't have said it better – and there were likely some of their children in the cast and audience that night.

This is hate writ large with cheap rainbow markers. Militant homosexual activists use psychological gimmicks and project their own hostility, paranoia, and malice onto Christians and conservatives. Nazi! KKK! (insert reactionary slogan here), like snitches in a schoolyard. Notorious baby pornographer Mark Truong's remarks are a classic example: "I believe in God, I just don't believe the church is correctly representing him. I think they're using God as an excuse for their own intolerance and hatred." [9] Thanks for showing us how it should be done, Mr. Truong.

GAY GODS

Liberal churches, which are willing to recreate the Church and God in gayer image, haven't ebbed the malice a bit. Now that homosexuals have more than they ever demanded, the true face of their animus is emerging, and their true goals. Nothing less than total submission of the Church and crushing of her cultural influence will do. Or an admission that God was very confused and has been converted – or transitioned.

Sadly, gay hostility toward religion forces students to oppose their own faith in public schools. Decades of propaganda designed to disenfranchise families has paid off. Parents are wearied from compulsory gay education trampling their child's emotions and spirituality. But gay commissars have issues with boundaries, and a collective case of monomania. Now their rancor is even focused on parochial schools, who defied them all these years. Emboldened by legal victories, they are like engorged ticks draining the rights of parents. Their goal is to make certain no child is left behind, in a state of happy innocence.

This is the endgame of a 2000-year-old crusade, with the Church on the *defensive* side. Homosexual rulers in Europe, Africa, and Asia sought to enslave Christians from the beginning.[10] Lists of gay demands are still remarkably like those old sex-cult religions. Incas took young boys to use as Temple prostitutes, dressing them up in female clothing. Mini-transvestites? Many ancient cults tended toward pederasty, and Judeo-Christian ethics were their only effective opposition for centuries. The enmity lingers.

The sword of the state makes gay-hate campaigns possible and profitable, using taxes of the very citizens they oppress. Well-armed by euphemistically named "Rights Commissions" they provide lawyers and funds for any aggrieved "non-heteronormative" person. It's blatant bigotry. Weapons are cocked, loaded and aimed at religious citizens everywhere.

Tribunals in Australia brought a "discrimination complaint" against Archbishop Julian Porteous, of Tasmania in 2015. His crime? He sent a pamphlet to *private Catholic* schools describing the Church's traditional teachings on marriage. For this effrontery, he was soundly denounced. Martine Delaney, an uninvolved, cross-dressing man, accused Porteous of offending and humiliating homosexuals.[11] Porteous' criminal-thought pamphlet includes shocking statements such as this: "Every man, woman and child has great dignity and worth which can never be taken away. This includes those who experience same-sex attraction. They must be treated with respect, sensitivity, and love." The good cleric wasted ink with his kind thoughts and good will, which were not reciprocated by gay extremists.

But Archbishop Porteous' misdeeds went beyond loving your enemies. He denounced political campaigns of legal discrimination against the Church as well. "Martine" seems to have no concepts of freedom of speech, religion, or irony. Apparently "Martine" is equally clueless of Australia's history of promoting freedom in other nations – even going to war against other types of fascism. Tragically, Australia has embraced a home version, as have as Canada and parts of Europe. America is pawing at the gates to construct their own legal dungeons for dissenters against Gay Doctrine.

Formerly Great Britain is apoplectic over the Anglican church sticking to its guns over gay marriage. After the Church of England sanctioned America's openly gay bishops, MP Lord Scriven asked the Ministry of Justice to "dis-establish" their 500-year-old Anglican Church. Mollifying gay thugs would include entirely dismantling existing British government. Queen Elizabeth would be required to enlist in gay servitude as well, as she is the Supreme Governor of the Church of England.[12]

Early war games against Christians include a 1989 dry-run on New York's St. Patrick's Cathedral. Reacting to Cardinal O'Connor's stands on family, birth control, homosexuality and AIDS, 4,500 protesters disrupted the mass. Screeching about O'Connor's "bigotry", activist Michael Petrelis either didn't know, or care, that the archdiocese cared for many AIDS patients. Foreshadowing the dark left censorship to come, the *New York Times* failed to mention grotesque details of condoms (possibly used) tossed at worshippers, and desecration of communion. This was about hating the Christian God, harassing his followers, and forcing them to conform. Cardinal O'Connor calmly counselled his flock to never respond with hatred, and Petrelis countered with threats.[13] Gay militants truly hate even their own, as they continue to savage Christian organizations. These are historically the only ones to treat and serve dying AIDS patients in many parts of the earth.

Gay aggression toward the Church is white hot now. Even academics should be able to see this – if they're not too busy creating new fields of study in honor of random homosexuals. Religious schools and businesses must endorse beliefs they find abominable. But they couldn't do it alone.

The campaign to disenfranchise Christians in their own colleges was recently upheld by the US Supreme Court. There are too many examples of hostility to list, but let's spin the wheel and choose a few.

ABANDON ALL THOUGHT

Gordon College faced lawsuits and funding loss over its ban on open same-sex relationships. Their accreditation was being "discussed" by thugs at the New England Associate of Schools and Colleges. This barrage began when President Obama ordered faith-based groups to support gay marriage, against their conscience. When Gordon meekly asked for religious exemptions, a cascade of hate was unleashed against it. Affecting shock, protesters feigned ignorance of Gordon's 125 years of Christian association, while attacking them for just that reason.[14]

Tufts, Middlebury and a herd of Cal State universities followed suit. Gay rights groups took an extraordinary interest in Bible studies over the last decade, insisting they be handed leadership roles in associations whose values they opposed. InterVarsity Christian Fellowships were harassed and suspended at SUNY Buffalo in New York, and elsewhere. After expensive litigation, some of the faith groups are now re-instated, but gay hit-teams continue their pogroms, with little fear a Christian will demand LGBTQ groups make him *their* president. They really should, just to see what happens. My guess is a real *hatefest,* and possible violence from this protected class of victims. Poor little Christians just don't have what it takes – deceit and aggression.

Academia can be a toxic pit for Christians, who are denied tenure and scholarships because their faith contradicts political narratives. Western media tends to obscure this abuse with misleading headlines, and missing information. Even the heartland suffers a suffocating uniformity of thought, marking them as cogs of the state. Same end, different means. By early 2016, gender-politics had reached Nebraska. The state ruled that even Catholic schools must allow students to play sports "based on their preferred gender identity." When a 90-pound linebacker breaks her pretty little neck, "diversity" specialists in Nebraska will hold themselves immaculate. Sexual sociopathology from sea to shining sea will not work out well for the rest of us either. You can lay money on it.[15]

Always creative, gay activists find endless ways to torment people who believe their Bible. Gay bigots are bullies, who are highly adept at self-righteous posturing and the fine art of persecution. Churches who minister to ex-gays quickly feel their wrath, as do any who help those fleeing the joys of sodomy. It's comparable to prisoners escaping a brutal army, who are shot to keep up the illusion of unity on the home front. Apparently gay thugs feel no one (including God) has the right to any opinions about them. Yet they have much to say about Christianity, and freely share it. Educational and corporate cleansing – it's happening in real time, here.

BAKE ME A CAKE

So many victims, so little time. Bakers seem to be magnets for gay sadists lately. Shopkeepers in Ireland are feeling the steel-toed boots of homosexuals, and their eternal stock of resentment. A male couple in Belfast County pushed a Christian baker to scrawl "Support Gay marriage," across a cake for them. Why not scribe the insipid propaganda themselves, or use a gay baker?

Sadistic lawsuits like this are manufactured to create ill will against Christians, and the historic precedents are troubling. This was a snare. Clear entrapment, but not clear enough for Belfast Judge Isobel Brownlie to catch on. She found against the bakery owners on the grounds that it caused "injury to feelings."[16] Since when do "injured feelings" become the responsibility of the state?

Abuse harmed more than mere "feelings" of the bakery's owners, Colin and Karen McArthur. They face bankruptcy, court costs, fines, possible closure, embarrassment, stress, and unpleasant publicity. The last is provided gratis, thanks to a hostile press. If this ruling isn't reversed, it alone proves that homosexuals subjugate straight Irish citizens. More simply, civil rights in UK are toast, and we're next up on the menu. Courts on both sides of the Atlantic now coerce religious persons to bear "injured feelings" every waking second of their lives.

Shoppers can blame homosexual bullies when prices skyrocket, once they add the price of a lawsuit or two. Who knew it was necessary to retain an attorney to make cinnamon rolls? And gay bigots are still agitating against Christians in their protracted Pastry Wars.

Spring 2016 found the season of gay-hate in full bloom in Longview, Texas. Ben Valencia and Luis Marmolejo sued Christian bakers, after they politely refused to make them a wedding cake. Apparently, their nuptials couldn't be pulled off without forced Christian labor. Gay plaintiffs (in these cases) have difficulty believing that "morality" and "faith" are actual things. Gay bigot Marmolejo proved this, when he claimed that he couldn't understand why the couple didn't violate their religious beliefs for *him*.[17]

Wedding cakes last year. Cakes with offensive political slogans last month. Mandatory giant penis cookies shooting rainbow sperm for school lunch may be next – and why not? Few citizens retain the right to refuse any performance, demand, or product that random homosexuals dream up. This is an era of unparalleled abuse for Americans. Who is "discussing" why millions should be forced to deconstruct their religion to satisfy the sexual quirks of a few? Senators Barbara Boxer and Patty Murray did, as well as Hillary Clinton in her 2016 presidential campaign. What will they do when they run out of Christians and bakeries?

True goals in a military advance are often hidden, but the gay wedding bash is looking terrifically martial at the moment. Aggressive homosexuals started their incursions by blaming the church for all their problems – or their mothers. Mothers aren't much of a problem, because they either die or convert to their offspring's cause. Decades later, immature homosexuals still blame the church. The existence of Bible-believing Christians enrages Gaytheists, like the sight of a crucifix to the undead.

REPRODUCING SAVAGES

Let them speak for themselves. Gay sex columnist Dan Savage insists teens are dying because of Christian beliefs, although he had a tough time coming up with examples. Pathologically unable to get over himself, he endlessly curses Biblical scribes for not first considering him and his sex life when they inscribed it for humanity. What were they thinking? Theological pronouncements include this one by Savage, on Pope Benedict: He was a "Mother****ing Power-Hungry, Self-Aggrandized Bigot In the Stupid F****ng Hat." [18] He liked that one so much, he used it twice.

Somehow allowed access to an entire school of other people's children, Savage launched into an insipid hate-rant, demonizing Christian families and bringing some teens to tears. Advising them to ignore "bullshit" from Bible" he gave them all sorts of helpful information on his extremely relevant sexual penchants. [33] Savage is clearly zealous about the well-being of gay youth, although it may be merely to keep up a fresh supply. It's impossible to impute good motives to a man who viciously taunts Christian students. Savage is gifted at gay hate and he makes a great deal of money off it.[32]

Apparently most gay bigots are so well-heeled, they assume they will never need charity – as from the Salvation Army (SA). Gay activist, Bil Browning, libelled them as actively discriminating against gays and lesbians, although hundreds of homeless homosexuals may be using their shelters at this minute.[19] Browning encourages gays to withhold their plentiful funds from SA, because they would not be allowed to serve with them. The SA doesn't give a sex test for aid, but employment is reserved for those abiding by the Salvation Army's doctrine. That excludes all manner of religious and sexual behavior, and not just Browning's. When did he or any gay organization reach out to the larger, straight world anyway? Where do they feed the poor, or take kids off the street (and not just into their beds)?

Europe, if anything, is far worse. At least in Britain, where the path to bad intentions is paved by gaystapos demanding "their" church do "their" nuptials, "their" way, or else. The wealthy Drewitt-Barlows, a gay couple from the U.K., must dearly love their local Baptist Church.[20] The hyphenated darlings were suing their brothers in Christ in 2014, to force them (against tradition and Christian doctrine) to do their bidding. Because we all know that churches were made for gorgeous gay wedding backdrops. What else?

KEEPING MY RELIGION

Assuming the entire world will submit to gay demands, it must be a great shock when things go south for them. Crusaders for Western homosexual mores in Uganda and Malawi were treated to a taste of their own poison in recent years. It left them almost catatonic with rage and disbelief.

After Uganda's contentious "anti-gay" bill in 2014, a magazine there listed names and addresses of prominent homosexuals, seeming to invite violence. Gay spokesmen were rightly enraged, yet failed to note that Ugandan gay bashers were possibly inspired by their own bitter crusades, waged against American conservatives since the 1970s. Names, addresses, phone numbers, IRS contributions, political supporters, places of employment, and even family members of conservatives – are all publicized by gay thugs, who never forget a perceived political slight. Classic homosexual hate tactics were now turned back to bite them. Rather than learn a moral lesson, gay militants laid Uganda's decisions at the feet of the same Christians they had battered for years.

Russia has proved another tough act for gay bigots. Accustomed to easy marks in Western churches, they are now meeting their match. Expecting to stride fearlessly across people's backs, they forgot America isn't the entire world. Groups of the faithful (some armed) blocked gay parades and events in Russia, shouting down the speakers. Militants seem shocked when treated in the same contemptuous manner they've dished out for decades. The land that took on Napoleon, Hitler, and baby raping Chechnyans now face masters of bitter and hysterical political theater on a global stage. Stunned over failures to submit to their demands, homosexuals used the usual arsenal: claims of trampled human rights and wailing "persecution."

Whistling for Western liberaldom to muscle in only caused Russians to bristle and further entrench. Yury Lushov, Moscow's mayor in 2010, bluntly called public gay events "satanic acts." Vladimir Putin, Patriarch Kirill (of the Russian Orthodox Church) and a host of political and spiritual leaders in Russia seconded his opinion.

Response to gay aggression is ramping up censorship in China as well, where gay relationships were proliferating on TV, social media, and the arts. In 2016, the Chinese government sent out a notice as part of a national curb on "vulgar and immoral" content. *"No television drama shall show abnormal sexual relationships and behaviours, such as incest, same-sex relationships, sexual perversion, sexual assault, sexual abuse, sexual violence, and so on."*[21] Christians had nothing to do with this. How will gay activists spin the fact that their lifestyle is offensive to many cultures?

Anti-Christian bigotry is not only irrational, it's suicidal in the long run. Judging by demands, gay imperialists want a revived form of the fabulously gay Roman Empire. With few exceptions, the gayer the Emperor, the more intolerant and cruel to Christians. Edward Gibbon, who wrote *"The Decline and Fall of the Roman Empire"* noted this connection. Speaking of the first fifteen emperors he asserts, "Claudius was the only one whose taste in love was entirely correct."[22] By "correct" he meant heterosexual.

Warm feelings to the Rainbow Troops for trashing our history, attacking our beliefs, and interfering with our families. Thank you for teaching us approved methods, body parts, terminology, and sex paraphernalia. Feel free to slap us around any time!

KIDDIE PROP

All budding tyrants gun for schools and kids first. Our public schools are fast becoming gay recruitment centers, thanks to special interest groups who prevailed over actual stake holders (parents and students). Children are sprayed with gay hype like weeds in a lawn. They not only lose their rights, but must forcibly celebrate their subjugation. Congress and statehouses naturally collect students with "correct" opinions on homosexuality (after they grow up to preferentially become professors, judges and senators).

Gay pedophiles and their press entourage made a stab at the kids in the 1990s, with a flood of pieces in respectable mainstream publications. In 1995, the *New Republic's* "Chickenhawk" veered close to sympathy for NAMBLA members. It bore a jaded sophistication, with no sense of revulsion over NAMBLA's child-hunting mission.[23] Similar pieces appeared in other mainstream magazines, until a horrified public made them back off.[24] What we are experiencing now is the redux, Kiddie Rapists II, returning with huge production crews. If you have children, they are considered de facto members of their cast.

Because children have no natural interest in venial matters, and homosexuality does *not* happen naturally, gay pushers rigorously teach it. Chief architect and lobbyist for kiddie-sex class is the American Anti-Defamation League (ADL), who boasts of helping teachers promote gay life to millions of little ones. Once an honorable organization dedicated to stopping anti-Semitism, the ADL now feeds the egos and election of progressives, while hiding behind an outdated moniker. Suckers may still give the ADL money and feel they are doing something righteous, but they have become every bit the wealthy, privileged haters they once fought.

Pimping the minds of our kids is the Gay Lesbian and Straight Education Network (GLSEN). According to GLSEN, providing a "safe environment for GLBTQ youth" ensures the comfort and creativity of all students.[25] But by "safe" they mean championed. The stifling atmosphere dictated by homosexual agitprop will prove unsafe for everyone. Organizations such as GLSEN are recurring nightmares kids can't escape, or turn down the volume.

Virtually any assertion from LGBTQ reps is mindlessly adopted in schools, because there is no counterweight, no voice of opposition. Homosexual hucksters, such as the ADL and GLSEN, also encourage gay teachers in all grades to openly share their lifestyle with students.[26] Wasn't that what Anita Bryant predicted 40 years ago?

A GROOMING ROOM OF MY OWN

Bullying" and "victimization" are the golden calves of this cult of child inductors. What are the magic words? "Bully!" Victim!" Repeat 12 times while dialing the American Civil Liberties Union (ACLU), and all your wishes come true. Once in, gay agents *bully* and *victimize* recalcitrant students. Often those are religious children. A generation of straight kids is being forced to work as adjunct gay activists, but they won't be getting any of the special favors. Now there are grave "Days of Silence" in public schools. Not for terror victims, but generic solidarity with transsexuals or gays.

While not usually a formal requirement, what are children expected to do when they want so badly to be accepted? It's a calculated ploy to suck kids into something they don't understand, and probably feel very uncomfortable about. Another word for GLSEN's work is "grooming."

This little jingle was offered at a 2015 Iowa conference for high-school students (purportedly to stop bullying). "People suck. They don't give a f— about you. People thrive on smashing our pride to the ground. People that suck, f— you." [27] Iowa Governor Terry

Branstad put his name on it. Co-sponsors of this, and similar waste products, include GLSEN, ACLU, the Human Rights Campaign (HRC) and Gay-Straight Alliance. Proud corporate sponsors include Nationwide, Office Depot, and Principal Financial Group. Even the Episcopal Diocese of Iowa was complicit in flipping off conservatives. [28]

You can thank the powerful non-profits above (covertly working with Federal agencies), for plundering your child's innocence. But America has a long way to go to catch up with the entrenched school pedophilia in the UK or Australia.

Homosexual hucksters in Australia are as embedded as ticks in schools. Children are conscripted like little soldiers and asked to chant, sing, make posters, and otherwise parrot mindless gay glorification rites. Bi-sexuality is dismissed as meeting a person and saying "you're really nice to me and I like you. That's what being bisexual means to me."[29] Yep, they nailed it. Although this is not a direct campaign to accept pedophilia, it softens them up for the kill. Pre-pedophilia, grammar school level. Christians have a habit of being opposed to it.

Bad as that was, Australia's politicians and teachers are keen for even greater sexual modifications to kiddies. Religious schools are expected to comply with their goals, which include this gem (my emphasis): *"Sexuality should be included in all curriculum relating to health and personal development. Diverse sex, sexuality and genders need to be normalised and all states and territories need to develop material which will help to combat homophobia, biphobia and transphobia."*[30] Note the inappropriate pandering, disregard of civil rights, and fascistic tone. Every Australian child is now bullied by immature, agenda-driven adults.

With Europe so tolerant of homosexuality and pedophilia, it comes as no surprise that the EU steamrolled gay education into schools. In 2006, Spanish researchers insisted sexual diversity be included in "early childhood education in order to promote its social normalization."[31] A few years later, thousands of adults marched in Madrid, demanding "affective-sexual diversity" in schools, which they openly described as "a political instrument to normalize homosexuality." By 2013, this was literally echoed word for word in US medical journals, as if they thought it all up themselves.

Why is gay rhetoric never questioned by these geniuses? It's easy to follow the bread crumbs left from biased Spanish academics, all the way to the American Medical Association (AMA). In their policies for LGBT issues, the AMA now takes non-medical stands to push homosexuality in children. AMA policy (H-65.979) asks youth organizations to *"reconsider exclusionary policies that are based on sexual orientation or gender identity."*[32] Why? Is it easier to rubberstamp anything from Europe than to research or think for yourself?

Making something socially acceptable doesn't make it less spiteful or evil. Child sex trafficking has been the norm in Thailand for centuries – should we accept it as well? Certainly, it's more "diverse." We've evolved our own forms of abuse, vicariously using children to champion and play out adult lifestyles and fantasies.

MEDIA STAGE MOTHERS

Western media giants are the gay movement's pushy stage mothers. Without their tender nurture and running interference, there would be no gay marriage and no harassed Navy chaplains. "Caitlyn" would be only an embarrassing family secret, possibly showing up in a psychological case-study somewhere.

Most of the largest press and networks worked hard to see this day, although it isn't clear what they hope to gain by it. Common tactics are half-truths, misleading interviews, ignoring the big picture, slander, and presenting things with no context. For example, in the run-up to the 2014 Winter Olympics, media claimed that gay parades had been effectively "banned" in Russia. But there were no Pride events there until Western activists imported the concept. Public gay parades are recent inventions everywhere, belonging to no national tradition or culture. Although they are legal in many free nations, they are sometimes culturally offensive. Patriarch Alexey II, past head of the Russian Orthodox Church, claimed that Gay Pride events were merely "propaganda for homosexuality." Russians are experts on propaganda, and call it when they see it.

US News pasted a verifiably false 2011 headline on Rick Perry's "Fringe Views" about gay marriage, claiming a majority of

Americans had "a different take on gay marriage" than Perry and other GOP candidates.[33] Yet, in 2011, US voters had rejected *every* proposition to legalize gay marriage. It existed in seven states, only because courts and legislatures imposed it on voters.[34] Biased and unreliable, the Rainbow News Service presumes readers are ignorant enough to swallow their dissimulation. This includes their fictional, unreferenced statistics supporting homosexuality.

Google (the world's most valued company) hosted a Chrome browser honoring Christian-reviler and gay-sex columnist Dan Savage. His *"It Gets Better"* program pushes gay teens to never question their lifestyle, in spite of parental anguish, and the fact that they are much more likely to kill themselves than straight kids. At least two boys Savage enlisted to help make his anti-suicide videos took their lives, shortly after. One was only 14.[35] This isn't an accusation against Savage or these organizations, but they clearly couldn't help these boys. Google et al, are part of the *problem,* working arm-in-arm to keep sexually abused kids far from those who may offer them hope. For these confused and tormented youth, *"It Just Gets Worse."*

Robert Stacy McCain is an expert on media fixation for virtually anything prefixed by "gay." McCain summed up the embarrassing sycophant syndrome of liberal media. "Journalists today cannot report about homosexuality, they must only advocate, endorse, praise and celebrate homosexuality." [36] This reduces reporters to the role of parroting propagandists for gay-rights.

Common media also actively suppresses the depth of gay hatred, perversion, and violence against their neighbors. The "Observatory on Intolerance and Discrimination against Christians" documents anti-Christian incidents in Europe, which generally come via Muslims, homosexuals, and the State. None of those are officially listed as "hate groups", even as they indulge their inner felons.[37]

Robert Oscar Lopez observed the rise of the Rainbow Reich from both sides, and remarks how ably they are aided by the press. He describes the LGBTQ lobby playing hard in England, France, and America because those are major centers of world power. After establishing laws protecting homosexuals (only) from all forms of hostile criticism, gay zealots began courting influential culture shifters: *The Guardian, Libération* and *The New York Times.*[38] These grand dames of the Fourth Estate displayed a senile susceptibility to flattery and prejudice, and are still eating from the hands of LBGT cadre. Lopez notes that through their help, "Ligbitists" (his name for LGBT activists) are "poised to play offense" with no need for defense.[39]

AMERICA'S PINKED-UP SOLDIERS

Homofascists are feeling smug. They've gained the power to project their sexual fantasies out of the closet and onto the tarmacs and firing fields of the great US military. Persecution has been particularly harsh in the armed forces, where serious Christians were used for target practice. Ex-President Obama hath made it so, due to his great spiritual illuminations on the matter. Imagine the possibilities when homosexuality is no longer constrained to Pride Parades, but unleashed on the real world.

We've had previews under our past Commander in Chief and his appointed ones – officers replacing the hundreds purged in an ideological bloodbath. Made in Obama's image, these newly minted officers shared simultaneous epiphanies on the role of gays in the military. It's uncanny. LGBT theory replaces military study, according to some retired officers who are free to speak. It is sucking up undue amounts of time and resources, which weakens us in war. Unfortunately, the only battles that matter to many in DC are sex wars.

Defense Secretary Ashton Carter (under Obama) no longer tolerated mere "acceptance" of gay service members. He demanded shock and awe for the 3.7%, by rigorous observance of June's "Gay & Lesbian Pride Month" initiated by Bill Clinton. Another month for gay adulation was bestowed in 2015. Latest addendum is November, commandeered by transgenders as their self-proclaimed month to be Even More Special. Can you hear our enemies laughing?

This insignificant minority has done absolutely nothing worthy, *as a separate class,* to bestow them a full 1/6 of the year to be worshipped. (I am not referring to their service, for which they deserve praise with other soldiers). Apparently, they get a new month for each letter tacked on the LGBTQI+++ acronym. Only black Americans are even close to being so honored, but for historically documented mistreatment, and while they served. This is national *offense* – not defense.

Gay designs on America's military were evident at least since 2007, when they staged mock outrage and disinformation campaigns against General Peter Pace. The General had ventured his personal opinion (in a non-official capacity) that homosexual relations are immoral. He made no effort to change policy. Pressure on Congress caused Pace to be "vehemently denounced and condemned" for failing gay compliance.[40] Pace was the Chairman of the Joint Chiefs of Staff – one of the most powerful positions in the world's most powerful nation. But we folded like wet panties against the hot steam of gay spite. Shortly afterward, the General was demoted – the first Chairman of the Joint Chiefs of Staff to *not* be assigned a second term, since the position existed.

Pace's downfall was expedited by the nastiness and unbalanced power of gay militancy in Washington, and he is not the only brass to speak up. Retired Army Maj. Gen. Patrick Brady accused former President Obama of "emasculating the military" in preference to homosexuals and women in combat. An anonymous Coast Guard crewman claimed most of his drills are on "things like diversity and preventing sexual harassment." Are we in danger of an imminent straight, male, Anglo-Saxon invasion? "It's becoming a joke, this country is in trouble" the reservist warned.

The rest of the poor schmucks toiling in our military who aren't sodomically-gifted, won't be getting any special favors soon. But that isn't the only insult the Brave New Brass dealt them. As part of multipronged bayonets in the backs of Christian soldiers, they denied religious expression for troops, and extended this even to Chaplains. They're treated like naughty boys and girls caught using wicked words from a Book of the Enemy (the Bible).

There are dozens of cases of pettiness, slander, and harassment against Christians. Col. Christopher Downey is one victim of the Gender-Non-Specific Army. Downey asked a lesbian couple in 2014 to refrain from kissing and "grabbing each other on the butt" which is prohibited (for all species) at public Army dances.[41] Upholding military decorum brought Col. Downey humiliation, various ad hoc criminal charges, and removal from service. Downey earned three Bronze Stars and seven Air Medals, but had not been informed the US Army was now a gay recruitment center, where regulations don't apply to lusty lesbians.

Who does this to people headed for war, and just to make political points? Christian apartheid emerged from the united efforts of a few radical homosexualists, Islamists, Marxists, and atheists. They comprise only a sliver of the Armed forces. After years of begging "tolerance", these activists revealed it was just a ploy. If the girl-groper who destroyed a fellow soldier's career is a clue, many homosexuals have little tolerance – and no gratitude, or loyalty for those who helped them climb the ranks.

Britain, which has tolerated child rape for decades, is seeing the practice continue with bigger boys now. In 2013, men in groups of seven, gang-raped young male soldiers "in a deeply degrading manner" according to charges.[42] At least 25 military, homosexual assaults were reported in two years, and there may be many more. True to course, newspapers didn't denounce the crime directly, nor was there any mention of homosexuality. They couched these awful crimes as instances of "bullying" and "hazing" as if they were naughty children. The *Times-UK* used this title, "Soldiers accused of gang rape in "routine" bullying."[43] Making a minor charge of *bullying* is an oblique means of promoting homosexual rape of their soldiers. Labelling it as "routine" implies its normalcy.

As homosexual unions are honored and promoted, Christianity is simultaneously despised and attacked. If the two are compatible, our governments are making certain they will not remain so. America's religious fighters are humiliated by enforced fawning over a subpopulation they may personally find revolting, yet are still forced to bunk with. Obama's appointees treated our soldiers like cultural units in a chess game, where the prizes were anything but military success or national protection. Give them a few armies and who knows what they will do next?

But if the last few years of America's pinked-up soldiers have been a teaser – it's beginning to look like an adult horror flick.

4

"HOMOPHOBIA" IS A HOAX

Like most of us with a rudimentary understanding of English, you may have been puzzled when the faux neurosis "homophobia" was first lobbed into a conversation. Huh? Cobbled together, the Greek words mean only "fear of the same." "Homophobia" is an empty charge, full of sound and fury, and meaning less than nothing. Construction of "homophobia" was part of a verbal craft-project meant to shut down intelligent conversation. If you're using the word, that means it worked.

Homophobia's de facto meaning is "what to blame when homosexuals don't get their way" and is acted out in the real world, all the time. It's the cleverest ploy to hamstring resistance to their cause. "Homophobia" is kept alive by a set of lies. Predicated on the myth of victimhood, the term has lost all meaning (except to the government and bureaucracies, which don't need any). Homophobia is a political construct used to justify something which is senseless. Because, "victim." Because, "homophobia." Whatever.

LAMENTATION, DARKNESS AND WOE

Gay lives are an endless chain of tragedies, dreariness and cruel hardship, they insist. In this chorus, homosexuals are tragically oppressed and unfairly hated. Children spit on them in the street. They've blamed their parents, fraternities, history, literature, God, schools, culture, comedians, language, mean kids in school, the Church, genetics, conservatives, poor psychology, bad medicine, opposing opinions, and inability to find Manolo Blahniks in a men's size 13. There's no end of tragedy brought on by those horrible, "homophobic" people who vote Republican and do other evil deeds. Woe is they.

Reality sings a different tune. Homosexuals are among the most successful persons in virtually all spheres of influence in the West – far more than the average religious family that many of them detest. With no or few children, they can focus on their careers and making life miserable for conservatives. Gays are often in positions of authority and prestige, and disproportionally swimming in dough. Census data and research proves their relatively posh lives, but you can easily make a simple count of any 100 top (fill in the blanks) and there will be far more than the 3.7% who fall somewhere along the LGBTQI+++ spectrum. As a class, the wealthy and elite of all orientations support even the most radical gay agendas. Inversely, they tend to detest traditional Christianity – and a good proportion do so with extreme prejudice.

Because "homophobia" doesn't exist (except for molested altar boys and such, who have good reason to fear gay men) – it can never be refuted. It's a basic rule of logic. Insinuations of *hate,* disseminated by the gay community, are so convoluted that they could never be intelligently studied. And would selfless LGBTQers lie? Why not? Homosexuality isn't founded on the Ten Commandments. There is no valid scholarship or psychology to back up the endlessly looping, self-contradiction that is "homophobia." No classical research supports the existence of this dread moral state, and anything written over the last few decades is a moot point. Useless because Politically Correct thinking is obligatory in colleges, where questioning "homophobia" is a bullet to the head.

Ghastly attacks of "homophobia" are attributed to several things, but lack of compassion is the charge most often lobbed at the accused. We can accept on face-value testimonies that their life has a certain amount of ostracism and pain. While admitting things are difficult, most deny that any of this is caused by their own lifestyle or choices. Surely a gay man or woman prefers to be loved and accepted by everyone unconditionally. Who doesn't? But this doesn't happen for any of us, unless you're a Pomeranian puppy. You can't force love or acceptance, although LGBT activists are trying mightily. Perhaps to escape self-reflection, or the need to change, gay academics and militants project their anguish on someone else. Scapegoating others to avoid dealing with your own issues is the entirety of "homophobia".

In the real world, adults try to agree on how to best live together. Some of them have beliefs and religions forbidding homosexual behavior – for *themselves.* No one chooses their religion merely because it rejects homosexuality. But exporters of the doctrine of "homophobia" insist that it must be the only reason we would keep any faith at all.

OCCUPY LANGUAGE

Successfully pulling off the *homophobia* ruse, various activists are cranking out dozens of new possibilities. One of these is the dismantling of language and common meaning, which colleges around the world gleefully do to service homosexuality, Marxism, and other totems. Proof that homophobia is a modern invention is at anyone's fingertips. I used a few older software programs to research this book. None were over a dozen years old, and not one listed "homophobia" in their dictionaries, either in British or American English.

Anyone can make a meaningless phrase, but it takes effort and time to move them onto mainstream use. With friends in high places and low character, it happens much faster. "Homophobia" is undoubtedly on children's spelling lists now, as it's a required subject in many states. Imagine the gay-friendly beginning readers (1960s style): "Dick and Fred see Jane. Jane does not like Dick.

Jane is Homophobic. Spot bites Jane – good dog." Expect to encounter many new socially prescribed taboos.

Launching these idiocies into public consciousness, the daily phobia is picked up by social media or cultural change agents. New words to entrench gay occupation may be something like these:

"Prefam": Ready-made children, through surrogates or adop tion.

"Stroles": Straight and servile beings.

"Gayspeak": Party line put out to defend all things homo sexual.

"Truth" - Anything but…

Our poor, mind-numbed tots are sitting ducks for social experimentation, and are drilled from birth to fear offending those in power. "Homophobia" is one of the few mortal sins left for them at schools. Homofascists introduced the new "Scarlet Letter", and it's a flaming "H." Transgressors are punished by the priesthood of a sexually fueled inquisition, who pressure teachers and school-boards to serve them. Alms must continually be paid to "victims" of homophobia in the forms of grant money, promotions, and the special status of *never* being questioned. .

"Homophobia" is an intellectual black hole absorbing all light and attempts to observe it. Objective questions are forbidden, because they are proof of – "homophobia." (Much like the drowning of New England's witches was seen as proof of their own sins). Reason is always taboo in discussions of homosexuality. Since it appears to work against all skeptics, "homophobia" has become the magic mojo for Gay Voodoo. Academic witch doctors are allowed to curse and intimidate all non-believers exhibiting signs of "homophobia" and drive them from their sects.

Opposition to gay promotion in schools, is punished by peer rejection. Jaded adults running the show know that it's a fate worse than death to teens. Hyping fears of catching "homophobia", makes our schools look like a dress rehearsal for *Lord of the Flies.* Indoctrination and threats of leaving the herd follow our students into university and beyond, where it's self-propagating. Adults frozen in perpetual infancy will seek the approval of others, and are unable to make vital decisions on their own. Thank the great Homophobic Panic of the 21st Century for this.

It's not unusual for entire nations to be jerked around by something that doesn't exist. Europeans blamed Jews for the Great Plague. Plain Salem girls in 1692 believed that attractive women communed with witches, or their husbands. Not so long ago, the Chinese People's Army convinced millions of uneducated youth that people who wore glasses should die. Some South African men rape toddlers, believing it will cure AIDS. All are convenient lies for political empowerment or personal pleasure – much like the campaign against "homophobia."

At some point, shame-saturation will take hold and "homophobia" will stop working its magic. (After hundreds of accusations, loss of freedom, prison terms, court cases, miles of code, job terminations and heavily censured books, films, music, term papers and articles.) "Homophobia" will lose its power to terrify, just as indigenous people lost their awe of white gods with gadgets centuries ago. The entire campaign proves we are no more sophisticated or intelligent now, and can be just as easily controlled.

RAINBOW-SPRINKLED RANCOR

Submissive pushers of the rules of homophobia are most deserving of contempt. Knowing it does nothing to benefit them or humanity, these straight teachers, politicians, and celebrities appease the mobs before they reach their own doors. They are true "homophobes", serving militant homosexuals out of fear, but not from genuine belief.

It isn't "phobic" to hold your own opinion, regardless of threats and ostracism. Such men and women are rare. Because courage is catching (like the Red Square protestor) all oppressors fear these people. Under the new hate-crusade banner of eradicating "homophobia" they snare and attempt to silence the few who fearlessly speak their minds. Even if they are kind, peaceful, and reasonable – they are not well tolerated in a gay-centric world.

By extraordinary coincidence, we are living the combined nightmares of novelists Aldous Huxley and George Orwell at this exact moment. Overlords in Huxley's "Brave New World" imposed a falsely gay society (in the traditional sense of the word). Now, our sitcoms yuck it up over the adorable little gay fellas and their harmless antics. Orwell divined a time (in his novel "1984") when language would become meaningless and humiliating. We are bringing this dark vision to life too, and the following chapters will count the ways.

5

HISTORICAL & LITERARY REVISION (first fatality, free-speech)

Dystopian nightmares are studded with slogans and hyperbole, but not by chance. Propaganda takes planning and hard work. Slogans and jargon are immeasurably useful to those who hope to rescript history as well. Tyrants use them as tools to rationalize oppressive regimes, and academics create lovely theories to help prop them up. Eventually, politically expedient speech finds its way into new legislation, textbooks, and mission statements.

Scholars needing original source information about anything touching on historical homosexuality are finding the way increasingly gated and chained. A website with translated speeches by Nazis on homosexuality comes up with dire warnings from supposed security site, Web of Trust (W.O.T.): "This website is unsafe", abandon all hope, and so on. Apparently, knowledge is perilous. Pro-family and pro-life sites are treated similarly. Unsafe to leave the lockstep, leftist herd. Electronic thought monitors like these exist to protect a specious gay narrative – not the safety of users.

I'LL HUFF AND I'LL PUFF...

Well, there are always books, especially old ones. Those are tougher to limit – but not impossible. Book stores generally self-censor to dodge unpleasant gay activists screaming down their aisles. Public libraries subjugated themselves to political correctness years ago, and answer only to their most martial clients.

When Fairfax County High School students tried to donate conservative books on homosexuality to school libraries, all 40 of them were turned down because they didn't meet "school standards." Standards were just dandy for books currently parked on their shelves, which promote the lifestyle to children. Conservatives visiting the 2011 Printer's Row Literature Festival in Chicago asked visitors which of eleven authors they'd like to see banned. Sarah Palin was the most detested at 36%, and other conservative writers earned another 50% of bannings. Bill Clinton, Michael Moore, Marx, and Obama weren't nearly so threatening. They gathered fewer vetoes than Hitler, who logged only 0.05% of the votes![44]

Publishers may be most affected by gay cultural terrorists, because stapled to every militant are at least two attorneys. When Scott Lively and Kevin Adams first attempted to publish their bombshell book *"The Pink Swastika"* in 1995, they had difficulty finding someone to dare take them on. It's readable and well researched, so the non-conformist content was the only problem. A year after its publication, specialized squads had formed solely to manufacture disinformation against *Pink Swastika,* questioning every quote, citation, and statistic.

Gay inculcation in schools hastens the death of personal beliefs about romance and procreation. First it was hip to be promiscuous, sophisticated, and irreligious. Next it was taught that it *must* be so, particularly to children, the ever captive and helpless audience. People may have a problem with that, but "people" don't matter much. When are parents ever asked their opinion over curriculum in schools? Students are now marinated like pieces of meat in Queer Theory, Gay Explorers and other idiocy.

Pioneer homosexuals used a combination of stealth and deceit to get their cannon balls rolling against all the little straight kids. Most academics don't require deceit though, as they are easily drafted by a few slogans and any career threat. These are the major players for gay cultural dominance. For example, unfortunate students of Michael Johnson Jr., at Washington State University, are required to "acknowledge" various oppressions, including "heterosexism."[45] This newly hatched concept was created by queer theorists. Because it would tank in the world of open ideas, people like Johnson use his pitiful students to acknowledge "heterosexism" into reality. It's gay academic magic.

College students have been forced to interpret virtually everything (i.e. mutton, plasma physics and architecture) through contrived relations to Marxism, imperialism and patriarchy. Recently "gender studies" joined the club, which attempts to cast a veneer of respectability on gay life. *Gender* is code for Anything but Heterosexual, although it occasionally references (genetic) women.

DON'T YOU (ZIM, ZIR, EM) DARE

Playing with words is one of the more benign forms of domination. Non-sexual terms "queer" "gay" and "faggot" were commandeered by homosexuals, and we allowed them to dictate their use. Now pronouns make the front lines of this battle. What began as a biologically backed triumvirate (he, she, it) is joined with at least five more gender designations. "Zim, Hir, Zir, Em" and "Per" are nonsense words referencing *nothing*, but they have cases and objects, which people are now required to learn. It's a form of harassment against people who have better things to do with their time.

Selena Lester Breikss, of Washington State University, threatened to fail students for using the terms "male" or "female" in zir/per/his/her exalted presence.[46] Scripps College, University of Tennessee, and various outposts in Oz forced dozens of new pronouns on their scholars too – perhaps as some kind of hazing ritual to see if they are servile enough to remain students there.

One newly-coined term is "heterosexualist", implying male-female relations are merely another obscure, specialty relationship, which needs to be catalogued. When the suffix "ist" is added to the end of a word, it means to follow or master a philosophy, profession, or system (i.e. Marxist or cellist). Several dictionaries add that "ist" often refers to political movements, and make it clear that you can't be born as any kind of "ist." "Heterosexualism" will likely creep into fifth-graders' spelling books to confuse them even more, as they mature.

California lawmakers now require public schools to teach "Gay Social Studies" to children of all ages. They're going to have to clean it up to avoid reading like hot porn – or perhaps that's the idea. Luminaires include Harvey Milk, who was *very* kind to street boys in their hour of need. Harry Hay, activist and early supporter of the "North American Man-Boy Love Association" (NAMBLA) is another they will learn to admire, to pass their classes. Curious students may check out some of the brilliant insights of other NAMBLA pioneers as well. Life is certain to improve in California thanks to these efforts – at least for those on sex-offender roles.

Sodomy enthusiasts insist that normalizing gayness for the kiddies will insure no one is "bullied." They pretend that a monstrous invasion of a child's innocence and budding sexual curiosity (or lack before they showed up) is nothing. Worse than bullying, it's intentional abuse, engineered to keep a small percentile of creepy California adults happy. Or gay. The real lesson for kids is that 3.7% of the population is "special" because of what they do in bed, and that they can be "special" too. One way they do this is by trashing heroes of the past and repainting them pink.

Our students are raised in bigoted political constructs at this point and not much else. Unless you are in a gay bar or a San Francisco city council meeting, the average person is NOT gay. By definition, it is neither normal nor natural, even if teacher is now forced to say that it is. Straight students trapped in this power struggle have no choice but to submit and play intellectually dead, if they wish to graduate. Conservative and Christian kids are forced to learn the language of their oppressors and agree with what they know is utter nonsense.

For virtual prisoners of America's schools and universities, there is no escaping the iron claws of reality-revisionistas. Or as columnist Donald Douglas so colorfully put it: "It's never about just basic truth with the homosexual left. It's gotta be some bizarre, deranged cooked-up lie designed to eradicate the existing "heteronormative" hierarchies of "homophobic" society."[4]

COMING OUT" WHEN YOU'RE DEAD

Hey kids, let's play hide-and-seek for homoerotica from the grave! Shakespeare and Bible-quoting Lincoln won't be spared. John Milton certainly wasn't. In a 2015 research paper, Christianity's most revered poet is slandered as a "A Queer Poet in a Queer Time."[48] Milton is the author of our greatest English epic and religious, poem, *Paradise Lost.* His work, marriages, and love affairs (with women) shout a healthy heterosexuality. The man was also an outspoken Puritan, who claimed to live "aloof from vice."

Nothing in Milton's life implied he was gay, except in the minds of demented academics. Sifting through his elegy to a dear male friend and finding the word "intimate" was enough for them, although it was common enough at the time. Milton's appraisal of politics of his day sadly applies to the gay supremacists we now face. He describes an "epidemic madness and general defection of a misguided and abused multitude".[49]

No one is off-limits. Virtually all revered, accomplished persons were either gay, bi-sexual or definitely thinking about it all the time. This is the take-home from higher education, thanks to "Queer Studies." None of the giants are shown the respect of being taken at their word, but sifted and deconstructed for links to gayness, as it was the Holy Grail. It's a projection of a universe circumscribed by their own genitalia. Scholarship is shriveling with it.

Celebrated men and women of yore are shoved through the meat grinder of sex-reassignment via "gender" studies as well. History wizards are sent forth to magically change the past into a sordid, gay-rewrite based on their own fantasies. Existence of spouses, children, religious standing, witnesses, or scandalous hetero affairs (with shockingly lurid love notes) – none of this is enough to spare them from the sex-maddened revisionist.

For individuals proving impossible to recast in a gay image, their work is still presented as brimming with lurid, gay innuendo. Artists are described as using "heteronormative imagery" if they fail the gay litmus test. Somehow, it's laden with homosexuality – even when it isn't. All creation is painted over with a toxic, rainbow oil-slick, and students are required to regurgitate this on demand. Because underneath it all, everyone is really gay after all; they just haven't discovered it yet. This is why Queer Studies and Queer Theory were devised, to help them along the shining path.

Until modern times, charges of homosexuality were considered a seriously *hateful* move; one that could get you arrested or killed in a duel. Reputations were ruined that way, and it tended to piss people off – especially if untrue. Fencing matches are unlikely to happen now, but there are still lawsuits. Gay revisionists are generally wary enough to wait until their marks are thoroughly dead before they tell children of their wondrous, possibly gay deeds, and newly discovered exploits. With no living witnesses, who could deny it?

Gay propagandists create a parallel world to accomplish their aims. So few, using so many, to accomplish so little. Einstein hasn't been dead long enough for progressive pimps to ravage his reputation, but give them a few years. They'll have a Unified Theory of Homoeroticism driving physics if enough of them get PhDs.

BENDING SINISTER

Homosexuality was generally mocked or only alluded to in Western literature, but few writers seriously tackled the subject in fiction. Vladimir Nabokov is an exception who can't be easily shot down.

Nabokov was one our greatest 20th century writers, and a brilliant thinker as well. No amount of spin and tap dancing can change that. Gay hate machines haven't dismantled Vladimir yet, because their worst charges of either "right winger" or "religious. . ." (fill in the blank) don't apply a wit. Nabokov biographer Brian Boyd insists he was "profoundly indifferent" to religion, and he is best known for his 1955 novel "Lolita" with its pedophilic protagonist.[49] Hardly church fare.

But an earlier Nabokov novel, *Bend Sinister* (1946) is still steaming gay gladiators. Like Orwell's "1984", it's a dystopian tale of enforced uniformity and state worship. Protagonist Adam Krug struggles with the usual: propaganda, his conscience, and a nasty antagonist, "Paduk", the dictator. The novel takes a *Bend Sinister* (or left turn) when Adam's young son is kidnapped and violently murdered by gangs of criminal homosexuals.

Nabokov clearly implies that not only is Paduk gay, but also appears to take some pleasure in the boy's death. Certainly, he had a hand in it. Mirroring our times, Adam had resisted social and political pressures to promote something he found repulsive; Paduk's leadership in this case. But he also fought an overlaying homoerotic fascism of the state, which eventually destroyed the only thing he truly loved.

Certainly, the average homosexual isn't a vicious child killer, but Nabokov just didn't like them. This was in the 1950s, when people still had the right to choose whom they associated with, and what they wrote. Living through both the Russian Revolution and the rise of Nazism, Nabokov specifically chose homosexuality as characteristic of an extremely evil regime.

Liberal critics outdo each other, making a case that Nabokov had emotional issues or family problems, or was just "homophobic" – their snake-oil cure for the inexplicable. When the novel is mentioned or summarized, sources like Goodreads and Wikipedia fail to even note this major element of homosexuality. Some writers now insist the man was gay, torturing his words into some kind of fabricated confession. Letting his title speak for itself, Nabokov explained that for him *Bend Sinister* was "a distortion in the mirror of being, a wrong turn taken by life".[50]

New York City has taken a sharp left-turn as well. Our greatest metropolis is in full thralldom (as of 2017) to their nouveau-powerful transgender minority. Decrees for proper Trans-grammar use are issued from City Hall, which apparently is their fiefdom. Men, poorly dressed as women, must be met with a hushed and reverential awe, as if encountering gods. Wayward pronouns, unmerited giggles, or eye-rolling can net residents up to $250,000 in fines and other punishments. That should run anyone with a modicum of intelligence out of the Gay Hate Authority. Mayor De Blasio, who initiated this abuse, should have fun with what's left. He has it coming.

Psycho-drivel is part of a global fairytale we must all engage in, or they'll send the wicked witches from the Department of Justice (DOJ) after us. Even their employees aren't safe, or at least not during the Obama regime. DOJ workers received brochures "requiring them to verbally affirm homosexuality regardless of their personal beliefs" according to a 2015 Fox News report.[51] Truly sinister was this line; "Silence will be interpreted as disapproval," along with the demand to "place pro-gay stickers" in their offices.[52] It's reminiscent of North Korean military parades, where officials showing "lack of enthusiasm" were put to death. We don't know where this is headed, but it no longer looks like America.

Another branch hacked away at is the Holocaust. Gay historians assert that between 1939 -1944, multitudes of gay men and women were persecuted by Nazis, although police records show lesbianism was not even a crime then.[53] Showing true genius at exploiting other people's tragedies, gay revisionists came up with (drum rolls and lights please) "The Homocaust." Numbers of gay victims swing from 15,000 to "millions" depending on the author. Millions of Poles were murdered in reality– where is the Polocaust?

Homosexuals were never forced to wear pink triangles on the streets, as Jews wore yellow stars. Pink-triangles were also issued to rapists or child molesters, yet "Homocaust" promoters claim homosexuals were treated "even worse" than Jews.[53] Some academics claim that most jailed homosexuals were also Jewish, which was a far worse crime to Nazis. As the United States Holocaust Memorial Museum explained: "It should be noted that Nazi authorities sometimes used the charge of homosexuality to discredit and undermine their political opponents"[54]

IMPERIALISM, THY NAME IS SODOM

Aldous Huxley should be canonized patron saint of beat-up conservatives by now. He divined this assault on family and sanity long ago in his novel, *Brave New World*. He just didn't think they would wear so much makeup. Gay activists are now busy reconstituting the history of almost every nation on earth, as well as attempting to dictate culture. Isn't this what all imperialists do in their spare time?

The Obama administration placed flamboyantly gay ambassadors in nations who find the lifestyle repulsive. Cardinals in the Dominican Republican fiercely objected to the placement of openly gay Ambassador James "Wally" Brewster. He and his male "wife" hurled insults and otherwise intervened in domestic Dominican affairs, all to better his sexual peers. Natives accused us of imposing America's sexual morality on the Dominican Republic, which was absolutely true.[55]

The US State Department boldly proclaimed its policy under Obama: "Advancing the Human Rights of Lesbian, Gay, Bisexual and Transgender Persons Worldwide: A State Department Priority." [56] It may have been their only priority. American spokesmen suggested the Church in those nations was standing "in opposition to human rights." Gay couples sent to represent America far exceed their representation anywhere on this planet. It may be enlightening to determine how many US Ambassadors were not gay, and what that percentage signifies.

Deliberately offending your host nation is a clear inversion of "diplomacy" and just stupid. We now send diplomats merely to force LGBTQ policy on others against their will. *The New York Times* generally emblazons their wedding announcements for them. Hanscom Smith married Lu Yingzong while he was US Consul General in Shanghai, in 2016. Same-sex marriages are illegal in China.[57] Smith followed British Consul General, Brian Davidson, who married Scott Chang in 2014, in Beijing. Chinese officials were not amused then either.

Robert Oscar Lopez relates how he was approached by a French journalist who asked him about coming from a nation considered an ally, but which "forced homosexual ideology" on them.[58] Diplomatic strategies for most of the world don't include making certain homosexuals are having a good time. Even Pope Francis noted the imperialistic tide covering gay ideology in 2015, and he has not been unkind to homosexuals: "There are also ideological colonializations of the family, different paths and proposals in Europe and also coming from overseas. Then, there is the mistake of the human mind — gender theory — creating so much confusion. So, the family really is under attack."[59] Our gay export policy is ill advised.

Ugandans had their own dark past with pederastic rulers, and they still remember them. King Mwanga burnt at least 30 young men alive in 1886, because they were Christian and rejected his sexual advances. Although he had at least 16 wives, he also raped various boys at hand. British LGBT activist Edwin Sesange blamed the entire slaughter on "missionaries." Making a case that Africans were natively "gay", Sesange considered martyrs only collateral damage. "Today also marks the anniversary of the introduction of homophobia in Uganda, and a condemnation of a traditional African way of life," he claimed in 2014.[60] Uganda still commemorates Christian martyrs to homosexuality every June 3rd, with great fanfare. This drives militants mad, because historical narratives where homosexuals are the bad guys must be scrubbed. History be damned.

African gay rights group SMUG, was even more bizarre in its definition of "rights" and who should be allowed to have them. Claiming sexual psychopath Mwanga as a "traditional African," SMUG makes a case that raping and burning people alive is normative, and apparently good for Africans.[61] Joseph Kony and Boko Haram aren't close enough for them? Other history websites helpfully scrub all reference to the sexual orientation of King Mwanga, or attribute their martyrdom to anything but religion and sex. Encyclopedia Britannica (online) didn't even hint at the king's homosexuality. Wikipedia editors laid it down to disobedient "male harem" boys, as if they were defense lawyers for old King Mwanga.

6

CENSOR AND ABUSE OF THE NON-COMPLIANT

Frank questions and disapproval are now verboten when it comes to homosexuality. Every sentient adult knows this, and has likely experienced it – but they are welcome to lie to themselves if it makes them feel better. No American movement has perfected self-censoring and auto thought-control so well as the "anti-hate speech" crew. Truly, money and politicians have achieved great things.

Conservatives who stood on their convictions have suffered horribly though. Behold the insane depravity directed at conservative leaders and spokesmen on the following pages. Quaint little idioms of their denouncers are often too vulgar to print, but this hasn't kept them out of the Senate. Oddly enough, no one accuses these activists and their supporters.of spreading "hate" though it oozes from every syllable, and breath.

FIRST DRY RUN – ANITA BRYANT

Anita Bryant was the first public test case for gay abuse. Campaigning against a 1977 Dade County ordinance over "gay discrimination" – she questioned the end goals of the measure. Advocates claimed gays were being denied fair housing and employment, especially in teaching positions. Media failed to report that homosexuals could teach in Dade County, but were required to keep their sexual preference out of "show and tell" time – exactly as straight teachers have always done. Neither were gay people living in tent cities before this movement.

Bryant strenuously opposed adults discussing their sexual proclivities with children, which is what this boils down to. Only teachers making public pronouncements on their sex lives would ever be affected in any way. This was too obvious for American media to catch on. Gay militants made one of their first power moves, and Bryant checked them. She did it alone, and was crushed on every side. The following 40-year onslaught of venom and intimidation was a clue to America's future, as well as the character of the gay movement's leaders.

Decades later, virulent hatred for Anita Bryant is hardly explainable unless ascribed to demonic possession or dementia. Homosexuals and their acolytes left thoughts on a YouTube video of Bryant being struck with a pie in 1977. Of 4,336 public comments, most were vulgar, violent, threatening and used (apparent) real names. No shame over their enthusiastic and self-righteous contempt. Following are a few tidbits from one of many online, gay hate-club rallies against Anita Bryant (names and some obscenity are obscured here):

> *DG: "I would have thrown acid in the b**ch's face instead!!!"* [62]
>
> *SS: "Nothing but s**t ever came from her ignorant face. I'd love to see some given back to her. C**t."* [63]
>
> *TG: ". . .So F**K Anita Bryant put the B**CH in prison make her F**KING PAY runner up pig"* [64]

Gay hate, it never ends. Imagine such a dismal, irrelevant life, that a juvenile attack almost half a century ago is the zenith of your existence. Posters mentioned the joy they feel replaying this video. Still stuck on *hate,* but too dull and self-referential to admit it. A case could be made that these venom-bloated bigots are not the norm, but sadly, it won't hold up. No forum of even mild-mannered homosexuals and their liberal supporters is much different. Perpetual hostility is the norm. Gay activists are unspeakably obscene as a rule, and rarely civil. Voilà, the Joy of Gayness.

Bryant has since proved spot-on in her analysis. A modern Cassandra, she saw the pending deluge of vitriol if we continued congratulating gay militants for their sex acts, while ignoring their aggression. Bryant reacted to their nascent power move in the 1970s, and had her tongue ripped out. Her predictions that gays would be forcing churches to marry them and adopting their children were prophetic. "Ludicrous!" her enemies shrieked in 1979, and then did exactly that. Media who hoisted Bryant's rope said nothing important or intelligent. As usual.

LON MABON

Scape Goat II (at a national level) was Oregon's Lon Mabon. Almost 20 years from the Bryant lynching, a younger generation was unaware of gay vitriol against perceived opposition. Yet few dared venture opinions on homosexuality outside of a pulpit or personal discussions in quiet corners. The national atmosphere was similar to mafia entrenchment after a successful Teamster riot.

Then along came Mr. Mabon and his Oregon Citizens Alliance (OCA), fielding conservative petitions in response to this ethical deep-freeze. Some were successful, driving Oregon's *gayngsters* mad. Liberal judges made certain the mistakes of the lowly people were rectified in favor of gay promotion though, and nullified their votes for decades. Mabon met gay and judicial aggression head on.

Since Bryant's crucifixion, few had openly confronted or criticized homosexual encroachment in the political arena. Offering Ballot Measure 9 in 1992 touched off a sharkfest. Mabon's petition dared touch upon the holy phallic cult, which (per liberal mythology), must not be blasphemed without horrific retribution. Fighting words from Measure 9:

> *"This state shall not recognize any categorical provision such as "sexual orientation," "sexual preference," and similar phrases that include homosexuality, pedophilia, sadism or masochism. Quotas, minority status, affirmative action, or any similar concepts, shall not apply to these forms of conduct, nor shall government promote these behaviors."* [65]

Mabon's efforts were met with met a perfect brimstorm of hate, with zero tolerance for faith or tradition. Leftists raged as if he had sacrificed their children and made their bodies into bratwurst. Reaction was hilarious (in a comedic-farce sort of way). Leftists mobilized in tabloid tradition, with headlines like "A Clear and Present Danger." In Portland's *Willamette Week* (1998), Patty Wentz described Mabon as a homophobic woman-hater. [66] Really? Rapes and murders were their daily bread, yet most of these journalists had never worked up a tear of lament – until Mabon. Ignoring the genocide of Kim Jong-Il and Robert Mugabe, they focused on a conservative Oregonian as the epitome of all evil.

Mabon and the OCA were treated like crash-dummies in the drive against conservatives. Gay-rights activist, Catherine Stauffer, showed up at an OCA meeting in 1992 as an obvious plant. Refusing to leave, a member escorted her out, giving her the excuse to claim "assault and battery." Thus commenced decades of malicious lawsuits – and Oregon courts proved they were up to snuff. OCA, Mabon, and others received large fines (for them, not having the means of their persecutors). Some they refused to pay because the charges were unjust and trumped up. Mabon eventually went to jail amid much fanfare, while Catherine Stauffer was canonized in Gaydom, a virtual saint in the Pantheon of Malice. Journalist Patty Wentz was rewarded for her smears with a series of high positions, including spokesman for Governor Ted Kulongoski (2007) and the Oregon Health Care Authority.[67]

Measure 9 is exaggerated to this day by liberals, as if they had survived the Great Plague. It's worked its way into legendary status, where Mabon is the beastly bigot whom brave gays and friends withstood – like Beowulf. Nothing could be further from the truth, which could be said of almost all LGBTQ lore. Vitriolic treatment of Bryant and Mabon left indelible scars on the psyche of the nation, while gays boast the Mabon family was run out of Oregon.

Supporters of California's pro-family Proposition 8 were similarly treated with mass scorn, greatly amplified by media. This gave militant gays yet another religion to hate, because Scientologists also supported Proposition 8, which would limit marriage to men and women (one of each).

Targets of gay-hate include all serious conservatives who have an audience, or who may possibly ever gain one. It isn't necessary to oppose homosexuality to be a recipient of gay death-rays – but most venom is stored for speakers and writers who dared to venture public opinions on the lifestyle. Using science, history, the Bible, interviews, news, science, and statistics, a handful of counter gay-supremacists scrutinize the gay narrative. Questioning homosexuality in its bloody glory, they found it wanting.

99 FLAVORS OF HOMOSEXUAL ABUSE

Beggars for "tolerance" a few years back, gay activists now lead the world in censorship and legal harassment. For instance, heavy gay handlers are steamed over the term "Gaystapo" and it may be a bit much. *Gay Stasi* is more exact, but not so catchy. If we called them choirboys, would there be fewer swarming schools or ratting on co-workers? When people live in fear of even whispering their true thoughts in public, the *Gaystapo* lives.

Victims of gay thug tactics are increasing by breadth, depth and type. In the past, they had to pick their marks carefully. Someone a little extreme, maybe wealthy, but always religious and white. With large chunks of the nation still reading their Bibles, and stubbornly sticking to family values, hate-appeals were low key and specialized; work on liberals first, next hit the schools.

Fortunately for them, few students have the courage to question orders any longer. Like cogs, they coast in neutral from elementary school to the grave, doing the bidding of the 3.7%, or other self-appointed Lords of Sanctioned Thought.

THE DAILY PREVARICATOR or *THE GLOBAL RAT?*

Without help from an enforcer-press none of this could have happened. Western newsrooms gush on as if nothing were more threatening to mankind than a gay joke. No doubt threats to their jobs are real. Virtually all major newscasters are in a lopsided servile relationship with the LGBT community. It's a weird bondage act with punishment, humiliation, and termination for those who have offended the self-chosen ones. Gay crusaders never had to even work up a sweat in their campaigns, since the press works as an advance army for them.

Even in the camps of the most manly, sports broadcasters are intimidated and tossed about like dog treats. There are dozens of examples, and probably more we'll never know. Evil Tweets brought the ejection of Canadian broadcaster Damian Goddard, for his non-standard issue belief on marriage. Football analyst Craig James was fired by "conservative" Fox News, for defending natural marriage *in his own political campaign*. They claimed he was "polarizing." Tut, tut.

Editors at most major news networks have a clear liberal bent, but vary in degree of censorship. Using their Tyrants-101 checklist, radical homosexualists target not only journalists, but celebrities, politicians and cultural icons. When major media scrape up the gumption to question their special ones over crimes or poor behaviour, they generally do it anonymously. Writers' names are replaced with "staff" or "reporter" to avoid retribution.

Social media is the big prize now, so this battle is fiercely fought there. The website "GoFundMe" shut down at least two Christian defense projects, which were, ironically, about highly publicized cases of *religious bigotry*. You can't make this up. Bakers Aaron and Melissa Klein and florist Barronelle Stutzman were denied basic civil rights in trumped up gay slander cases. "GoFundMe" administrators apparently felt the world needed a little more injustice. YouTube and Facebook actively squelch conservative opinion if it ruffles too many gay feathers, as well.

Owners of the Henager Drive-in theater in Alabama, felt the fist of mighty Facebook censors in March, 2017. Just 24 hours after announcing they would not be showing Disney's *Beauty and the Beast* because of an exuberantly gay character (in a children's film) – their Facebook page vanished.[68] Yet even physical threats against Christians are rarely removed, or noted on these social platforms.

Considering their teensy numbers, gay activists are given a heavy priority, or we wouldn't be hearing from them at all. Unequal consideration of homosexuality adversely affects many respected institutions, like the Catholic organization "Fathers for Life." They posted scientific studies warning that because of traumatic childhood abuse, gay parents are more likely to suffer anything from eating disorders to suicide.[97] For outing this research, some anti-virus programs (O2, Symantec, etc) blocked them from the eyes of the world in 2013. Who knows how many pro-family and pro-life websites they nobly "protect" us from? [69] Corporate execs are welcome to their opinions, but equating conservatives to a virus is just silly.

One of this millennium's first dry runs against media rebels was Dr. Laura Schlesinger, a moderately conservative talk-show host, into morals and other antiquities. Schlesinger managed to avoid major controversy for decades until she crossed the pink line. In a 2010 show, she allegedly claimed homosexuality was a "biological error" and "deviant" – but this may have never happened after all.[70] Dr. Laura's real crime was holding traditional family values. Furious that a popular celeb would deny homosexual superiority, a Hiroshima blast of gay malice was leveled at her. At 3.7% of the population, this should have gone unnoticed, but her remarks were amplified by gay echo-chambers in the press.

Schlesinger backed off and placed a contrite apology in *The Daily Variety* begging "forgiveness" of the gay community for hav ing an expert opinion. Her humiliation was useless, as no group is as petty as gay militants. Dr. Laura still has gay fans, despite Joan M. Garry of the Gay & Lesbian Alliance Against Defamation (GLAAD). Garry attempted to hold Schlesinger responsible for GLAAD's endless resentment: "The anger Schlesinger's words have caused is too great and too profound to simply go away after a qualified admission of some guilt." [71] How do they repeat this garbage with a straight face? Years later, the doctor was still receiving hate mail from enraged homosexuals.

FEARMONGERING FOR FUN AND PROFIT

Lying, cowardice, and mob rule aren't the only gifts "anti-hate speech" laws have bestowed on us. They also bring financial ruin and real rejection. Politicians fail elections and others lose promotions, once the dreaded "H" word descends on them. Photos of bedraggled conservatives hauled into court are becoming routine, and we are in danger of becoming accustomed to it.

Corporations like Starbucks used company profits to support gay efforts in their worker's names, as if they were indentured servants. Home Depot demands employees work surrounded by gay pride posters through the month of June. One complained that he is "forced to observe and promote LGBT month [as Home Depot] seeks to redefine morality, and therefore effectively defines religion." [72] Other businesses "request" their workers wear gay symbols and other obligatory forms of support. This is disrespectable and humiliating.

Many Americans find the only safe way to vent over speech monitoring is to anonymously rage in forums. A response from on online reader to the daily gay indignity: *"I'd rather wake up in a slime filled container with wires sticking out of me than be inundated with this psychotic faggotry every fu***ng day."* [73]

Gay thuggery increases with social acceptance. Katy Faust described how supporters of traditional marriage in the Obergefell vs. Hodges (gay marriage) court decision were treated – like Ebola culture on a fork. Interviewing with *USA Today*, Faust defined what all conservatives who filed amicus briefs in that case agreed on: that marriage between one man and one woman is in the best interest of children and society. These unrelated groups experienced nasty blowback from gaydom. Faust explained that in the current political climate, "it's easy to understand why children with gay parents might not feel comfortable voicing misgivings" about their childhood. [74] Publicizing their current mistreatment isn't tolerated well either.

Jonathan Rauch is a stereotypical gay-rights warlord, who comes out smelling like a fascist by any other name. Droning on in the patronizing manner to which gay spokesmen are accustomed, Rauch dictates which rights he is willing to leave us and which the 3.7% plan to seize. Acknowledging it's a bit nervy to ask the masses to give up their "historical understanding of marriage" Rauch is full of tolerance and understanding.[75] He assures us he wouldn't ask that centuries of moral and cultural tradition be "relinquished overnight." They are beneficent, willing to bequeath legislatures and courts "a while" to kiss our human rights good-bye. After the Good Fascist/Bad Fascist gig, Rausch gets down to business. Christian "homophobes" will not be *allowed* to "discriminate" while quoting the Bible." [76] Like all agitprop, it's confusing, open-ended and vague. The 3.7% have no intention of "asking" for rights of belief, religion, or expression to be stripped away. Rausch and gang make it clear; they intend to just take them.

Americans suffered under an administration serving only a sliver of the population, but only those who rock the rainbow feel that heat. Former Atlanta Fire Chief, Kelvin Cochran, is one of them. After publishing a devotional book, allegedly critical of homosexuality (self-published and on his own time) he was fired. Cochran's supervisor, Mayor Mohammed Kasim Reed, originally opposed gay marriage as well – but quickly converted.[77] Perhaps the Mayor feels that since he was forced to submit, his underlings must as well.

WALK SOFTLY & ASK A PROGRESSIVE FOR PERMISSION TO SPEAK

An aggressive and indulged LGBTQ movement in both continents boasts a high body count of conservatives. Dr. Julia Gasper and Dr. Hans-Christian Raabe are just two of them. Americans may never have heard of Gasper, and the extreme left is doing their best to obscure her existence in the UK. Gasper is a rebel academic who refused to stay safely within party lines. Her extensive research on gay pedophilia terrified entrenched politicians, who apparently feel obliged to protect the practice. As someone to make an example of, Wikipedia labeled Gasper "right-wing. . . homophobic and transphobic" – biased blather, proving the unvetted internet encyclopedia is nothing to take seriously.

All political parties across Europe are wetting their bloomers over fear of offending random homosexuals. In 2011, Dr. Hans-Christian Raabe became another sacrificial lamb to gay power. He was dismissed from the UK Advisory Council on the Misuse of Drugs, for his unrelated but "embarrassing" views on homosexuality. Who was embarrassed? Raabe's opinions were only an issue after an attack from gay ex-MP, Evan Harris, who was seething after he lost his seat to a Christian Conservative in 2010. Left-wing journalists then "lynched Raabe" and attacked him specifically because of his Christian faith.[78]

The upshot of this is that homosexuality has become an untouchable topic of near mythic status. Pedophiles and pederasts are scrambling under the same lead blanket of legal protections sheltering generic homosexuals from all scrutiny, at this moment.

Meanwhile, whistle blowers, investigative journalists, and legitimate and serious academics who uncover child abuse in the gay movement are severely censored and silenced.

Agressive homosexuals now engage in quasi-military type occupations, involving propaganda, draconian punishment, and public contempt. Brendan Eich, cofounder and CEO of Mozilla, was one of their campaigns. Eich was pushed from his own company in 2014, after squealers sent gay activists after him like a pack of rats. Eich's sin? He donated $1,000 to California's Proposition 8 campaign in *2008*, which limited marriage to a man and woman. Gay fascists refused to live with the will of the people, who passed it by a huge margin. Apparently, they've hated anyone associated with Measure 8 ever since, and they have a list. That's almost a decade of gay retribution. Mozilla insiders claim Eich was kind and fair to everyone, but it wasn't reciprocated. Gay hate cannot be placated. Feed it a few martyrs and it only grows.

Eich's treatment was so shockingly unfair that even liberals were appalled. He made a serious mistake, but not the one he apologized over. He should have realized that aggressive political lobbying for homosexuality may be toxic to well-being, camaraderie, and civil-rights at Mozilla. Making this observation qualifies as "hate-speech" at this moment, but no one is standing up for victims like Eich. Silicon Valley peers haven't reassessed their strident gay promo-codes that push people down and under. The DOJ hasn't done a thing to address Eich's loss of rights or livelihood at the hands of treacherous and ungrateful gay employees. No one is holding them accountable.

HOLLYWOOD CENSORS FOR HOMOSEXUALITY

Gay & Lesbian Alliance Against Defamation (GLAAD) is a media watchdog to promote gay values. They have an actual blacklist, naming naughty conservatives and Christians who are disobedient to their betters. This is schlepped around to news and media outlets, who must take it *very seriously.*

Even "conservative" Fox News bows before the will of mighty GLAAD, which takes snippets of quotes out of context, and with creative editing, defames their foes.[79] GLAAD and other gay leviathans are aided by the wealthy and celebrated, who make oaths of loyalty in promo-pieces. It's an act of cultural extortion, and most of the media understand this. GLAAD also hosts a "Studio Responsibility Index" which rates (censors) major studios, making certain that "images of homosexuality" are correct and suitable. Instructions are issued for news organizations, such as their *"HIV & AIDS in the news: A guide for reporting."*[80] Dozens of "guidelines" are pitched by GLAAD on how to properly report on gay issues.

What news room uses a guide on medical issues from homosexuals, instead of doctors? Probably the one you watch. If they need instruction from the subjects they report on, they aren't journalists. And you thought news was objective? Not since Henry the VIII – only the powers have changed.

7

SENSITIVITY TRAINING – OR HOW TO SMILE WHILE ON THE RACK

With the Feds planning weddings so well for homosexuals, this frees up resources to find new ways to harass conservatives. Classically, these operations were launched from institutions where they left garrisons in the form of "diversity" departments. Anyone remotely acquainted with this euphemism knows it's generally a place of subtle bullying, humiliation, and white-collar abuse. Selected races and sexual activities are praised, and the rest forced to quote meaningless drivel in their honor. It's more than bizarre. Once again, the 3.7% or so are running most of the show. Occasionally women, the disabled, or racial minorities are addressed – but that's just for show.

Neo-haters aren't the first to come up with this brilliant, low key form of torture. Constantine forced Romans to "voluntarily convert" to Christianity or die, almost 1700 years ago. Muslims in Pakistan, Nigeria, and elsewhere are doing the same to thousands at this moment. While Western "sensitivity training" surrounding homosexuality may not include imminent death – it is in every way a forced conversion and a new religion. Creeds and attitudes are dashed, and believers are "saved" from bigotry. Old gods are dumped and the born-again must be sufficiently zealous in following articles of faith or *diversity doctrines*. Hallowed be Thy Pronouns.

Shaming is the true purpose of re-education, whether in Chicago or the Gulag. Agitprop professionals know they can't change deep beliefs through belittling, patronizing, or even torture. Those are merely a show of power. Mocking and shaming softens up victims for more serious attacks to come. Germans whipped up resentment and envy, leading to genocide. Before Progressives resurrected the thing here, the Chinese had almost perfected political "conversion" or re-education, via work-camps, fines, and propaganda. Chairman Mao used staged slander and humiliation campaigns to ready his victims for the kill – and not just metaphorically

Thanks to anti-hate speech laws, this is all making a comeback. Hysteria and accusation are at fever pitch, and portend the Maoist People's Picnic from hell. Cone hats and Marxist songs are ditched in favor of indignant slogans: *"Hate is not a family value"*, blah, blah. Still the dark, Goya-esch, circus of the monstrous is in full session wherever they hold this subtle form of mental tor ture. Appreciation of homosexuality is inflicted. We must hear and see it in amplified volume, until we sing its praise to make it stop. This is a psychological tactic straight out of a prisoner-of-war camp. Or hell.

ASK NOT WHAT HOMOSEXUALS CAN DO FOR THE COUNTRY . . .

Unquestionably, the largest captive (adult) audience for diversity experimentation is the US government. Federal employees make up between 4.1 to 15 million individuals, depending on how they are classified. [81] All souls are compelled to take part in the Federal Gay Games that the Obama administration opened, although other leaders bestowed their blessings as well. To join, applicants must leap high ideological hurdles, and train on endless tracks of "Diversity" programs, lest they be eliminated.

Decrees from the White House and Pentagon demanded all hands on deck for their pro-gay social experiments. We can only imagine how "special" the armed forces might become someday. Will unbecoming camos be replaced with satin jackets – or sado-motifs? Pressure runs painfully deep against military conservatives to buckle and join the Dantean floor show, or leave. This isn't a fair choice. A 2011 report claimed the new policy on gays was such a high priority that soldiers were approached with this even in Afghan *battlefields.* [82] Oncoming bullets are ignored for "sessions on respecting gay rights" in accordance to the US Department of Defense, and various chiefs of each service. What exactly are our soldiers being prepared to do?

Like other propaganda, the term "diversity" has come to mean the exact inverse of the original word. No longer does it stand for open arms or minds, but for favoritism and cronyism – and few there be that find it. Only those with a retinue of attorneys and street brawlers are rewarded by designation as a protected class. Statistically, that is likely to not be you. Most glaringly, "sensitivity" sessions are a hostile, adversarial action against a person's will, whether backed by state or private group. Victims risk fines or imprisonment for disobedience. That is rare in the US, but less rare in Britain and Canada – at this point.

CORPORATE GAYNGBANGING

America's biggest corporations will do almost anything to keep up with cultural trends; the businesses Leftists pretend to hate, but play like a cello. Few Fortune 500 companies missed a chance to crumple helplessly at the feet of gay anarchists, and meet their every wish. One of those was an assortment of Christian heads on a platter. Obliging the shrillest of the 3.7%, most corporations reacted to gay threats by dissing Christian clientele and herding all employees into sexual training camps (AKA, diversity classes).

They also buckled to gay extortion with piles of silver. The U.S. donor community, for example, has invested substantially in LGBT causes. The Tracking Report on LGBT and Queer Grantmaking reported that in 2014 alone, private U.S. foundations dispersed over $153 million in LGBT-related grants, nearly half for advocacy. Individual philanthropists contributed millions more. One donor group, 'Funders for LGBTQ Issues', called for foundations to increase their giving to gay causes to $200 million annually in 2017.

Hatemongers are like bouncers at the gate of all professions, checking for outdated ideology and theology. Thanks to the machinery of political correctness, all upwardly mobile must profess faith in the Great Gay Way. This is not merely cultural pressure, but a real threat, with professional, economic, legal, and possibly even physical consequences. Americans (and their businesses) have almost totally surrendered to militant gay bidding. Rare holdouts become cultural hostages and are treated with bitter public contempt.

Possibly the most productive turf for gay militants is through hiring practices. They hit pay dirt when the Equal Employment Opportunity Commission (EEOC) ruled in 2015 to extend Title VII of the Civil Rights Act over something it was never intended to touch: gender and orientation. Now, homosexuals and transgenders profit from legislation intended to protect against sex discrimination in hiring. "Sex" originally meant women. Real ones.[115]

Haunts of the traditional and manly are coopted into backdrops for coming-out parties as well. Who would have thought that Chris Culliver of the 49ers and Miami Dolphins Don Jones would be sent to re-education camps, like naughty children who snickered at their betters? Details of their crimes and misdemeanors: Culliver in 2012 for "laughing at homosexuality in NFL locker rooms." [83] *In the locker room,* like some film noir nightmare. Jones had the audacity to be shocked by a make-out session between burly men on the field. *Shock* is on the list of banned emotions for straight people. American's once plucky citizens are groaning under the noxious shadow of the Gay Watchtower. Yet complaining about this sadistic treatment is also proof of "hate" in an ironclad argument of self-reinforcing, circular stupidity.

HRC & SPLC, BRINGING YOU SENSITIVITY – WITH A TIRE IRON

One flank of white-washed fascists is led by the oxymoronically named "Human Rights Campaign" (HRC). The "largest gay rights organization in the world" is concerned with their tribe only, but in typical grandiosity, purports to speak for all humanity. HRC is an elitist advance team for those blessed with same sex attraction. Demonizing conservatives and dismantling Western ethics, they don't let rights of those dull rubes stand in their way. HRC boasts an actual "enemies" list, on which many of the consigned (conservatives all) are proud to appear.

Sociopathic contempt for traditional and religious people fairly drips off the HRC website. It's a gay-centric universe with more spite for conservatives than the Inquisition ever had for Galileo. Without a shred of humor or humility, HRC describes goals for the nation like these: *"Demanding diversity training on both gender identity and gender expression."* We must also *"Demonstrate support* [for transsexuals] *at the highest levels of management."*[84] All tradespeople must now be experts in fine nuances of LGBT "expression" and able to identify gay species, phylum, subspecies, classes, hairstyles and so on. Emotional travails of trannies now supplant all needs of humanity, and there will be no laggards.

Since "transitioning" is the newest gay fad, it behooves us to be raptly absorbed in all things "trans". We have nothing better to do (being straight and all). Insisting work supervisors receive diversity training "based on gender identity", the HRC demands remedial and continuing Gay Ed. But wait – there is always more. A comment left on HRC's site informs us that we'll *all* be transitioning soon, because "Everyone transitions" when transsexuals come out in the workplace. [85] There you have it; homosexuals are of such intergalactic importance that we simultaneously "transition" with them. Who knew?

Veiled threats in HRC directives use intimidating Police State verbiage, such as ensuring "compliance" of all employees. Warning of the "consequences" of failure to comply, their pages are littered with dark innuendo. They emphasize that their suggested "policy change" may "mitigate risk." Risk? Do they have gay firing squads yet? [86] Failing this, they stipulate a web of fines, censures, shaming, and possible delicensing to fall on noncompliant state assets – or those entities which were once known as a "business."

Leftist lawyers calling themselves the Southern Poverty Law Center (SPLC) staked a claim on America's kids since 1991. Knighting themselves Lords of all Sexual and Moral Matters, they took it upon themselves to bestow their vast wisdom over K-12 schools. SPLC's *Teaching Tolerance* magazine reaches 400,000 teachers of children – they have claimed. Their lesson plans and documentaries advise to create classrooms that "celebrate the LGBT lifestyle," particularly in history and English classes. [87] Why should teachers be doing that?

Among other things, SPLC has no discernable relation to either the "south" or "poverty." They do have plenty of flush lawyers – the better to sue you with my dear. This Leftist bully is worth an est. $340 million, and spawn of the same seed as the ACLU. In 2015, they dragged tiny Jewish counseling center Jews Offering New Alternatives to Healing (JONAH) to court, using four informants against them.[88] JONAH had defied homosexual edicts that no one escapes their clutches, ever. This is similar to Muslim anti-conversion fatwas, and perhaps they were their inspiration. Terminology is even the same, as several states now ban "conversion therapy" for unwanted homosexual attraction.

Cloying self-righteousness is a common tone in sensitivity sessions over homosexuality (alternating with histrionics, displaced guilt, threats, and projection). Diversity guidebooks are often obsessed with gay life, with the rest of humanity used as a mere backdrop. Sensitivity training is an action of mass bullying and shaming. It is unconstitutional and should be offensive to anyone who believes in human rights. America's kids have been raised on this poison and are deeply indoctrinated at school to honor and serve the 3.7%. It sounds a little like a marriage ceremony – or the John Wayne Gacy School of Child Rearing.

8

ARE WE IN PYONGYANG YET? BIGOTRY OVER SEXUAL PREFERENCE

All hail, saints Kennedy, Kagan, Ginsburg, Sotomayor, and Breyer – our demigods of intimacy! Gagging us with rainbow hankies and matching handcuffs, the anti-Christian movement is euphoric. The US Supreme Court (SCOTUS) codified gay marriage as a right in 2015. This would be fine if homosexuals intended to leave the rest of the rest of us alone. They don't. Reaction to the SCOTUS decision just proved gay-haters never will be mollified. They want their Christians *and* circuses – with buttered popcorn.

Even liberal press such as *The Guardian* took note, ribbing that the first "Supreme Court Gay Week, day one, has concluded." Thanks to the zeal of biased Justices like Ruth Bader Ginsburg, we now live under a rat's nest of oligarchies, committed to selective oppression. Justices just handed a gold-plated Glock to these militants, after stamping a bullseye on the backs of conservatives. As alarmist as it may sound, try denying virtually any homosexual demand. Wait for the tantrums and subpoenas, attended by swooning media lackeys, and tap-dancing attorney generals.

Hate in the service of Gay Nirvana precludes concern for liberty; that's just for the little people. Gay zealots and their liberal devotees clogged courtrooms with dozens of indictments against Christians recently; merely for being Christians. Homofascists crafted these charges against their spiritual foes even before the

SCOTUS pasted gay marriage into the Constitution. Now it's likely to wax into thousands of accusations and other creative forms of torment.

Every tyrant despises religious liberty and freedom of conscience, whatever their cause. Religious rights are foundational to all other liberties, and they know it. The militant gay movement wants them gone. They may get their way, if entire branches of the US government continue to function as gay nannies. African American scholar George Yancey discovered this was a goal, from his work focusing on racial prejudice. A leftwing respondent in Yancey's research revealed a common fascistic attitude: "*We should put in place mandatory extreme prison sentences for anyone or any group that attempts to take away civil liberties guaranteed by our constitution.*"[89.] They meant gay rights, but emphatically not religious rights.

Since the SCOTUS determined that homosexuals have a right to marriage, the Church has been dumped directly on the firing line. Hate makes these creatures so myopic that they are willing to deprive millions of their civil liberties, for no clear reason. State legislatures and governors also stick it to the little straight guy, by disregarding and reversing his vote on family matters. Routinely. The SCOTUS gay marriage rout was preceded by decades of courtroom contempt for the will of the people, which has been clearly announced at the ballot box.

Objective onlookers should have gotten a clue by now; a weensy and undeserving minority has the power to nullify your vote. The Score as of 2017? Gay lobbyists, 10 – average citizen, 0.

BUREAU OF PRETTY LITTLE BOYS

Homosexual aggression is aided by authorities who are well rewarded by the wealthy fringes. This is burgeoning in America and Europe where we never expected it. Apparently, we don't learn easily from the past. Once again, we are being conditioned to give away our freedom, our children and our sanity. Romans and Germans didn't pay much attention to what was happening to them either, as it leached in by degrees.

Greeks took this to extremes. Pederasty became an official state institution and was common with the upper classes in ancient times. Older men mentored young boys and regularly sodomized them, with full knowledge of parents and even under State *regulation.* A Bureau of Hot Boyz next? They weren't too nice to women either, who had far less rights, regardless of class. This is the full-blown fruit of gay legislation in state and school.

Liberals supporting gay Promo-Ed haven't thought this out well. Would they mind their child faced with a class like "Pedophilia in Action" with live demonstrations? What is to prevent this, if you have no say at all? Mocking Progressives might consider that there is no safety net for anyone, if the Constitution succumbs to their blows. It's already outmoded. Laws are now based on histrionics, Twitter counts, and extortional threats of suicide (similar to breath-holding by toddlers). Anything could happen.

Look at Fairfax County school district, where lone board holdout, Elizabeth Schultz, voted against sexual deconstruction of their children, in 2015. Ten of her peers ignored hundreds of enraged parents and agreed to "undefined special protections for transgender students and employees" including bathroom invasions.[90] Why? Because of federal threats, and interference by Virginia AG Mark Herring. "If we don't implement policy according to the federal government's whim" Schultz explained, "they are going to come and take our Title IX money, our students with disabilities money, our free and reduced lunch money."[124] Now Feds steal kid's lunch money in service of homosexuality?

There is no valid excuse left for the existence of the gay-rights movement at this point. Couple's benefits such as adoption, property laws, and insurance coverage granted homosexuals equality for years. They thrived for decades in the West, with minor restrictions on age, consent, nudity, and public sex acts. Most of those restrictions they ignored anyway.

Contrast this to demands that conservatives modify life around "feelings" of homosexuals and their diminutive judges. Constitution be damned. No one stopped them from renting halls, ordaining clergy, and creating churches in their own image (with great help and sympathy from the IRS). City Halls recorded gay civil unions, and neighbors let them live peace. But it was never enough. The old Church was dragging her feet again, snubbing social fads and stubbornly grasping her 3500-year-old creeds.

Gay beefs with the word of God go back at least to Moses, although they attribute it to neocons and TV preachers, who are closer targets for their bile. Did they gratefully accept the largess of Christian-majority voters, who enacted rulings everywhere, solely for the benefit of homosexuals? Less happy and more vocal than ever, gay political goons turned against the very moderates and conservatives who, for the most part, never opposed them in any way.

GAY COLONIALISM

Desire trumps every other human right in much of the world, according to the Gospel of Gayness. Vietnam is a dark, oppressive land, where women rot in prisons for teaching Sunday School, and minorities are starved. But never fear – Vietnam is stepping into our shiny new world where life is much brighter for trannies!

Recently, they passed laws easing restrictions for the sexually undecided. Why would you need food when you can change genders so easily? Coinciding with Vietnam's great leaps for gays, were a series of vicious crackdowns on religious rights. Christian human rights lawyer Nguyen Van Dai was seriously beaten, his belongings stolen, and he was pushed into the sea. [92] Even the UN's High Commissioner for Human Rights was alarmed by the "recent spate of violent attacks on human rights defenders" in Vietnam.

By no coincidence, the Obama appointee to Vietnam was a homosexual. You know how hard it is to find good ambassadors anymore. "It's a dream come true," Ambassador Ted Osius gushed of his new assignment, where he worked tirelessly pushing rights for transgenders and ignoring dying prisoners.[93] Now, if those religious people would just lop off a testicle or breast, they may be deemed worthy of human rights by the US State Department.

There is immense power for the keepers of this racket. One result of US support for gay activists in Nigeria directly led to withholding aid for thousands of Christians, who were subsequently slaughtered by Boko Haram. These policies were crafted under Hillary Clinton's reign of terror, and continued under John Kerry – until public opinion forced them to back off. We can thank the hate-mongering mission at the Obama-era White House for the world's first sexually-induced genocide.

Letters by gay ambassadors and an envoy to the State Department in 2015 described how Obama admin trade agreements were all about LGBT: "We know firsthand that U.S. interests are best served when we pursue policies that also advance our [homosexual] values. That's why trade policy is among our most promising tools." [94] Specifically, they pushed the Trans-Pacific Partnership (TPP) and the Transatlantic Trade and Investment Partnership (T-TIP), which are detested by people across the earth. Like everything else related to gay totalitarianism, they employed legal and financial tactics. Cash is their Big Carrot and lawsuits their Big Sticks.

Barrack Obama seemed riveted by the demands of a meagre minority in a mutual aid and fawning society. Issuing public statements and lectures, he preened over all things gay with great pomp and circumstance. If the ex-POTUS were merely neurotic, few would care – but his infatuations became solid law. Since the unveiling of America's first "Gay President," most executive agencies have been at the disposal of queer activists before all others.

GAY-SEX CZAR JARRETT

Ex-White House advisor, Valerie Jarrett, called for a ban on so-called "conversion therapies" for the no longer happily gay. Forcing people into life-long homosexuality is now federal policy, which made that administration a lot like the mafia – only kinkier. Jarrett presumed to speak for all humanity: psychiatrists; counselors; churches; pastors; priests; rabbis; doctors; researchers; scientists; current and former LGBTQIs and their loved ones. Possibly their pets. Conversion therapy can have "potentially devastating effects on the lives of transgender, as well as gay, lesbian, bisexual youth" Jarrett gushed, with virtually no proof.[95]

There was no rational reason for this promotional surge of queerness, unless Obama is secretly stuck in the closet, or homosexuals have all the money. Most likely, it was just another swipe by leftist haters at conservatives and the church. And what hater wouldn't ramp up the venom when the White House invites him to a box seat at the Colosseum and makes you his new BFF? (As this book goes to press, there is a change of guard in the US, and Democrats are vacating many seats of power. Whether the new administration is clever enough to replace crusading gay bureaucrats, who will make their lives hell, is yet to be seen).

Obama's administration wasn't the first to hang foreign policy on how flattering you are to homosexuals, but it's a first here. There was Trajan, Hadrian, Caligula, and Nero previously. After a full flush of legal victories, Homofascists should be sated with the blood of their enemies. Not happening. Human Rights Campaign (HRC) luridly warned in 2015, that businesses had some nerve to request religious conscientious exemptions to "gay" anything. We should all be thrilled to serve them in any manner. Tracking all attempts to protect religious rights, HRC, SPLC and other gay garrisons, paint such possibilities in alarming tones. They slyly call these protective bills a "license to discriminate" or evade paying tribute, as they work to neutralize the rights of Christians.

TEMPLATE FOR CORRUPTION

Gross exaggeration of the gay population is yet another Leftist intimidation tactic, inflating their numbers like a pack of puff-adders before they strike. But progressives don't have to worry. They earn loyalty of gay militants the hard way, through mammoth political payoffs. Gay string-pulling is so rough in Washington that it manipulates major domestic and foreign policy.

Liberals refuse to acknowledge crimes and misdemeanors of gay politicians, such as profoundly corrupt, ex-Congressman Barney Frank. Frank's Democratic Party peers found no fault with the 16-term politician: Neither abuse of privilege; nor allowing a lover (convicted child-porn aficionado) to pimp from Frank's home; nor fixing legal "problems" for male prostitutes; nor engaging in a little paid action himself. Frank wasn't even questioned too harshly. His dirt was swept under the rug of "humanitarian" causes, which appears to be a new tag for paid sex.

Au contraire, Frank shot to Congressional heights, where he experienced moral immunity for decades. But he didn't just enrich a few gay boys, he was busy screwing America. Using his considerable influence in the House Financial Services Committee, Frank helped place ex-lover, Herb Moses, in Fannie Mae.

Shortly after Moses was ensconced, incentive pay for executives more than quadrupled, rising from $8.5 million to $35.2 million a year.[96] Nepotism was working great guns. Frank covered and denied all wrong doing for Fannie Mae, even after it imploded oozing billions of tax dollars with it. Thousands who lost homes and businesses can thank Frank, who was charged with oversight of "all components of the nation's housing and financial services sectors." [97] Including Fannie Mae.

Contrast this to horrified shrieks when conservative politicians are caught with their pants down. Radio pundit Debbie Schlussel mused on the difference in how Democrats and Republicans treat wrong-doers in their ranks. Republican Congressman Donald Lukens (caught in a sex scandal in 1989), was summarily removed, forced to attend sex offender classes, take an AIDS test, and face an ethics investigation. Nothing similar exists for gay Democrats, except a very old script. "Meanie bigots" and "wah, wah, wah," all the way home. Democrats circled the wagons for Frank, and his apotheosis continues, with big kisses sent from the press.

Frank admits the inequity and tacit agreement media have with both progressives and gay politicians. "I was a gay man who enjoyed a media silence that [conservatives] had been denied" he admitted. [98] Frank retired in comfort to publish his memoirs, and deny serious new charges – such as how his House Financial Services Committee failed to stop Hillary Clinton selling 20% of our uranium deposits to Russia. Or because he undoubtedly knew the buyer (ARMZ-Uranium Ore) contributes millions to her gay-friendly Clinton Foundation. "There's no way you're going to tie me into this," Frank said to Breitbart News, sounding remarkably like James Cagney in "The Public Enemy." [99]

Dozens of politicians have since joined the crusade to harass Christians and conservatives in the United States. Washington State Governor Jay Inslee leads a fierce campaign against human rights of religious people from his governor's mansion in Olympia. Not only does he pounce on free thinkers in Washington, but punishes other states by restricting trade or travel – should they stray from gay doctrine.

HATE-FRONTS HRC, SPLC & ACLU

Co-founded by anti-Christian bigot, Terry Bean, the Human Rights Campaign (HRC) is a trio of non-profit agencies. Bean and this hate-group savaged, threatened, and sued Pastor Scott Lively for noting that many homosexual men are pederasts. Ironically, Bean was arrested in 2014 for felony sexual abuse and making porn with a minor boy in Portland, Oregon.[100] That's quite the coup, since it's notoriously difficult for a homosexual to get arrested in Portland, known for bikes, beer and gay pride. Part of a proud tradition, former mayor Sam Adams (D) seduced his male, teen page, whom he had mentored (Greek style) with no real reprisals in 2005.[101]

Cursing those powerful rich Republicans who push little ones like him around, Bean made his millions. He was a major Democratic Party bundler of funds from the wealthy. Generous to Obama, all doors in the White House were perennially open on his many visits. HRC is a back door to gay cronyism among the wealthy and elite, soliciting top Fortune 500 companies and their big bucks. Among them are Apple, Google, Microsoft, Chevron, Northrop Grumman, Bank of America, Pfizer, Coca Cola, Citi, Lexus, and dozens more.[102] They represent the military-industrial complex, banking, investment, culture, travel, oil, entertainment, technology, and media. What's left? Through cash and praise, knowing or ignorantly, America's largest corporations support child rape, oppression, and hate.

Persecution is even nastier from the Southern Poverty Law Center (SPLC), a monster hate-machine with most turrets aimed at Christians. This once noble group could be inspiration for *Lord of the Flies,* and is a classic study in irony and corruption. Originally founded to take on racism and anti-Semitism, SPLC was one of the first to foster the "anti-hate" meme and seems to have patented it, as it is so very lucrative for them. Decades later, SPLC is rotted into a bitter, partisan hate-group, putting out virtual hits on their political foes, and raking in vast sums for it. Joined at the hip to progressives in power, the SPLC has grown in support, funding, and in political heft.

Maintaining a list of "hate groups" consisting of conservatives and religious people, the SPLC essentially extorts those desperate to stay off. There's good reason for their fear. Although non-profits shouldn't be counseling the Feds, the SPLC does – especially so during the divisive and racialized Obama administration. It's a mutual win/win. SPLC gains more rank and cash, and Feds have new ammo to oppress and criminalize their political opponents. Which is how the SPLC (perhaps inadvertently), sent an assassin to the Family Research Council.

Flying topmast in the Most Hated lists of the SPLC, is the Family Research Council (FRC).[103] This pro-family group is targeted because they are Christian, support the family, and speak publicly on social issues – all unspeakable crimes according to the SPLC. FRC ventures opinions on homosexuality as it affects Christian families, of which the left has decided only they are allowed to comment. The SPLC slanders and demonizes conservatives so darkly that some of their deranged followers have gone mad with hate.

One of these was gay leftist, Floyd Corkins II, who used SPLC's hate-map to find "anti-gay" people and kill as many as possible. This handy "map o' hate" functions as a hit-list, with names and sometimes even home addresses. Because someone may want to drop in for tea – or a shotgun sometime. And that's how the SPLC racket runs. There was the FRC dead center, with all coordinates. Fortunately, an armed guard (who was shot) subdued the hate-crazed Corkins before he fulfilled his mission. Not that the SPLC would enjoy seeing anyone rubbed out or anything. Admittedly no one, not even a hate-front sucking donations from the gullible, is fully responsible for another's action. But personal responsibility is a conservative belief, *not* a progressive one.

Following in the steps of the "happy-face killer", Corkins brought Chick-fil-A hamburgers to smear on his victims' faces. It was a political statement (something like "everything I needed to know about snuffing conservatives I learned at the SPLC"). Chick-fil-A company was another target of far-left groups at the time.[104] Corkins' rant and motives fit hate-crime criteria in every point, but Feds didn't charge him with it. No wonder, since the SPLC likely trained the very FBI agents investigating Corkins. This thinly disguised propaganda mill (working exclusively in the interest of the Democratic Party) took no responsibility for their almost successful hit.

Outrageously bigoted SPLC also labeled Dr. Judith Reisman as an "anti-LGBT conspiracy theorist. Reisman was considered the foremost academic expert in pornography, child abuse, and pedophilia in the 1980s and 1990s, although SPLC mocks her credentials. Reisman is still an expert on pedophiles, and SPLC is still protecting them via policies of attacking family-protective organizations. Now, they've taken to targeting anti-terrorist bloggers and politicians, including mild Muslim reformers, such as Maajid Nawaz. Thanks to their efforts, ISIS and other Islamic hate fans can find them easier; but perhaps they will show up at local SPLC offices for directions first.

SPLC informs the Justice Department and other Feds who they will, or will not, be hating in the future. Utterly unqualified to make pronouncements on these issues, this crusading PAC now lists "conversion therapy" as a hate crime. This means no human being in the US may seek counseling if they are an unhappy homosexual. SPLC, a true hate-titan, would rather see you die than escape a lifestyle you no longer desire (see gay suicide statistics).

RAINBOW BALL: BYOM (BRING YOUR OWN MACHETES)

It's a big Debutante Ball for haters, and most of the US government showed up in advance to lend a hand. Gay militants decide who gets in. Charioteers of radical homosexuality are tactically fascist and push for totalitarian-style legislation. It's all about self-promotion. Me, me, me, and whoever I want to screw at the moment — but not you. Inclusive humanity is never the concern of gay-related ordinances, which is an indication of their true social worth.

Stirring up hordes against the Church and waving little rainbow pitchforks, mob action continues via courts and federal offices. Why? Perhaps Judge Douglas Wilkins (MA) can explain. In 2015, he ruled that a Catholic academy must hire an openly gay employee who had clearly lied to them about his lifestyle and beliefs. Would Wilkins extend his favors for child molesters in a day care? There are places where not every employee is suitable. Or is it illegal to even think that now in Massachusetts?

Freedom of conscience and religion is being trivialized, and we are fast losing our rights. We lost them because few dared question homosexual hegemony and lived (as a public presence) to tell the tale. Even dissident homosexuals are targeted. As in most totalitarian systems, asking for justice brings dire consequences: Don't make noise or demands; be invisible; attend your required diversity classes. Smile, and perhaps we will leave you alone. Ah, the lovely ambiguity of anti-hate laws, based on thought-crimes alone! First this was only de facto, working through social pressure and simpering college students. But in its noisome legal glory, liberal bigotry has truly arrived. Government now uses gay pandering as a political litmus test, while Christians swat away subpoenas like horseflies.

Even the powerful are unable to defend themselves against gay fiat. Texas Governor, Rick Perry, opposed gay marriage for years, earning him the everlasting enmity of the gay community and their leftist servants. They struck back. Even as chief executive of Texas, Perry was punished for not considering homosexuals before all life forms. When Travis County DA, Rosemary Lehmberg (D), was charged with drunken driving and wouldn't step down, Perry refused to fund her office. That's what Governors do. A grand jury in liberal Austin convicted Perry of doing his job (vetoing bills and expenditures, allowed there since 1876), calling it "abuse of power." Charges were dropped because they were fictional, but not before Perry was arrested and nationally humiliated.

Feds now hold summits for "lesbian farmers," offering incentives based solely on sexual orientation. A person of indeterminate sex was employed by USDA (Department of Agriculture) to explain the new purpose of agriculture: "We are trying very hard to change people's mindsets."[105] Referring to a farmer as a "white, rich male" he/she proved that USDA appointees in the Obama administration had likely never set foot on a farm. Worse than the glaring unfairness, is the scope of politically motivated sycophancy. Historically, it has too much in common with bloodbaths that began with rearranging farmers and land. See Stalin, Pol Pot, Mao, South Africa, and Zimbabwe.

Homosexual despots particularly abhor the Church, and they share this ugly habit with almost all authoritarian states. Gay tyrants seem highly inspired by economic assaults of the type North Korea and Soviets unleashed on Christians (before they had power to openly kill them). After years of crushing Marxist regulations against Christian businesses in North Korea, the Church was underground or dead. We have our own budding tyrants, and some of them are LBGTQ leaders. They aren't even hiding their hate, or intentions, at this point.

Amusing things happen on the path to the Great Gay Valhalla though. In Iceland and elsewhere, some Old Norse pagans are up in arms against gay marriage. Resenting intrusions into their (pre-Christian era) traditions, they remain focused on nature and fertility. Homosexuality fails massively on both counts. Commentary from an Odinist organization, such as this, was fierce: "We cannot coexist. Either traditional society will be maintained, or homosexuals will be allowed free reign to assault children."[106] Pagans are unlikely to feel much repercussion, because they're a fierce lot who don't subscribe to "love your enemy" and so on. Gay power-grubbers prefer nice Church people, who can be slapped around easily.

But this is the Great Gay Path to paradise, and they have plans for us all. Pastors have been threatened, fined, censored, and arrested for preaching "unapproved" sections of the world's most read and published book — the Bible. Many of us find fascism and force hateful, but leftists have successfully used them to bully the masses since at least 1789. Not that militant LGBTs ever took all this "hate" business seriously. That was just to gain legal standing against conservatives.

Presidential candidate Hillary Clinton made it clear she was campaigning for not only for homosexuality, but against Christianity. Delusions of grandeur marked her 2014 speech as she chided the Most High, letting him know his cultural codes and biases on moral issues, will just "have to be changed."[107]

HATING FREE-SPEECH IN CANADA

Canada leads the ex-free world in fining and imprisoning people for their thoughts – since at least 2002. That year, Dr. Chris Kempling was suspended as a school counselor due to his "unacceptable criticisms of same sex-marriage" found in a personal letter to a regional paper. Kempling lived a Kafkaesque legal nightmare many years after that. He was banned from speaking on homosexuality, and has been disciplined, fined, and threatened.

Canada is now one big no-go zone for free speech in the name of gay rights. Parents and clergy were preemptively shut down to stop them from protecting their children.

In 2010, Canadian teachers were asked to discuss gender identities and sexual orientation, because allegedly "more students have same-sex parents." Duhh?? There are far more Native Americans, and heaps of Scots and French. Statistically, more people have herpes in Canada. Where is the pro-STD curriculum in grade school? That would be more rational than allowing sexual psychopaths to mess with the minds of Canadian kids so they can harvest them later.

Kathleen Wynne, fabulously gay Premier of Ontario (see her at all the Pride parades) was Education Minister at the time. Her fingerprints are all over crime scenes known as Ontario schools, where 3rd graders learn the joys of "anal intercourse" and "vaginal lubrication." And why? How else will they get kids this small to have vaginal or anal intercourse, unless they know what it is and how to do it? There is no other explanation. Canadian government is all-in for this, and supports the dark side at this point. Ontario's former Deputy Minister of Education, (Ben Levin, under Wynne) was sentenced in 2015 for creating child porn and plotting to sexually assault children. Other crimes include molesting his daughters and flooding K-12 sex-ed classes with his sadistic fantasies. But the Canadian government thought so highly of Levin that he was trotted across the country, as an "expert." [108]

One child molester in jail is meaningless. Dissenting parents and pastors are in danger of imprisonment, and they are far more likely to be dragged before lions in Canada. Broadcaster and attorney Ezra Levant is an outspoken critic of rampant child abuse there. He was repeatedly found guilty of "defamation" for revealing grotesque corruptions of the Canadian government. Because Canadians who lie in print, or in office, can't be called out as "liars." Those silencing you may not be described as "oppressors." Men who promote raping children must not be labeled "child molesters", but prevail in court. Justices unleashed on Levant in a December 2016 Appeals Court said as much – insisting that "malice" against anyone or anything was illegal in Canda.[109] But only for conservatives, because they are the only ones being arrested there. Liberal hatred remains perfectly safe.

Prime Minister Trudeau is a virtual LGBTQ proxy. Under his term, Ontario's children are now met with posters of gay threesomes getting it on, in their subways. This alone proves how little Canadian authorities care for their innocents. But homosexuals there never fear they will be traumatized by encountering actual diversity in real life. It's been eliminated. Free thought was sacrificed at the altars of Gay Rights Tribunals, like vestal virgins before an orgy. Political expression is limited to a list of acceptable possibilities, and Canadian imagination and courage is withering with it. Even conservative Americans are harassed at the border, their property confiscated, and sometimes denied entry. If freedom and justice were diseases, Canada apparently intends to firmly remain inoculated against them.

UK, MAKING PEDERASTY GREAT AGAIN

Our northern neighbors may be following Britain down the paths of Gaytopia. England turned its napalm toward conservatives at least 50 years ago, about the time a White Paper on cultural policy debuted (1965). Culture Secretary, Jennie Lee, in *A Policy for the Arts: the First Steps* claimed her goal was to make Britain "a gayer and more cultivated country." Now she may have meant "happier" which also applies – but "gay" for homosexuals was common, even then. Cary Grant used it to explain his dress in a 1938 film. Seeing how her Labour Party has tirelessly striven to empower not only homosexuals, but also pederasts, one does wonder.

The once "green and pleasant" island is boiling with gay hysteria, after campaigns to beatify buggery and lesbianism were imposed by harsh censorship. No Western homosexuals have enjoyed that type of immunity from crime. And as part of a coming-out process, England's gays are leaving a cultural wasteland behind them. Christian tradition must be relabeled, removed, unspoken, struck, banned, unpublished, and unelected. Yet gay demagogues enjoy the fruits of Judeo-Christian civilization, even as they work to destroy it. Will a future Queen begin life as a prince? How far will leftists push this thing, before they are collectively vomited out? Gay militancy is to cultural freedom what ISIS has been to the Syrian Church. They just use money and attorneys instead of missiles.

In the rest of Europe, conservatives are backed against a wall as far as they are willing to go. Some erupt in anger, while others quietly work underground, thanks to bizarre, third-world style laws against free speech there. Many saw it as a hostile takeover, and are psychologically arming themselves for a counterrevolution. Robert Lopez wrote about this in the *Manif pour Tous,* a grassroots movement of revulsion after President Hollande created same-sex marriage for France, in 2013. Lopez describes radical homosexuality diminishing Europe:

> *"It no longer makes sense to speak of an LGBT "community" or "movement" but rather a world-historical lobby, a specific cadre flush with money, positioned strategically close to the same centers of power that oversaw empires in the nineteenth and early twentieth centuries: Washington, Paris, and London."*[110]

THE POL POT SCHOOL OF FAMILY VALUES

Massachusetts is working furiously to keep up with the Canucks in tormenting and abusing their children. Even legislators in liberal land were shocked by sexually explicit (gay) matter distributed to minors in their schools. In 2015, State Rep. Rudy Mom (a Cambodian emigre) was so horrified by sexual trauma being imposed on students that he said it "reminded him of what the Communists had done to people back there."[111]

It's a tsunami of an accusation. By "the Communists" he meant the Khmer Rouge army. In Cambodia, at least one-quarter of Cambodians were murdered by them, and most survivors tormented, forcibly moved, imprisoned, traumatized, and starved. Family bonds and marriage were especially despised, and almost annihilated by Khmer armies, who made laughing, mercy, and pity *illegal.* Some of this contempt is shared by 21st century gay warlords, as they attempt to deconstruct natural family structure and traditional marriage for their own purposes. Paralleling gay abuse is the stunning absence of coverage in cases like this. Only local papers and a handful of conservative media mentioned the situation in Massachusetts.

Deny the fascist tendencies of gay extremists if you like, but once they attain a certain height of power it becomes indisputable. The unleashing of ex-Mayor Annise Parker on the unfortunate citizens of Houston was one of these public manifestations. Openly gay Parker subjected Houston to an abject campaign of self-interest in 2014. In a draconian overreach of self-presumed powers, she subpoenaed a number of the city's pastors, demanding contents of their *sermons*. At issue was Houston's "equal rights ordinance" allowing transgenders to use any potty they pleased. Not only did pastors find the invasion of privacy intolerable, they addressed safety of women. The chance that a rapist or child molester could toss on a skirt and become "transgendered" for an hour, eluded Parker and her side-kick, City Attorney David Feldman. Apparently, they mistook Houston for a Roman Circus. Eclipsed by their little crusade was the safely of an entire city.

American conservatives live in a parallel reality to the bogus gay narrative. Many of these families sense they are being forced underground as well. Former US diplomat, Todd Huizinga warns of the dangers gay zealots pose in office. A career diplomat for 20 years, he leveled serious charges at them. "I think the LGBT ideology is implicitly totalitarian . . . it is going to destroy freedom" he cautioned in 2016.[112] Huizinga contends that only by heavy suppression can LGBT groups impose their counterintuitive, fantasy ideology on others.

We may not be shooting Christians who fail to reverence homosexuality, but we've already borrowed North Korean terminology. Kim Jong Un has the "insufficiently enthusiastic" face firing squads, while gay militants and their retinue drag non-compliants to court, or have them demoted for the same offenses. Egos of both appear to run on the same scale, and share a tendency to resentment and spite. But the rainbow uprising isn't threatening only conservatives, it's inspiring potential enemies as well.

Building up to the Crimea/US stand-off, Russian President Vladimir Putin suddenly found religion, and sharply criticized the West because of our lack of respect for it. He appears to be crafting state doctrine as defense of Russian values vs. moral excesses of the West. Specifically, our glorification of "genderless and infertile" homosexuality was his rallying cry.[114] Putin views gay extremists as being as much a danger to the Russian people as Islamic ones. The LGBT movement is "inherently anti-democratic" he charged. Gay crusaders are too busy with their law suits and sex toys to notice.

Nearing the end run of a long campaign to disenfranchise conservatives, homofascists are jubilant. Like football hooligans, they gloat in the ruins they made, planning another hit whether their team wins or loses. It's not what their enemies *do* but who they *are* that enrages gay thugs. Therefore, the only way to appease them is for conservatives to not exist.

9

SCIENCE IS DEAD! LONG LIVE GAY MYTHOLOGY!

Scientists in the 21st century are conditioned to quickly surrender to organized hate, just like everyone else. More than a decade ago, psychologists Nicholas Cummings and Rogers Wright warned that their profession was eroded by intellectual arrogance and zealotry, and dominated by social-activists.

American Psychological Association research was less than worthless, they claimed, because only "predictable, socially driven outcomes" were permissible. After this thought-crime, peers refused to publicly associate with them, although Cummings had been a past president of the organization. Privately, doctors admitted that they feared the gay lobby and "loss of tenure, loss of promotion and other forms of professional retaliation."[115]

Gay militants showed the world that scientists aren't so clever; they haven't been able to defend themselves against blinding attacks of gay bigotry any better than pastors or actors. Biological sciences are being sent back centuries, as they scramble to accommodate fantasies and fads. Phony scholars diddle with data, trying to prove gays are "born this way", with celebs like Lady Gaga making their background music. It's a sad day for science.

SIMULTANEOUS CHOICE AND GENETIC TRAIT – BECAUSE GAYNESS IS MAGIC!

When gaystapos rushed the American Psychiatric Association, (APA) in 1972, demanding their predilection be scrubbed from the list of pathologies, they hadn't yet come up with "homophobia." Like a gang of Luddites, they whined and harassed the assembly, claiming that homosexuality wasn't a disease, but their freely chosen lifestyle. When this argument was no long useful, they asserted that homosexuality now is an innate or genetic trait, which they did not choose, although there is no evidence for that either. Research be damned.

Proving bullies generally get their way, gay guerillas took on the American Psychological Association in 2009. Guess who won? Fulminations this time were over their report on gay-to-straight therapy entitled "Appropriate Therapeutic Responses to Homosexuality." Gay spokesmen had problems with the words "Appropriate" "Therapeutic" "Responses" and "Homosexuality." "Therapeutic" implies there is a problem. Thousands of people who seek counseling for the "non-problem" of homosexuality are insignificant in LGBT-land. Therefore, there is no need of a "response." Dr. Joseph Nicolosi noted the glaring absence of experts making this decision: "Remarkably, the APA rejected, for membership on this committee, every practitioner of sexual-reorientation therapy who applied for inclusion."[116]

Affirming in the same report that gayness is a "normal and positive variant" of human sexuality wasn't enough to mollify homosexuals. Scientists distanced themselves even further from the right to an opinion, by hedging that there is little evidence that "gay-to-straight therapies work." But here's the kicker; those doctors believed other people had rights! At least in 2009. Their paper allowed that people should have the right to receive counseling for whatever they like. It concludes "We take the perspective that religious faith and psychology do not have to be seen as being opposed to each other." [117] Unfortunately, radical homosexualists don't share their vision of peaceful coexistence.

Objectivity of science fails in dictatorial, fear laden regimes – and it's tottering in America now. Marianne LaFrance, former chair of Lesbian and Gay Studies at Yale University, insinuates that heterosexuality has a "cause" and is to be questioned. Are biology and physiology doomed? Now even the hard sciences are endangered. Almost all measurable, empirical reality is at risk, when bureaucrats such as LaFrance work as anti-science troglodytes. Scientists will be shamed for believing in such things as chromosomes in the LGBT Inquisition.

Genetics are under danger of extinction as well. Because gay couples long to be true parents but physically cannot, they demand we redefine all physical reality for their cause. Formerly this was diagnosed as something like schizophrenia, but now scientists take orders from such. In the world of Queer Science, "men" can have babies because they are in fact women, who believe they are men. It's like Alice in Wonderland – with a mustache. If botulism could "identify" as Merlot, would they drink it? The irrationality of "gender flexibility" is not only befuddling – it's lunacy.

Instead of using their talents to cure Multiple Sclerosis, scientists are enlisted to make 3-parent children. Early in 2016, the National Academies gave a green light to conduct clinical investigations on this, as long as was used only to help women with genetic disorders reproduce. But leftist blogs such as the Daily Beast interpreted the news with breathless excitement via gay-speak: "Biological Same-Sex Parent Babies Could Be a Reality by 2017." [118] And that's all folks. This is not being pushed because of sick babies or mothers. Consider who pulls the strings and follow the money.

The almost infinitesimal transgender population is parking itself across research journals as well. A recent Lancet article claims a major problem in the study of "transgender medicine" is a "paucity of high-quality data" and claim they need more research and funds. Why – is it a disease? Transgendering is a cultural/political construct, as proved by the draconian laws required to keep it artificially alive. Even the term is new. It's imported and taught – as a non-native, unnatural, drug-induced, and medically-dependent state. Doctors explained why they needed research on testosterone therapy for transgender men. It includes effects and risks such as "acne, alopecia, reduced HDL cholesterol, increased triglycerides, and a possible increase in systolic blood pressure."[119] Why not spend millions on avoiding skull fractures when people jump off cliffs? It's the same concept; a rescue operation for bad choices with extreme consequences. But for the poor straight suicides, we won't all be paying.

Efforts to sideswipe science create phony journals and research to spread the Gay Gospel. When gay militants demanded the Royal College of Psychiatrists produce statements that homosexuality is innate, (in 2014) they were slapped down. There is no proof of that, yet many fabrications exist. Social scientist Walter Schumm claimed that at least 150 legal and social science articles accepted statistics from the gay community that were patently false. They repeatedly claimed as many as 28 million children were being raised by same-sex couples in the US, with this number cited in endless loops, but never verified. When someone bothered to check "the true number was found to be closer to 200,000."[120] Tiny little math errors….

Axe-grinding homosexuals are to science what Godzilla was to Tokyo – because real science cancels out Queer Theory. Researcher Julia Gasper documented connections between pedophilia and homosexuality, as well as the academic and scientific acrobatics used to deny it. Gasper relates this to Soviet-style "Lysenko-ism, the prioritizing of ideology over scientific enquiry." [121] Politically charged research polluted science under Stalin, and always came up with the results he demanded. Nothing is new under the sun.

QUEER SCIENCE FOR KIDS

Hundreds of studies verify connections between childhood abuse by members of the same sex and homosexual behaviour later in life. Denying this means we must reject and repress decades of science. Radical homosexuals are willing to do that and more, to cover up the damning evidence that their lifestyle sucks – for them, their children and the rest of us. Censoring evidence keeps those caught up in LGBT hell from the information and tools they could use to either cope or escape.

Most odious of the effects of gaymania is pandering to child molesters in the social sciences. It's one thing for adults to go collectively mad if they wish, but children need protection and someone on their side. They are fast losing both. In the APA's own journal *Psychological Bulletin*, a 1998 study criticized "the common belief that child sexual abuse causes intense harm, regardless of gender."[122] They recommended exchanging terms such as "victim and perpetrator", for the morally neutral "adult-child sex." That is not "morally neutral" and clearly their intention was to normalize pedophilia.

Mary Eberstadt found that 1999 was the last time the word "pedophilia" was used in the American Psychological Association website. Even that instance was in response to a letter from a "right-winger" objecting to their pro-bono work for child molesters.[123] After a dustup in 1998, the pedo-pushers in the APA continue to publish in the same vein, so it's obviously a personal interest. Anyone working in a university is likely aware of this. Buggering little boys and molesting little girls is positively trendy now.

Child-sex enthusiasts not only remain in academia, but are highly promoted. and often run the place. Such is gay activist Gilbert H. Herdt, Professor of Human Sexuality Studies, and a founder of the National Sexuality Resource Center at San Francisco State University. From there, he spawns "research" that is seriously pondered, via letters after his name. Herdt appeared as far back as 1988 in pedophile promotional materials, with a gloss of academia. One was the Dutch *Paidika* whose mission statement included this: "The starting point of *Paidika* is necessarily our consciousness of ourselves as paedophiles."[124] Ethics are so low at our universities, that men like Herdt make public policy, and influence generations of students. Pedophiles are heavily represented in departments of psychology, sociology, anthropology, and sexuality at colleges in the West.

Prestigious science-repository PubMed posts at least 15 papers by pro-pedophile Bruce Rind. He posits that child sex abuse (CSA) victims aren't badly harmed, and that most of them secretly like it. In scientific terminology, of course.[125] NAMBLA and other kiddie rapist corps were giddy, and widely quoted his results. At that time (1998) the entire nation was enraged, precipitating a Congressional condemnation of Rind's paper and conclusions. That was then, before the Democratic Party sponsored radical homosexuals into many offices. Now Rind is mainstream science. Rind's 2016 paper is titled: *"Reactions to First Postpubertal Male Same-Sex Sexual Experience in the Kinsey Sample: A Comparison of*

Minors With Peers, Minors With Adults, and Adults With Adults." [126] Didn't Kinsey have fun! It's your government at work.

BAD MEDICINE

From the early days of Grand Poobah Pedophile Alfred Kinsey, gay doctors and scientists have done their best to legitimize child rape. One of Kinsey's acolytes was Dr. John Money, who "fixed" a simple, botched circumcision on one male twin in 1967. Entirely removing the boy's genitals, the doctor convinced his parents to raise David Reimer as "Brenda." I'm sure it was *totally* unrelated to his fascination and research with gender reassignment. An utter disaster, David/Brenda was severely depressed. After desperate attempts to repair the surgeries, David killed himself.

But that's not all Dr. Money did for the Reimer family. Later, it was revealed that he molested both twin brothers, forcing them to commit sex acts with each other at *seven,* which he photographed (for science of course). Official reports failed to note any of this, except the inexplicable death, which is hard to pass off – or his brother's schizophrenia and suicide shortly before David's. Money described man/boy sex as "sexually expressed friendships" and covered his tracks with fictional reports of his glorious success. "The child's behavior .... so different from the boyish ways of her twin brother" he brazenly lied to his colleagues. [127] He wasn't challenged until a Rolling Stone exposé in 1997.

Was the lowest blow to this family a lack of justice and outrage? Dr. Money was never arrested, nor lost his license, but was celebrated and feted – with 65 awards, degrees and honors. New Zealand's Prime Minister even named an art museum after him. Notorious child abuser Money was professor of *pediatrics* at Johns Hopkins University before he died in 2006. Universities are keeping up the grand old tradition, and have not yet repudiated work of these creatures, nor barred their doors to them.

Thus, the advent of contemporary "trans medicine" was birthed in bad medicine, swaddled in misery, and delivered by sadistic liars and pederasts. Trans movements still use Dr. Money's helpful terminology such as "gender role" to obscure the perfectly clear sex of 99.99% of us. He also eased the way for future pedophiles by exchanging the word "paraphilias" for "perversions." Academically now, there are no "perversions" – yet more kids than ever are being raped and emotionally harmed for life.

Only because these men spent years in universities, do their findings carry weight. PubMed and the APA hosting their research is part of the reason children now learn anal sex techniques at school. Even years ago, this type of indoctrination worked. Serial baby rapist Peter Truong described his childhood abusers in a prison interview as "very convincing" showing him psychological studies, articles and books. "It's not bad," they insisted, "it's good for them" he mimics his indoctrinators.[128] Truong and his own abusers would have been thrilled to have the APA, a plethora of universities, the NIH, and the most powerful nations of the world lined up to help him in his endeavors. He was just born a few years too early.

TRANSITIONING FROM REALITY

Following at their heels is the play world of transgendering. There, new realties and dimensions break forth into singing, by merely appending the prefix "trans" to anything. More gay magic! Embattled feminist Germaine Greer is finding it black magic, as she fought for sanity in the UK. She and other nonconformists are accused of "problematic" and "hateful" views on transgendering. Greer criticized equating women's accessories with being an actual woman, and the hatestorm may never stop. Thousands of people in the UK petitioned to shut her up. Not surprisingly, this contempt occurs at universities, where gay doctrine is hallowed.

A UK study reviewed and conducted for *The Guardian* heralded poor prospects for happiness after surgical alterations for gender reassignment. Scientists found no strong evidence that sex-change operations could improve a transsexual's life at all. Worse, they discovered that many transsexuals remained severely distressed, and some became suicidal after their operations.[129] This should surprise no one; because self-maiming was considered a sign of mental illness until we suddenly decided it was liberating. But keep in mind, this study happened a dozen years ago, when there was relative freedom to even discuss such things. Political gay dominance is so strapping that even scientific inquiry wilts before it now.

A monster Swedish study, published in 2011, followed 324 people for decades, who had sex-reassignment surgery. They found that trannies had increasing mental and emotional difficulties, particularly by a decade after surgery. Suicides in this group were almost "20 times above the comparable nontransgender population."[130] Rather than step back from the entire thing, activists assert that mean people must have caused all their problems. If doctors proactively warn patients to avoid the surgery, they are mocked for their concern. Transphobic! Tran-exclusive! If this continues, medicine, archaeology, anthropology, and even forensic science are down the toilet. How will these morons identify a body without using the words "male" or "female"?

More dangerous to children are puberty-blocking drugs that delay maturing, while their parents decide what they will be when they grow up. These cause serious consequences, as doctors experiment on them. There is little to no research on the effects of powerful hormones given at early ages (10-11 for girls and 11-12 for boys). Not only do they block natural processes, but pump them full of cross-sex hormones, estrogen for boys (or transgender girls) and testosterone for girls (transgender boys).[131] They begin this when they claim a child is "mentally and emotionally prepared" – which is mad.[184] A 12-year-old can be tormented for hours over what she wears to school, and she is "emotionally prepared" to maim herself and switch identity for life? Also, there's the matter of "legal consent" which minors generally can't give. This protects kids from human traffickers, statutory rapists, and now endocrinologists.

With rates of suicide skyrocketing for adults under reassignment surgery, we have yet to discover what they will do to children. As of 2015, the FDA hasn't approved hormonal treatment for "gender dysphoria" (confused kid syndrome) for good reason. Hormones are class-3, controlled substances, with serious side effects.[188] Medicare and Medicaid are not required to cover "gender transition procedures" because experts cite high risks and low success rates. Yet individual doctors may not refuse these "treatments" without litigation from our ultra-gay governments. Hormones used to hijack nature are associated with hypertension, diabetes, blood clots, hysterectomies, leukemia, depression, heart attacks, arterial stiffness, stroke, and cancer in adults. Spironolactone is touted as one of their best drugs, yet warns of 57 major side-effects.[132] These same drugs get athletes tossed from Olympic competitions.

The American Psychiatric Association (APA) has also dropped all protocol and objectivity. Slogans are immediately accepted as medical fact (i.e. gender dysphoria) and no one is too mad or too young to be maimed or shot up with hormones. APA's bible, the DSM, states that while schizophrenics may have "rare delusions of belonging to another sex," "transgendering" is not an illusion. They claim the person "feels like a member of the other sex, rather than truly believes that he or she is a member of the other sex.[133] Delusions will now be rationalized to accommodate Gay Theory?

A man I knew feared his food was poisoned for years, and almost starved because he believed it. Yet the DSM-IV claims that "psychiatric disorders" are no reason to avoid "sex reassignment therapy" unless they are the cause of a patient's "gender dysphoria." Doctors still don't know what causes schizophrenia. As they constantly rearrange their definition of "gender" how could they ever determine the cause of "gender dysphoria"?

For adolescents, sex-change hormones end bone growth prematurely, and interfere with their brains. Do we really need duller transvestites roaming the streets? "The bottom line is we don't really know how sex hormones impact any adolescent's brain development," pediatrician Dr. Lisa Simons said in an interview with PBS.[134] Brain damage is unlikely to stop doctors from damaging children in this political climate. As in all things homosexual, children's health takes a backseat to gay supply, while possibly leaving them sterile and seriously disturbed. But the show must go on.

GO AWAY BIG, BAD SCIENCE!

Science was held hostage for years by political correctness, but gay activists are losing patience and just lining it up for a firing squad. Scientific method? Bang! Impartiality and transparency? Bang! Quantifiable evidence? Objectivity and disinterest? Two shots to the head! Bring in the new queens of science: Opinion polls, sob sisters, riots, and leftist dogma. Reactionary sexual doctrine (with gay bias) is our newly assigned Universal Field Theory, and if you want to keep your head (of a science department) you better get yourself schooled.

Science once weeded out bias and personal interest by researchers. Wave goodbye to all that. Australia's *Independent Newspaper* allowed a gay activist to review 1997 research, that concluded there were "strong correlations between male homosexuality and paedophilia." [135] Ridiculing the report with no counter-evidence at all, the shill ended his tirade with an account of his partner vomiting on the article. This suffices for gay science. It should also come as no shock that most research coming up with absolutely "no evidence of child abuse in lesbian/gay families" is written, conducted and/or analyzed by homosexuals. Usually all of the above.

In possibly the most perfect example of Orwellian doublethink yet, gay studies reported that conservative families were proportionately more likely to "harbor repressed homosexual" tendencies than others. [371] Why would they say that? Because members of these families stubbornly preferred the opposite sex. In Gay Creation Theory, absence of homosexuality is only more proof of its existence. Because gayness is everywhere. It's the stuff of creation, the missing link. One day they may tie all human knowledge together in a Grand Queer Theory.

Nonprofit B4U-ACT is an organization established to support "minor-attracted" clients (new buzzword for pedophiles). In 2003, they offered to serve as a research gateway for the APA committee that classifies mental disorders for the DSM-V. A spokesman and registered sex offender from B4U-ACT made this kind offer to the doctors.[136] Does it matter? Should Bill Clinton do research on cute interns? Considering this is a major war over family and the effects of gay parenting, such "findings" should be suspect. Nanette Gartrell defines herself as an "American psychiatrist, researcher [and] lesbian activist," giving her a several dogs in this fight.[137] Yet, she poses as an objective lead researcher for the "US National Longitudinal Lesbian Family Study (NLLFS)." Who could believe her conclusions? (other than the editors of the Archives of Sexual Behavior and the National Institutes of Health, who publish them as solid fact).

That's how science is conducted in the 21st century, making the inquisition look measly. Even Christian psychiatrists bow before them, as they did at their 2012 "Christian Medical and Dental Association" conference. When the fabulously gay Archbishop Gene Robinson cancelled his place on a panel on Sexual Identity Therapy (SIT), the entire thing collapsed at gay delegates' demand. The topic (SIT) became controversial by the inordinate amount of free air-time a few homosexuals were given to vent their grievances, and less attention given to other delegates, science, or facts.

SPRINGTIME FOR MILITANTS

Science has never proved homosexuality beneficial nor superior. Only the reverse. But that may change in the future, because institutions can be bought or threatened. It happened in 1972 at the American Psychiatric Association's meeting, where militants originally threatened their way out of inclusion in the Diagnostic and Statistical Manual of Mental Disorders (DSM). Apparently, psychiatrists don't train much for hostage negotiation. After screaming and general gang tactics, the APA suddenly saw the light. They had been wrong all along. Dawn arose, and with it the normalcy, yea the surpassing and wholesome goodness of gayness. This went unremarked, because it didn't affect us much at the time. It was still Glasnost and springtime for militants, who calmed down a bit before sharpening their axes.

Booster-group GLAAD showed their true colors (not a rainbow) when they menaced the press on how they were to discuss transgendering, in a 2012 press release: Journalists and others in the media must note the "approved changes" around the term "Gender Identity Disorder" (GID) which will no longer be used. GLAAD continued to make editorial demands on journalists: "It is still unacceptable for media outlets to lend credibility to anti-transgender activists who continue to draw false connections between being transgender and certain behaviors."[138] With the ACLU on speed dial, they have ways to make science-writers behave.

Making male/female virtually interchangeable means scientific data must be dumped. They have this in common with Soviet agitprop. Research was suppressed that wasn't in lockstep with materialism, Marxism or whatever they were fixated on at the moment. It's rather terrifying how closely Queer Science follows Soviet oppression. Stalin started an anti-genetics campaign in the mid-1930s, and the gay lobby has their own going. He particularly despised genetics because its discoverer, Mendel, was a Catholic priest. Sex chromosomes can't be changed, and are present in virtually every cell in the human body. Complete "transitioning" would require a full body transplant, yet "trans-deniers" are politically savaged. Gay slogans are worms eating the body of science.

Another face of gay-hate comes in the form of inequity in healthcare. Homosexuals have every benefit given to heterosexuals and far more, per capita. Corporations, institutions, and especially universities hawk special deals for their miniscule numbers of gay clients. Health dollars often cover gender-reassignment surgery where more common surgeries and procedures are excluded.

While the HRC trumpeted the University of Chicago (UC) as a "Leader in LGBT health-equality" – students there are far from equal. The college has paid for "Gender Affirmation Surgery" since 2013, but UC health-plan students learned that ER services are not covered (in 2016). Hetero? Your sexual issues don't matter. Even routine newborn care and "related physician charge" is denied, because babies are insignificant in our Queer Universities.[139] It's a form of booty from student funds.

Under pressure by queer ideologues, the US Food and Drug Administration (FDA) caved to make the nation possibly much sicker, by lifting bans on gay blood donors. Fully 77% of US AIDS cases stem from male-male sex.[198] Testing is quite accurate, but HIV/AIDS can't be detected in early stages. The FDA requested in 2015 that male donors refrain from sex with men, a year before donating blood. This was unacceptable to some gay men, who may be devastated over your preference to not die a slow wretched death. Leftist rag Thinkprogress.org echoes this in their screed "How The FDA's Revised Blood Ban Caters To Religious Anti-Gay Beliefs."[140] Zack Ford conflates the science of epidemiology with religious conservatives in this screed, which belongs in the archives of the Flat Earth Society.

Everything connected to the lifestyle has been declared taboo, and this includes frank discussion of HIV/AIDS, a horrific curse with millions of victims. AIDS was branded by the gay community long ago, because it was primarily spread, hosted, and kept alive by their sexual excesses. Privately they'll admit it, but fiercely attack any outsider who makes the connection. This muzzles scientific and medical professionals, as they attempt to help them.

Homosexuals have a love/hate relationship with the disease, because the only known cure for HIV is to end random, promiscuous sex.[175] This is intolerable in the gay universe, or they would be seriously discussing it. Anything limiting geography of the hallowed penis is unmentionable, and the World Health Organization (WHO) best remember.

Even MDs with expertise in epidemiology run the pink gauntlet of censorship. Urologist Dr. Paul Church warned that "two-thirds of all new HIV/AIDS infections in the U.S. are the result of men having sex with men," and that half of all gay men are likely to be infected with HIV by age 50.[141] Being on the Harvard faculty hasn't shielded Dr. Church from vendettas for this factual revelation. He was dismissed from his positions and expelled like a criminal. Personal attacks were lobbed from both Harvard Medical School and Beth Israel Deaconess Medical Center, where he worked nearly 30 years. Apparently, they have no gratitude, nor interest in health.

Rather than applaud Dr. Church's efforts at ending disease, they placed him under a gag order, and eliminated him when he wouldn't shut up. "This is almost a fascist effort at mind control" Dr. Church said of the bizarre censorship he encountered. Almost fascist?[142] Fascism is getting positively trendy at Harvard. This isn't the first time Ivy League colleges sought out and protected fascists, but they appear to have no loyalty to peers either. Harvard et al, proved that the long arm of gay censorship is strong, swift, and completely free to throttle any who hesitate to join their cause. Health is far from their first concern.

British AIDS activist, Cass Mann, was diagnosed as HIV+ in 1985 and lived with it until 2009. He spent his last years warning outré homosexuals to change their ways in exchange for longer lives. Mann also charged the gay community with censorship – showing only "healthy, buff young men" — instead of images of AIDS dementia. He did this out of love and sincere concern for this scourge in the gay community, which is evident in his speech.

Response so far has been threats to shut down research, unless it reaches the desired conclusions. They could use their cash and anger against the AIDS virus itself, possibly finding a cure. Instead gay militants blame "religious, anti-gay beliefs" – because science is just so mean.

10

NUKING THE NUCLEAR FAMILY

Traditional families leave gay unions looking dreary by contrast, and for some reason that seems to enrage militant zealots. Their reaction has been to diminish biological families in any possible way, and to deny their validity, significance, and worth. While homosexual households are numerically measly, they have (per-capita) the most political and financial clout of any minority in the US. Yet, they are demonstrably the *least invested* in schools, family, and in childhood issues. Why are they calling the shots?

GAY BUT NOT HAPPY

When the University of Texas published a large study on comparative parenting in 2012, gay and lesbian families were left looking pretty shabby for the most part. Collecting data from 15,000 young adults between 18 and 39, they analyzed it according to strictly scientific method.[143] Then they had the nerve to publish it. *The New Family Structures Study (NFSS)* was a reflection of reality, as experienced by young adults from alternative families – but the answers were all wrong. It was not in accordance with gay doctrine, and therefore must be hotly disputed.

Slate, Huffington Post, and all the new Flat-Earthers took up the hue and cry against the results of *NFSS*. Several columns questioned motives of the research, rather than results. Stupid questions were lobbed at study architects such as, "why did you assume respondents' answers were true when they described their parents as 'gay'"? (As if mothers only faked lesbianism to irritate their kids). Scientists researching other subjects aren't forced to prove the identities, IQ, and political party of their *randomly* selected, *anonymous* subjects, who are giving their personal opinions and experience.

Children in gay households almost never live with parents in a faithful, stable relationship, whether they call it marriage or not. A classic 1984 study couldn't find one male pair that managed to keep a monogamous relationship for five years. Gay male couples in other research found 41.3% had open sexual agreements, with some restrictions, while another 10% had open sexual agreements with no conditions at all. Even those covenants were broken by 1/5 of those interviewed, and others engaged in risky sex with strangers.[144] That's bound to make a cozy home.

Adult children of even one homosexual parent are much more likely to have recently contemplated suicide. Specifically, 2.5 times more likely if their mother was a lesbian, and almost 5 times more likely with a gay father.[145] This joyfully natural and normal life continues to affect them years later. How do we know this? Science. Since common sense, history, and personal testimonies are trashed if they trespass gay mythos, we are left with science alone —and that is being altered for political expediency as well.

High rates of suicide weren't the only damning evidence of the comparative unhappiness of children raised by gay parents. Twenty-percent of those raised by lesbians and 25% of those raised by gay men reported contracting a sexual transmitted infection, compared to only 8% of those raised by biological parents.[146] Adult children of homosexuals reported more extramarital affairs, and other forms of unfaithfulness in romantic relationships. They are also more likely to be unemployed, or be victims of sexual molestation or assault. Boys had higher rates of delinquency and violence. Girls are more likely to become pregnant teenagers.[147] They tend to do poorly in school and suffer far more addiction. For the most part, these children were ravaged by their past, but are not free to tell anyone — unless by anonymous survey. That way the researchers catch all the flack.

Devastation for gay children continues when they dare leave the herd. No cult is fiercer than the gay community toward a straying man, woman, or child attempting to exit the gay ghetto. Robert Oscar Lopez is an example. His book *Japeth's Daughter's* chronicles his life and trials as a boy raised by lesbians. Lopez became opposed to gay adoption and marriage as he matured. He has called it a "crime against humanity" and a type of slavery.[147] Lopez flatly claimed that gay marriage, adoption, and lifestyle are "detrimental in every conceivable way" — especially for children. He should know.

Gay groups such as "Equality Matters" immediately targeted Lopez for silencing. They would have been far worse, but rules of PC etiquette require a grudging civility for fellow "victims" including Latinos. Thus, it took a full 26 months of harassment to remove him from his tenured position at Cal State-Northridge. Leading the pack was a demented grad student, who had issues with Lopez being given the freedom to speak on his own childhood. A number of faculty and students joined in a humiliating, reverse hazing-ritual, which is becoming a common LGBT campus event. Civil-rights at Northridge were flushed down the toilet by gay vigilantes in 2012.

Concepts of family are becoming so distorted at this point, they may cease to exist in a child's consciousness. This is intentional, and our schoolbooks prove it. Before they can even read, toddlers have this garbage shoved into their bewildered little faces: "Mummy and Mumma get Married", "And Tango Makes Three" and "King and King." John Erickson's book for older students exposes the belligerent, greedy bullies they hope to make your children: "Gay Kids! Sue Your School for A Million Bucks!"[148] Assuming they need no reason, (or one can easily be constructed) and to hell with other kids and teachers.

Should a school refuse their sodomic paradise brochures, gay operatives fume over being "banned." Likely, they know the difference between "banning" and "choosing" but hope you will be intimidated enough to yield.

GAY COUPLES NEED YOUR KIDS - PLEASE GIVE GENEROUSLY

Another statistic from the embattled NFSS is startling. Only 61% of those raised by lesbian mothers and a whopping 71% of those raised by gay fathers described themselves as "entirely heterosexual" (they are some variation of gay). Compare this to the more than 96% of those raised by intact, biological families who identify as entirely straight.[149] Now you've grasped the real raison d'etre of gay marriage- *to reproduce the lifestyle.*

Objective statistics proved what we already knew — that gay households tend to produce gay children. Stridently gay parents preach homosexuality as being valuable and superior, and their culture seconds that. Is it even conceivable that parental attitudes and example have no influence on children under their control for 18+ years? For this alone, militant gay lovers fought to adopt and gain custody of children who could never be biologically related to both of them.

Hostile gay couples who can't recreate, often resent those who can. Exceptions are when straight people do their bidding, as they did in ancient Greece, where homosexuals (men only) were almost enshrined. Other males were demoted as breeders— like some creepy, alien slave-caste. This still happens in places such as Afghanistan. Schoolgirl-shooting, Taliban terrorists are busy raping little boys, when they aren't throwing IEDs under buses. They make them dance first (the boys).

Needing children to perpetrate their barren tribes, homosexuals must access other people's children. They didn't have it so easy in the past. Authorities defended families from intruders and predators, however they presented themselves. Lesbians can always make a baby with a willing male, and many were married to men earlier. But gay men struggled before these glory days. Lopez described homosexual men from his childhood who deliberately broke up marriages and seduced the father, so they could gain custody of the children together.

After a taste of power, gay band leaders are now demanding

everything. All the kids, of all ages, all the time. Don't forget church schools, where they've already sent scouts and attorneys. No child left behind! After the First Gay President signed waivers and favors as fast as his little fingers could go, there seemed to be no end in sight. The SCOTUS is sending them bon-bons. (Update: Change of POTUS in 2017 – family futures rise slightly).

HOW DID WE EVER GET HERE?

It took disinformation, mandated gay studies, and legal terrorism to reach this point. By force of law, counselors dare not suggest a child is *heterosexual*. Their school mottos may as well be "Face it kid, you're a homosexual." This is patent abuse and psychological torment.

Assuming we survive this, a day will come when all involved will be justly despised for the experimentation done on this generation. It will make the involuntary sterilization and waterboarding of former times seem tame, as the scope of victims is so much greater, and more vulnerable. All this time, our governments and school boards function as procurers, enablers, and wardens of captive children.

Many gay rights organizations don't limit themselves to only adult legislative and work issues. Often, they have arms for child recruiting – but they can't just call it that. Instead they issue kiddie agitprop books sounding like vacation pamphlets to paradise. Conservative literature was notably banned over the last decade, and still is. This sort of thing was schlepped around libraries for decades. Even the children's magazine, *Highlights* is now a gay promo piece. A venerated publication since 1949, *Highlights* cracked with just the tiniest nudge (a few complaints by gay parents).[150] Since one of their publications is aimed at 0 to 2-year-olds, one can only imagine the sexual prodigies turned out in the future.

More ammo was aimed at confounding kids in 2017, when New York's Tonner Doll Company announced their intention to market a "Transgender Doll." This should confuse or terrify children. Will it have interchangeable genitals? Children are now surrounded by reminders of their suspect sexual identity — which, they are warned, is dangerously unstable and liable to exponentially change at any moment. Facts speak otherwise, which is why they are banned.

In 2013, researchers questioned results of a broad, two year sexual-identity study, "The Dubious Assessment of Gay, Lesbian, and Bisexual Adolescents" from the *Archives of Sexual Behaviour.* Authors claimed to find astonishingly high rates of teens professing to be gay or bi-sexual in their original assessment — but they couldn't account for over 70% of these self-professing gay and lesbian youth who claimed to be *entirely straight* only a few years later.[151] It may have taken the poor kids that long to realize they were being fatted for the slaughter.

Fads over gay parenting were created by a host of highly paid professionals. The rest of them are cowering under the rainbow turrets, in fear of incoming lawsuits. The biggest missiles were launched from Camp Obama Care (the Affordable Healthcare Act-AHA), and rammed through unvetted and unwanted. American doctors, administrators and counselors had a rash of revelations over gay households, when the AHA was first introduced. Six years into the *Affordable Care Act,* and most have completely remodeled their care and philosophy in line with who will be paying most of their bills. If the AHA is dismantled, will we still be left with its rotted carcass of gay entitlement?

Since 1930, the American Academy of Pediatrics (AAP) had either nothing to say about gay parents or were highly critical. That is until 2002, when they began to thaw under heat. Their 2013 report is now like a homosexual, how-to manual: support of civil marriage for same-gender couples; adoption by single parents, co-parents or second parents (regardless of sexual orientation); and foster care placement in gay households. Children must have vastly changed their emotional needs over the last decade.

Medical resisters are holding out in the form of alternative professional groups, which they are forced to create. Children's doctors created the "American College of Pediatricians" (ACPeds) to distance themselves from the cowardly and capitulating AAP. From their statement on gay parenting: "There is sound evidence that children exposed to the homosexual lifestyle may be at increased risk for emotional, mental, and even physical harm." But the good doctors don't stop with there, describing same sex-marriage as "inappropriate, potentially hazardous to children, and dangerously irresponsible…. whether by adoption, foster care, or reproductive manipulation." (ACPeds Position Statement, 2016).

GENIUSES, A TEEN CRUSH WON'T MAKE YOU GAY

Early teens often have an innocent crush on someone of the same sex, whom they admire or envy. Mine was Susan Witherspoon,* my dream idol for about three months in junior high. Obsessed over her beauty, poise and popularity – oh how I wished I could be Susan for one day! Just to have her clothes and the eye of all the boys. And that was it. No lurid sexual fantasies, and my entire life straight as a pogo-stick. It was the same phenomena that makes girls try to look like their favorite singer or model now.

When a teen girl hung a likeness of Sophia Loren or Natalie Wood on her bedroom wall (circa 1968) it wasn't as a sexual aid. She can thank God that she was spared the assaults of "gender specialists" and LGBT hunting expeditions, who cruise the earth posing as academics. 1960's Girl wasn't permanently branded a lesbian because of her wall décor, best friend, or love of mathematics. If she were cursed enough to be in public school now, at the very least she would leave with nagging doubts about her femininity and sexual identity. Conscription agents posing as counselors in diversity offices make it their life's calling. (**name was changed*)

PARENTAL CONCERN IS A CRIME

Child-sex programmers have been toiling away for decades, but few parents make efforts to protect their offspring. Watching the brave and battered parents who try may be scaring them off. It's just another effect of the unnaturalness of gay dogma. Even animals will try to protect their own.

Concerned father David Parker was arrested in 2005 for objecting to homosexual curriculum in his son's *kindergarten* class. For the towering impertinence of asking to remove his child from state-mandated sexual abuse, enforcers made an example of Mr. Parker. Informed his requests were "not possible" his fatherly insistence earned him accommodations in jail. Parker was publicly demeaned by Principal Joni Jay and Superintendents William Hurley and Paul Ash, whose contempt for families couldn't be clearer if they spat in their faces. Proving that in Lexington, Massachusetts, parents have no legal standing in the face of gay demands for access to their children.[152]

Since then, aggression by homosexual handlers has spread, and parents are the clear losers across the land. Yet all is well in Gaysville. Over the rainbow appears the promised land. The White House was well within conquered territory for eight years, and the American flag waved in tacky solidarity. We don't know what will happen next, but it isn't going well with many children raised in gay households. Marian is one of them.

REAL KIDS FROM GAY HOMES TELL ALL

While Marian's mom waltzed off with another man, dad experienced an instant conversion to homosexuality. Marian* describes a bizarre world where she lived with male lovers of her father, and not all of them found little girls repulsive. Emotional stability was impossible, because of her father's promiscuity (statistically most gay men are promiscuous, but we're not supposed to tell anyone). Even in the midst of a "monogamous relationship" daddy cruised for sex and sometimes brought his prizes home. Marian was exposed to sexual activity and disease at a young age, which may damage her health later.

(Marian is yet another who suffered in a gay household. She requested I change her name and details)*

"Little girls with two-daddies end up with no one" Marian explains. They can never experience a healthy daughter-father relationship, since it is partially grounded in gender roles such as masculinity and expectation of protection. "Men struggling with masculinity can't affirm either femininity or masculinity in their children," she said. Romance and chivalry, associated with antique Christian constructs and rigid gender roles, are spit out as well.

Women and motherhood were at least indirectly discounted as being unnecessary, insignificant, unattractive, and uninteresting by her father's choices. Instead of learning ballet, she lived with cross-dressing, minor recruitment, and voyeurism – all the things a young girl needs to know. Marian wasn't admired for womanly beauty or grace. Those qualities were lauded in drag queens though. Or a gay father may belong to that camp himself, forcing his daughter into a grotesque competition with him.

By the time Marian's father died, she felt free to speak out about her melancholy childhood. "All children love their parents and feel loyalty to them" she opened. "This kept me from acknowledging, even to myself, the ugliness in my childhood. My father was sexually abused as a child —which he admitted to me on his death bed. He described how he spent his entire life trying to forget, and also replace, the missing male love." As a child, he was innocent, but was an inexcusable parent.

Abusive parents come in all flavors, but it was sexual orientation and lifestyle that caused Marian's pain. Out of concern for children in gay households, she attempts to share her story with the world, but few dare interview her because of backlashing hate from the gay community. How many others won't speak for fear of losing family, friends and lovers? There is no movement to defend abused children in gay households, because of fear. This is true homophobia.

Sons (or otherwise obtained boys) in a male, gay household fare no better in the long run. They may grow up feeling the more acceptable and attractive of the species, but it doesn't protect them from abuse. These boys have no examples of true masculinity or what natural marriage is like. Denied motherly nurture and admiration, they may have difficulty relating to women. Little boys who are forced to turn to men for all their needs are likely to continue as an adult. This is no problem for many gay couples, and they may be thrilled. Recent research proves as much. Advertisements for gay sex in Craigslist, taken from seven American cities, were analyzed. Many were seeking older, and fatherly men.[153]

Interviewing Alex, who introduced this book, was an eye opener. Born to a father who decided to go gay, presumably this momentous discovery happened after numerous acts of conjugal intercourse, and pledges of faithfulness to his wife. Heterosexual, married, and now a father, Alex describes himself as being "almost totally disabled" by his childhood. Memories are like porn movies with child extras. Alex was dragged to nude beaches and used like a prop to attract men for his father. He uses the word "survivor" to describe his childhood. Lack of concern over children is the biggest beef he has with the gay community.

We've known about the pernicious effects of divorce caused by absence of a mother or father for a long time, but gay doctrine insists we forget all about that. Breaking marriage vows and families is another issue gay militants want to bury. "Children need to be raised in stable, monogamous and lasting relationships with [an authentic] mother and father for security" Alex insists. Abuse from hetero parents is fair game for social workers and police, but no one reached out to rescue Alex from neglect and molestation.

UNUSUAL PUNISHMENTS

Lesbians aren't about to let militant gay men upstage them, and some are just as accomplished at home-wrecking. Previously, lesbians were limited to merely impersonating or channeling men. Now through the magic of science, they can maim, inject, or graft themselves and their children into gross, fantasy constructs of their desires. It's like a collaboration between Charles Manson and the Marquis de Sade. This isn't a blanket condemnation against all gay women, but the dominating female environment is naturally non-supportive to boys.

In 2011, the world heard from a lesbian family with a son who "always wanted to be a girl since he was three years old." I raised sons, and at three, I could safely waltz any of them into a women's locker room and they wouldn't even notice the difference. No honest pediatrician would accept the assertion of these demented harpies point blank. They lie. The kid's preternatural desire for girliness is from his mothers, alone.[154] Medea Dearest had already emasculated him as far as she could. What's next – kiddie castration? Who would want one of those awful things anyway? This boy was used as a trans poster-child, whatever is left of him. And his "mommies" are making a strong case that giving lesbians custody of boys is cruel and unusual punishment.

Aggressive lesbians of this type are busy rejecting the male presence in history, institutions, their personal lives, and in the worst cases, in their own children. Researchers found that boys raised by "two mothers" face hostility toward their masculinity within the lesbian community. Say it isn't so! Although there are plenty of hetero swine making headlines with this kind of thing, horrific gay abuse is tidily buried by our media, and rationalized by them as well. This includes the beating death of Jandre Botha, a four-year-old boy killed in 2003 by his mother's lesbian lover, because he refused to call her "Daddy." She could make adults do it, so what was his problem? Gay crimes receive little to no press.

Children like this are merely stage props in homes where men are neither needed nor necessary. Boys and girls who hate their sex don't grow up in a vacuum. Some force (parent, school, abuse, trauma, fear) is sucking them into this place. Assisting the abuse instead of helping the child is just evil. Every politician or educator who aids these bizarre child-experiments is guilty of child abuse as well. We seem to have forgotten that children who are sexually abused often repeat the cycle. This was a mantra only a decade ago. Now we told we must forget it?

Gay communities stocked with a high percentage of child abuse victims, have lasting and serious problems. Violence between same-sex couples occurs 200 to 300% more often than with straight couples, and children will witness this.[155] Denmark's huge, 30-year study of gay unions found that marriage tended to increase the life expectancy of gay men, but married lesbians faced even higher death rates. This effect persisted through a time of lower mortality for Danish women in general. And just like dysfunctional straight families, their kids will blame themselves for their parents' troubles.

Undoubtedly, many gay men and women are fond of the children in their homes, and some of them may even be their own. But that's not the point. The big fat taboo question is "what is the child's best interest?" Little ones simply don't much matter in the conversation about gay families and how marvelously "normal" they are. But they are far from normal, nor is there a convincing case that gay adoption or families are beneficial to any children. Intentionally creating a contrived relationship where children are permanently deprived of a mother, father, or both – is selfish and hateful.

Certain words spark rage in leftist and gay circles. Pro-family, Christian, morality, perversion, values, purity, monogamy, natural. These are served up with sneers and mockery. Anything related to Christianity or traditional institutions, (even indigenous cultures, if said natives are non-gay affirming) are the nemeses. Until the sudden promotion of gay marriage, "families" were loathed as well. Remember the patronizing remarks over "family values" a few years back? Ironically, some gay couples are now hell-bent on replaying "Ozzie and Harriet", imitating traditional families, and co-opting family roles of straight people.

Still, only miniscule portions of the gay population actually raise children, regardless of their claims and hype. Even those are unlikely (statistically) to keep up the facade. Same-sex partnerships are fleeting compared to heterosexual marriages. At least four research studies, and CDC data, reveal the average same-sex relationship lasts only two to three years, whether it's called "marriage" or not.[156] More than a century ago this information was widely available and reported in newspapers. Below is an example.

Hungarian Countess von Vaya raised her daughter, Sarolta, as the boy "Sandor" to convince her husband he had an heir. After a decade, Sarolta/Sandor was so "carefully trained to be boyish" that she couldn't switch back to femininity, after years of living a lie.[157] Papers reported in 1890 that Sarolta "arrayed in men's clothes, entered upon a career of wild extravagance and dissipation." She had as many as ten "wives" over her debauched, angry life. Posing as Count Sandor Vay, she seduced and married the teen daughter of a rich manufacturer and spent most of the girl's fortune before she was arrested. Sarolta ended her days in mental institutions and infamy, thanks to mama's early gender bending experiment.

There are many examples like this, but after years of being unchallenged, homosexuals believe their floorshow is the real thing. They insist we join them, or at least send over the kids.

MARK NEWTON AND PETER TRUONG

Real life accounts of children in gay households run from the perplexing to the tragic. Notorious pedophiles, Mark Newton and Peter Truong, were trotted out by Australian press as model parents. They couldn't get over themselves, finding this adorable couple, with a cute kid yet. Deranged baby pimps Truong and Newton purchased their son for $8000 (in 2005) from a Russian woman. It's the great gay path to fatherhood.

Adam* proved to be a great business investment and a source of pleasure. Pleasure too perverse and nauseating for most adults to bear, so courts avoided showing much evidence of their happy home. Truong and Newton groomed and molested Adam within the first weeks of his life, filming most of his wretched days with them. Living high, they jetted about servicing their "son" to rich pederasts (there seem to be plenty). Investigators were stunned by the "sexual sophistication and performance" this tiny prostitute was trained to do by his two "papas."[158] (**Child's name has been hidden by authorities for his privacy*).

Ah, but Newton and Truong couldn't have pulled it off without the complicity of the state and its media. Australian Broadcasting Corporation (ABC), notoriously aided and abetted this duo in their rush to convince the world that gay parents were perfectly normal. In a gushing 2010 interview titled "Two dads are better than one" reporter Ginger Gorman was cringingly deferent — close to feigning brain-death. Missing even a whisper of journalistic skepticism, Gorman shamelessly plugged them as misunderstood champions of gay rights. Raising chickens, cute little toys. "It's a happy, relaxed family scene, but it wasn't an easy road to get there."[159]

Newton and Truong mocked Gorman along with her readers. At one point, she showed a smidgeon of chutzpah, and skirted near the truth. Did authorities ever feel there was "something dodgy ... something paedophlic going on here?" she inquired. "Absolutely, absolutely, I'm sure that was completely the concern," Newton responded and shrugged it off like a great joke. [160] This wasn't followed with suspicion or assertive questioning. Sure, it's easy to see something like this in hindsight, yet if responsible adults had done their jobs at any point, this never would have happened.

Gorman was played. Groomed to accept all homosexual claims by her education, by her employers, and by her nation. "But I didn't know….I'm so sorry" she apologizes in a later column.[161] Gorman claims remorse, which is believable, but even then, she is retchingly sycophantic. In an inappropriate and sickening pivot, she simpers over various LBGT groups, inquiring over their travails. But she wasn't done with the excuses yet, and attacked those who sent her "hate mail" (the only example she gave wasn't even "mean mail"). With the last coup-de-idiocy, Gorman insists it all comes down to "homophobia." [162] She just can't stop. Gorman's rationalization of Adam's tormentors, and deflection of their guilt, makes her just another abuser. It is difficult to read such garbage.

Russia routed its entire foreign policy of adoption because of pedophiles like Newton and Truong. Americans and other Westerners (with our fondness of all things gay) are now considered suspect and disliked in many places. Gay-sycophant press wept great tears over evil "Russian discrimination" while never mentioning the perfectly logical reason they did this. American parents had been adopting and caring for Eastern European children for years. Homosexuals playing house just destroyed the possibility that many of these children will ever find loving homes – at least on this side of the pond.

Michael Cook of Mercatornet posited (for sake of argument) that perhaps only rare gay married couples end up as pedophiles. "But the ghastly story of Newton and Truong" he warns, "suggests that same-sex marriage will be the best possible cover for those who are." [163] Like an eerie harbinger, a dozen years before he was arrested, Mark Newton was stumping for homosexual marriage in California. He didn't like a 2000 Initiative which read (in its entirety) "Only marriage between a man and a woman is valid or recognized in California." [164] The thing failed, Newton got his way, and the rest is history. What could go wrong with two gay men adopting unrelated little boys? What couldn't?

Straight men don't generally seek to adopt children without a wife or woman, with a few exceptions. Nurturing isn't a strong point for most men, and they rarely work as child care professionals. Social workers, adoption agencies, and courts rarely handed custody to men – even fathers, for centuries, except in dire cases. Unrelated males are the biggest threat to children in their homes, according to police. Shouldn't it follow that widespread acceptance of gay adoption is a danger to children, and greatly increases possibility of their harm?

CORPORATE AMERICA LOVES THEM SOME DAN SAVAGE

Corporate America courts families on one hand, while sponsoring cultural terrorism against them with the other. Don't they even need our money anymore? Family-hating sponsors in the corporate world hand anti-family bigots the world on gold-crusted platters – as long as they keep the hate coming hot and fast.

Conservatives, take that! One is CBS, which tried in vain to host a comedy around Dan Savage's ugly contempt for nuclear families.

"Family of the Year" concerns a son who "comes out" (what else ever happens in Hollywood?) All the bad old normalcy is banished. Rainbows and angelic sprites accompany this "bright new chapter" when everyone "starts being real."[165] As per all homosexual propaganda pieces, reality and worth is leveraged on degrees of gayness, while traditional families are presented as absurd. Straight family members are inconsequential – little moons orbiting the blazing brightness of the newly formed star, "The Homosexual." "Family of the Year" met a well-deserved, natural death.

Distancing children from their parents (while pushing gender change), is a goal of the ACLU, the National Education Association (NEA), Gender Spectrum, and the HRC, as described in their paper *Schools in Transition.* It is absolutely terrifying in its secrecy, scope, and scale. Insanity abounds: "Age and grade level. . . should never be used to justify delaying or denying a student's gender transition." [166] Why the hell not? These are just highly-paid lawyers, not God Almighty. Worse is their caution to avoid "even inadvertent disclosures" (or secrecy) to non-supportive families. They hysterically warn that doing so places children in a "potentially dangerous situation at home." [167] What dangers? Avoiding interrogation about their sex life? Or the "danger" they may escape toadies for the ACLU?

Near the end of the 68-page *Schools in Transition* come a series of appendixes informing school staff how they *must perform* at the behest of the HRC and associated agencies. Appendix E is *Accessing transgender Students for Special education,* or how to track them down. The last sentence in this path to Pedophile Hell is an open threat of lawsuits, with the ACLU breathing fire and subpoenas down their necks.

DOLCE & GABBANA VS. SIR ELTON

Of a few honest gay celebrities, designers Domenico Dolce and Stafano Gabbana dared admit that they "oppose gay adoptions" and even said (gasp!) that only traditional families are the real thing. Gabbana told the Daily Mail in 2006, that he was opposed to raising children with two gay parents. Back then he could safely speak his mind, but the Pink Reich isn't tolerating that sort of thing now. Speaking to Italian media in 2015, Dolce dropped these incendiary comments: "You are born to a mother and a father. Or at least that's how it should be."[231]

The duo further enraged *Those Who Must Never Be Questioned* with their comments over babies conceived thorough artificial insemination, and the unnaturalness of it all. "I call them children of chemistry. . ." Dolce explained. Some things can't change, he insisted — which is evident. Yet the cloud of screeching, counterculturists lost it. Someone challenged their alternate reality, and it was one of their own yet. Fabulously gay Elton John had a fussy tantrum and got all his celebrity buddies in a huddle to boycott Dolce and Gabana clothing. "I shall never wear Dolce and Gabbana ever again" he promised. They never had enough tinsel for him anyway.

For speaking the obvious, the ex-couple were reviled, smitten and cursed — mostly by Hollywood. The designers were "pathetic idiots" and "mentally ill." All this abuse was reported as if it were extraordinarily witty, because it spewed from celebrities. Refreshingly, some Italian politicians didn't submit, describing Elton's team as the "Gay Taliban" and "thought censors." Apparently, the entire world isn't intimidated by prissy rock-stars, or other self-reverential celebrities. [169]

It's common practice for gay men to rent a uterus and buy human eggs. Depending on age, they may purchase anonymous sperm as well. Their only claim to them is through financial transactions, giving them the rights to a child's life. Isn't there something terribly wrong here? It has so much in common with slave auctions. Police also warn that some of these made-to-order children are created "for the sole purpose of exploitation." Children of gay parents are not all sexually abused, but there is always a forced "family" while missing the true parents.

Fear of homosexuals (homophobia) restrains criticism of gay households, even while they denounce heteros for the same thing. For instance, the head of the Australian Medical Association denounced a woman who gave birth through IVF at 63, as being "selfish."[170] Yet John and his lover David Furnish were respectively 65 and 49 when their last child was handed over. Elton indignantly uses these children as a shield to deflect questions, implying that concern over their welfare is harmful and bigoted.

Psychological harm done by hiding identity of birth parents is a subject for another book. Still it's a plague in gay families and screams for acknowledgement. Even the happiest adopted children seem driven to learn their genetic roots, but with lab-constructed babies, dad's identity falls to the paper shredder. Courts across the world are recognizing deliberate Parental Alienation as a crime.

Belgium's courts recently came to this conclusion as well. "*The right of everyone to the establishment of parentage is expected to outweigh the interest of the peace of families and the legal security of family ties.*" [171] Even the UN says as much in their *Convention on the Rights of the Child,* Articles 7 and 8: Children have "the right to know and be cared for" by parents, and to preserve their identity, "nationality, name and family relations" without interference. If recognized by national courts, this alone would undo most gay adoptions, and some of the more unnatural straight ones.

Part of the enmity Elton and his devotees felt for the Italians stemmed from their thoughtful stance on parenting. Gabbana ignited an uncivil war by revealing that part of the reason he split from longtime lover (Dolce) was to bring future children into a *more natural* family. Gabbana planned to use a surrogate to carry his child, and at least keep her in the picture. "It is cruel to take a baby away from its mother" he said to *The Telegraph,* in 2015. Which was obvious to the entire universe before "homophobia."

Chutzpah in the face of massive gay pressure was commendable, but sadly Dolce and Gabbana (D&G) couldn't keep it up. Life and business was apparently unsustainable after falling off the pedestal of gay approval. Both folded like teensy rainbow flags that had been spit on too long. Combined forces of gay hate and Hollywood sycophancy threatened to end the great D&G empire. Humbling themselves effusively before the gay gods was not enough. Less than a year later, D&G saw the light, and began creating agitprop accessories (with truly awful art) to promote homosexuality. Cartoons of gay and lesbian families beamed wildly from their handbags in an effort to win back the affection of gay lords and their patron saints—such as Madonna. It's penance for those terrible contrarian opinions they once held. And truly pitiful.

ASK THE BIGOT

Traumatized adult children of gay couples were utterly ignored at the legal circus known as Obergefell v. Hodges. While America's Supreme Court mullahs imposed gay marriage by fiat, two young women traveled from Melbourne, begging them to change course. Raised by lesbians, Heather Barwick and Katy Faust presented a "Friend of Court" paper in 2015. Barwick wrote "Growing up, and even into my 20s, I supported and advocated for gay marriage. It's only with some time and distance from my childhood that I'm able to reflect on my experiences and recognize the long-term consequences that same-sex parenting had on me." [172]

Faust was also raised in a stable lesbian relationship and claims both of the women who raised her "have my heart." Regardless, she learned to her sorrow that neither of them could cut it as a dad. Faust suffered under an imaginary family identity she felt forced to act out. "There's a lot of pressure on children of gay parents.... to carry the banner forward for them" Faust revealed in an interview. People secretly agreed, she said, but wouldn't "come out" for traditional marriage, because the relationship with their parents is too tenuous. Even pro-gay marriage spokesmen admit to intense political pressures surrounding this topic.

Faust appeared on talk shows and news outlets in the US, where she was met with shock and dismay. Flabbergasted progressives suddenly discovered the concept of family loyalty, although trashing straight parents is their favorite TV theme. Faust takes this abuse head-on. She laughs at the predictability and narrow-mindedness of liberals, and the pro-gay marriage camp. Labeled a "bigot" by people who don't clearly don't know the definition, Faust flows with the hate in her website, "asktheBigot.com."

GAY MARRIAGE– NOT SUITABLE FOR MINORS

In 2002, the *Journal of Gay & Lesbian Social Services* documented that gay and lesbian relationships resembled cage fighting more than domestic bliss. Between 25% to 50% couples had serious domestic violence issues. They concluded that "the gay and lesbian community is dealing with a significant mental health issue, one that is not being adequately addressed." [173] Gay marriages had already a proven a failure to provide safe, long-term shelter for children. [174] But perhaps Supreme Court justices don't have time to read much before they make their edicts.

As homosexual militancy wields disproportional political power, sociologists and psychologists have done a 180° pivot. In an aggressive tango, scientists step backward the entire dance. Gays are leading. Timidity of the courts to intervene in gay households is many times worse now than in the past. Officials are straight-up terrified of being pegged as "homophobes" by lodging a complaint against gay child abusers. Which would be no big deal if whistleblowers weren't punished more harshly than the people who rape little boys or girls. Mary, recovering from gay childhood, is quoted in the *National Catholic Register*: "For years we were silent because society had no idea we existed, and now a deaf society won't allow our voices to be heard."[177]

Unrelenting venom for traditional families is focused on conservative advocates more and more. Dan Savage called for the parents of Leelah Alcorn, a 17-year-old, transgender girl (boy) to be held responsible for his suicide. [178] Why not? When Savage gets away with his personal version of the Westboro Baptist Church by hurling curses and accusations at a grieving family, anything can happen.

Apparently, the Alcorns didn't support their son's transitioning, and were fearful of this very thing. Will Savage pony up for HIV treatments of the gay children he supports? Will he be held responsible for their deaths, if he encouraged the lifestyle that led directly to their demise?

OFFICE OF FAMILY REDISTRIBUTION

A friend told me a disturbing story of gay abuse about 10 years ago. Married to a frail, disabled man, the elderly couple were being driven by a male DHS worker in Portland, Oregon. She described how the man crept his hand up his disabled male client's thigh, while the couple sat paralyzed with humiliation and fear. After reporting this creepy molestation, nothing came of it, and she feared making further complaints. This isn't a blanket condemnation of social workers, but a personal testimony of "homophobia" at work. In Oregon, it's reaching critical mass.

Adoption is under threat because of homosexual aggression, as well. Affirmative schemes to benefit gay families deprive birth parents of choices they once had. Siblings, profession, and religion of adoptive parents often matter very much to birth mothers. Now they are being denied critical decisions about lifestyle. Are mothers still allowed to refuse meth addicts? Or is this happening because giving mothers a choice means they will likely specify a straight family? The Gods of Gaydom have prevailed, and once more the straight majority is screwed. Even the babies.

Proof that homosexual activists aren't concerned over child welfare came from India in 2015. Mother Teresa's beloved Missionaries of Charity orphanages were ordered to either place babies with single parents (including gay couples) or be forced from their adoption missions. Devastated nuns were ordered to ignore their conscience, along with ancient teachings of the Church. In the past, they matched children into solid, two-parent, traditional homes they thought best. India now emulates the West. They also cater to homosexuals, who desire children but don't care to create them the same way everyone else must.

Even liberal papers noted that hundreds of orphaned children will go unplaced if Christian orphanages close. This monumentally selfish demand will turn vulnerable children out to starve there. It's a move that may be advantageous to a certain type of person. Street children in India are sometimes forced into brothels, and even hung in cages to be used by strolling pedophiles. But we can't look down on India while it's happening here. Possibly India was inspired by the gay juggernaut thrashing through America. In the wake of the Affordable Care Act (Obama Care) many Christian charities met the same dismal fate, and for the roughly the same reasons.

Orphans and street children are at risk of human trafficking and rape. These are the hunting fields of pedophiles, and it is manifestly to their benefit to disrupt natural bonds and weaken the traditional family. Who gains from this type of legislation? From the original 1971 Gay Manifesto comes one answer: "We must aim at the abolition of the family." [179]

Fortunately for gay crusaders, many politicians find their bitterness useful. Common goals include castrating the church and family, leaving a cultural desert for them to replant. Meanwhile, children who want to feel happy and secure with their own mother and father are invisible. They are like little ghosts — placeholders in an ugly game for grown-ups.

FAMILY THUG COURT IN VERMONT

Case in point. Vermont lesbians Janet Jenkins and Lisa Miller split in 2003, when Miller left the relationship. Later, she converted to Christianity. Courts forced Lisa's *biological* child to visit Jenkins. This was years before Vermont legalized gay marriage, making the relationship equivalent to straight people shacking up. Two experts testified that the "little girl suffered from emotional trauma following court-ordered visits to Jenkins" and there were assertions of abuse.[180] Her mother, Miller, stopped the visits. Judge William Cohen retaliated, giving Jenkins full custody of the daughter of her ex-lover, in 2009.

According to documents, Vermont intended to hand over the girl because the ex "missed" her and had "grown accustomed" to the little thing underfoot. Kind of like a spaniel. Seems the sins of the birth mother were to reject not only one lesbian, but the entire lifestyle. Rather than donate her daughter, Lisa Miller fled the US with her child. Her Amish-Mennonite Pastor, Ken Miller (not related), is presently *imprisoned* for giving her pastoral counsel and aid. [181] Previously, this was considered sacred communication, not privy to courts or interference. But this was a *Big Deal*— a lesbian didn't get her way.

Pastor Ken supported Lisa's fight against state-sponsored religious bigotry, threats to her child, and massive denial of civil rights. They sent him to Federal Court, where the average person can't scrape up funds to defend themself. A jury of lowbrows found Miller "guilty", while the state rushed to make laws (after the fact) for some grounds to keep him in prison. Judge William Sessions III held Miller in Contempt of Court because he refused to *inform* on his own parishioners. Church members were terrorized and pushed to turn on each other, as if it was a cartel murder.[182]

This mob scene occurred years after the women's split. Clearly, gay marriage has been interpreted as open season on Christians; the courts may as well put up neon signs. Keeping with the Fascist theme, the state punished even well-wishers of the defendants. Under pressure from the US, people accused of aiding Lisa were arrested as far away as Nicaragua. Seeing she was allowed a long chain, Jenkins has been allowed to sue charities who asked for prayer or defense money for the beleaguered Miller, using the "Racketeer Influenced and Corrupt Organizations" statute.[183]

Courts didn't take motives of defendants into account, although these Amish leaders claimed their work was similar to the underground railroad aiding runaway slaves. [184] In Vermont, a change of sexual orientation is grounds for unfit parenting and prison sentences — but only when it's headed straight. And they showed those Amish people who's in charge, as Pastor Miller's family has been left destitute. Heil Vermont!

Jenkin's spite is apparently infinite and well-funded, because it never ends. In 2017, fourteen-years after the women split, another man paid dearly for befriending Lisa. Philip Zodhiates was convicted of international parental kidnapping and conspiracy, although in this case, the entire system is guilty of that crime.[185] *The Atlantic Magazine* missed a chance to stand for liberty when they summed up this charade as one of the "most bizarre plots against the growing normalcy of homosexuality in American society." [186] If this is gay normalcy, it is seedy and vicious. Even if Lisa was an unfit mother (which they did not find), courts don't give unrelated people offspring of their ex-lovers. This is corrupt and savagely creepy.

Judge Cohen, if a man grows fond of his neighbor's little girl, will you award him custody should they move? And why not, if he claims to suffer terribly? What if he once had an affair with her mother —or lived in the same home? What is the difference, dear Cohen? Your state motto is Freedom and Unity, but it's past the pull date. There is no "unity" and only lesbian sociopaths and federal attorneys appear to have complete freedom in Vermont.

11

PEDERASTY FOR FUN AND PROFIT

One of the most underappreciated qualities of homosexuality is their vast over-representation as child sex abusers. Herein lies true inequality. With straights outnumbering homosexuals by 24 to 1, busy gay pedophiles still manage to commit 30% to 41% of child sex offenses. [186] Let's put the nasty stats in a different light. Although only 1.4 to 3 % of men prefer sex with other males, 40 % of male pedophiles (they are almost all male) are *very* fond of little boys. [187]

Boys find it especially humiliating to admit they were forced or manipulated, and it is very emasculating. Dr. Robert Johnson reported as much back in 1988, when doctors could still discuss such things without losing their practice. "The vast majority of cases of male sexual molestation is not reported. As a result, these young men keep both the incidents and their feelings to themselves." [188] A New York study in 2008, found that 50% of trafficking victims were American boys, used by men.[189] Before the Gay Era, the Department of Justice (DOJ) concerned itself with child exploitation as well. Back then, they took the side of the children. The DOJ shared this in 1999: "Adolescent boy victims are highly likely to deny certain types of sexual activity" because of embarrassment and feelings of shame.[190]

Knee-jerk response to these facts is to find any instance of a straight child molester, as if all the big bad statistics must now melt away. While there may be as many straight pedophiles or more, they are *much* less prolific than homosexual ones. Gay pederasts often rape hundreds of boys compared to straight pedophiles, who seem to be less energetic in their sordid activities. To be exact, an average 150.2 boys are abused per gay male offender, compared to an average 19.6 girls by straight male pedophiles.[191] Math makes it obvious; homosexuals are light-years more likely to screw a kid, or try.

All homosexuals are not child molesters or rapists. People sharing the ugly facts above are not claiming this either, although it's the usual reactionary accusation used to deflect facts. But if you were to toss a membership application for NAMBLA into a gay parade, the odds of it landing at the feet of a pedophile are much higher than the general population. Kiddie-sex recruiters go ballistic when any of the above is mentioned, because statistics are so.... hateful.

PEDERASTS WITH PHDS – MAKING PEDOPHILES RESPECTABLE

UC Davis' Psychology Department, while trying to obfuscate unwelcome facts away, makes insipid remarks like this: "The distinction between homosexual and heterosexual child molesters relies on the premise that male molesters of male victims are homosexual in orientation. Most molesters of boys do not report sexual interest in adult men, however." And this proves what? Because men who molest little boys aren't turned on by big, hairy men, they are not *homosexual*?

Alternatively, a study of sexual offenders against boys in Behavior Research and Therapy found that most gay male pedophiles are sexually attracted to "males of all ages." In another study from "Archives of Sexual Behavior," some 86% of pedophiles described themselves as homosexual or bisexual. Admitted pederast Kevin Bishop said as much in a 1997 interview with the *Electronic Mail & Guardian*: "Scratch the average homosexual and you will find a pedophile."

Disproportionate numbers of academics identity as gay, and the rest seem mortified of crossing them. The sheer number of papers for norming child molesting is proof that the lifestyles are becoming closely related. Rarified halls in Cambridge echoed to these words in 2014: "a sizeable minority of normal males would like to have sex with children." *Normal* fathers would have clubbed them about then, but there were apparently none for miles. An article in *"The Journal of Homosexuality"* (1990) claimed the pedophile is no threat, but a family friend and "lover" of your sons. They shouldn't be viewed as a competitor, the author insists, but as a "partner in the boy's upbringing, someone to be welcomed" into the home.[195] Pearls of academic wisdom.

Ken Plummer, from University of Essex, wept great verbal tears for poor misunderstood pedos, and came up with this diabolical construct to deny children any voice at all: "Childhood" is not a biological given "but an historically produced social object."[196] Plummer, et al, don't believe in children, preferring to see them as organic sex toys. They greatly contributed to the halls of pederasty by insisting that pedophiles "are incapable of relations with adults" as a monstrous rationalization – because they *must* have sex. No child should begrudge them that! Undoubtedly, they were paid high fees for sharing these lofty thoughts to key experts in the field, at Cambridge and elsewhere.

Peter Righton was a child protection expert, social worker, convicted child molester. and academic. Those occupations are coming in clusters lately. Many people were aware of his proclivities, since he wrote on it between bouts of abusing vulnerable orphan boys and such. Nick Davies describes Righton's lecturing as "an attempt to "legitimise his obsession in a series of academic studies." Apparently, he did a bang-up job because he was never jailed. Instead, he was honored as consultant to Britain's National Children's Bureau and Home Office, where he led inquiries into *child abuse*. Righton (died in 2007) illustrates the risks of tolerating men in academia who rape little boys. There is a place for firm intolerance.

Greater danger comes from allowing pederasts to officially define "family" or sexuality for a nation. Plummer was head of the Sociology Department at Essex. Righton and peers contributed to a book called *Perspectives on Paedophilia* (1981), which made a strong defense of sex with minors. Published by academic imprint, Batsford, it was chock full of respected academics from top flight universities. Allowing pedophiles to have a have long run is beginning to be a habit in Britain. America, the faithful running-dog of pederasts, follows nipping at Britain's heels

Many who sit on boards or run gay rights organizations, end up in mug shots due to their child-friendly persuasion. Terry Bean (founder of Human Rights Watch) and San Francisco's Larry Brinkin are among them. Frank Lombard was associate director of the Center for Health Policy for Duke University, yet was caught offering his *five-year-old* adopted son up for sex to men. Ex-professor Walter Lee Williams (USC) even made it to the "FBI's Most Wanted" list, which is quite a feat. A lauded pioneer in the field of Queer Studies, Williams is an omen for where this is taking us.

Universities are ethics-free zones now, so they are safe places for kiddie-rapists to hold their club meetings. While colleges work to indoctrinate big kids and poison research, the juiciest, low-hanging fruit is in children's schools. Ripe for the picking.

K-12: READING, WRITING AND "BUTT-PLUGS"?

Obscene "dating" surveys were handed to Andover High School students in 2015, along with their lunches. Names, family secrets, emotional state, and even criminal acts were solicited —with sweets offered as bait. One local noted that the survey content could even be used against them in court. Blackmail fodder in the "Youth Risk Behavior Survey" must be seen to be believed:

"What do you feel is your gender?" "How old were you when you had sexual intercourse (oral, anal, vaginal) for the first time?"

They were also asked about violence committed by, or on them.[199] Note the assumption that minors not only have sex, but they are sexually sophisticated, and wish to tell adult strangers all about it. Subtly implied is the impression that such behaviour is normal. Promoters encourage kids to try a new sex or partner, as if it were no more than a cereal. Students are also learning extreme sexual passivity, as authority figures encroach on their emotional and physical privacy. Although this survey has been around since the 1990s, the CDC updates it every few years. Apparently, the interest of homosexuals is a very high priority at this point.

In September 2016, a gay, male couple from Minnesota killed themselves rather than face multiple charges of sexual abuse of their students. Boys had been encouraged to "come out" under their tender ministrations. These teachers plied them with alcohol, raped, and otherwise abused them. Being useful to adult predators is the *only* reason children are being pressured into making rash decisions about their sexual identity. Some version of this couple have access to most students in this country.

The American Civil Liberties Union (ACLU) aids adult aggressors in these endeavors.[200] Kids aren't given handouts on their civil rights, along with the assaults on their innocence and identity. Rest assured, no ACLU attorneys were sent to counsel straight children on boundary violations, when besieged by unsolicited sexual advice. They weren't offered "safe spaces" from adult panderers either. As MassResistance reported, the surveys appear designed to change children's attitudes and beliefs, rather than measure them. The ACLU has no right to do either one.

Nonexistent in the dark ages of determined gender, were the voyeuristic sexual assaults today's child must endure. "You too may be a homosexual" is the gist of it all. And if at seven you're quite set in your gender, they have ways to break you. Can you imagine this in a *Happy Days* rerun? Innocence was the reason they were *happy*, and not *gay*. Children are being forced to hear, see, understand, and applaud sex acts against their will. They are also preternaturally conditioned to accept homosexuality by adult authority figures, who are demonstrably the only ones to gain.

Judith Reisman reports how gay leaders panicked in the mid-1980s, as kids became terrified of catching AIDS, and recruit levels were dropping. Academics like Gilbert Herdt (San Francisco State University) determined that gay leaders must access schools, scouts, and other child "institutions" to keep up demand for young flesh.[201] Leaders enthusiastically trolled for "gay kids" in public schools, while Herdt counseled teachers to aid recruitment and limit escape. Adult-led groups should direct the adolescent first "into a self-affirming semisecret group, then by collective socialization into a 'gay' cultural system" Herdt wrote.[202] Lo, the humble beginnings of the now pandemic LGBTQ school clubs – an *adult* project.

Herdt was rewarded for his endeavors with a Guggenheim Award for Social Sciences in 1997, proving that right-wingers were right all along. Gay militants *are* working hand-in-hand with power-mongers of the world, and comprise a surprisingly large number of them. Newest sexual-deconstruction effort by Herdt is his book *Moral Panics- Sex Panics,* where he preemptively attacks people who are on to him. Patronizingly, Herdt argues against "political abuse" (or jailing pedophiles) and our unreasonable overreactions to having our children raped.

The amount of crap thrown at these kids is beyond belief. Goodreads (in 2015) boasted 654 books on "Gay Romance /Characters Attending High School/College" and 1,062 labeled "Best Young-Adult Fiction with GLBTQQI themes/characters." The "Trevor Project" offers porn romances for adolescents. *Puppy Love* is described as "perhaps the world's first gay BDSM coming-of-age novel." *Bare Me Safely* is all about gay sex with band boys, and helpful ideas (for the adult publishers) about boys picking up older men. Gay fiction, as well as "serious" academic work, promotes "intergenerational intimacy", because it sounds better than "dirty, diseased, old guys buggering teens and children."

Recruitment camps in schools are nothing less than gay induction centers. Students are confined, controlled, and vulnerable – like fish in puddles. Without their assistance, your teen would never in a million years know what a "butt plug" is. I didn't, and wish I could get the damned thing out of my head. But our lucky little scholars! They don't have to wait to hear the glorious details of gay sex, in flaming colors.

UK -GOD SAVE THE QUEERS

America's gay militia were inspired by the success of homosexuals and pedophiles in the UK, and apparently took good notes. Dr. Julia Gasper documented the connection in her book *Homosexuality and Paedophilia: A Reference Guide."* She asserts "nobody could write a full account of [pedophilia in Britain] unless they were willing to devote their life to a topic that is monotonous and unsavoury, to say the least."[203]

Gasper proved that despite efforts to protect the guilty, this information is still available. The good doctor returned from her studies with horrifying revelations; the UK is shot full of powerful, organized, pedophilic groups which are both fashionable and accepted. Gasper also accused British media of being "willfully blinkered" over major gay scandals, such as the "Scottish Stonewall Paedophile Ring." [204] Stonewall executive, James Rennie, was arrested in 2007 for such crimes as molesting a three-month-old male infant –which is almost inconceivable. Co-rapist Neil Strachan assaulted little boys as young as 18-months, while he was *HIV positive.*[205]

More damning is the continued funding of gay organizations as legitimate charities, long after they're revealed as mass crime fronts. Stonewall lives on as "LGBT Youth Scotland", where they "offer advice and support" to LGBT youth. "Youth" in Gayspeak includes adults up to 26. It is terrifying to imagine the kind of "advice" a man like Rennie and his seven charitable cohorts might offer. Was it how to insert an adult male penis in the rectum of a 14-pound child without ripping him to pieces? Another 200 pedophiles related to this group were arrested abroad, all gay.[206] Induction into homosexuality by any means is clearly the primary goal of many gay charities.

How does this become a tradition? With an endless supply of politicians charged with sex crimes. The Kingdom fairly crawls with them, like maggots on a corpse. Of 87 offenses by Councilors, MPs, mayors, activists, and candidates – the majority were by men who like little boys. Labour was so omnipresent, that pedophilia could pass as part of their platform.[207] (To be fair there was a sprinkling of Tories, one Lib Dem, a few conservatives, and a UKIP former Royal butler). Perusing pedo-politicians back to the 1970s, you will find a notable difference; there was far more interest in molesting members of the opposite sex then. At this point, they may need special Parliamentary wings in British prisons.

Demonstrably, the cultural push to legitimize and even glamorize gay life has its consequences on children. When politics are deeply embedded with child molesters, laws are inevitably bent to suit them. Beatrix Campbell acknowledged as much in her work for *The Guardian,* in 2016. She accused virtually all bodies bearing responsibility for children – police, churches, schools, and justice system – as complicit. [208]

Britain already functions as a state-sponsored child brothel, with public awareness of the boy-sex thing going back to before Thatcher's time. With the majority of perpetrators belonging to the Labour Party, they have stolidly refused to move against each other. Even after official enquiries were held, Labour Party faithful denied all, claiming all these rapes, and children's accusations were merely a "myth of the Far Right."[209]

Once a quiet English town, Rotherham is now a byword for pedophilia. Although their molesters attacked boys and girls, we heard no hint of male victims in the news. Rotherhams's children fell prey to a deadly combination of intersecting Political Correctness – abject fear of criticizing either homosexuals or Muslims. Habituated to pederasty for decades, and trained to ignore it, officials had no impulse to do a thing when the last batch of child rapists showed up from Pakistan, Somalia, and points southeast. Like their gay brothers, these Muslims were assigned to a coddled criminal class and blithely ignored.

The Telegraph reported on this extensively between 2002 and 2006, but their findings were either ignored or slighted. Eight years later, a 2014 headline read "Rotherham sex abuse scandal: nobody at the council needs to resign, claims deputy leader."[210] Well, well. In 2017, Rotherham police investigators exonerated themselves yet again, concluding there is "no case to answer."[211] Pederasts will be pederasts – but many will also become MPs, editors, mayors, and police commissioners. Even Rotherham's ex-Mayor, Barry Dodson, was charged with child rape.

Social workers and police admit they won't investigate sex trafficking there because they fear being labeled "homophobes." [212] There you have it, from their craven little lips. Adults charged with protecting the nation are completely beggared by the fabrication of "homophobia." They have reason, as they watch a multitude axed before gay orthodoxy. Magistrate Richard Page was removed from his position at family court, for claiming that "children do best in the custody of a mom and dad" in adoptions. "To punish me and to seek to silence me for expressing a dissenting view is deeply shocking…..illiberal and intolerant" he stated.[213] Poor Magistrate Page was under the impression adoption was to benefit children. Not anymore.

Bodies are still being counted from a 20-year pederasts' orgy in group homes and orphanages in northern Wales. Of those victims, one committed suicide, one was convicted of murder, others have been killed; and hundreds claim their lives were destroyed. Witnesses and whistleblowers of major scandals have also been murdered. Arson is popular, and one of their victims was a three-month old baby.[214]

No one seems too interested, except passing conservatives, such as Sir Ronald Waterhouse, who compiled a vast report in 2000. *The Telegraph's* (2011) obituary for Waterhouse claimed all his recommendations were implemented, but few rapists even lost their jobs. Almost none were incarcerated.

But that isn't the worst of it. Kids treated so treacherously are likely to be angry, violent, depressed, or suicidal. All of us must live with the effects of unconcerned, slothful, or criminal officials. At this point, Britain is so saturated with unpunished child abusers; they may as well fence it in and consider it a huge pedophile colony.

UGLY RAINBOWS DOWN UNDER

In Australia (an extension of homosexualized European Union), a new program under the guise of "anti-bullying" does just that. Bully. Children. Ramming adult concepts and aberrations down their tiny throats, children as young as six are mentally raped by their teachers, principals and "guest lecturers." Apparently, homosexuality is now the most significant subject in Western civilization. Their mantra is, "Gender isn't quite as simple as whether you're male or female" (an actual poster in elementary schools there). Adults who create this garbage are fully and maliciously aware of the developmental level of an 8-year-old.

A much hyped "anti-bullying" campaign rationalizes this crap. Apparently if you are not gay at 6, or don't find it even comprehensible, you are a "homophobic bully." Posters in K-12 schools are a cross between Doublethink and porn teasers: "Gross! Being Straight is totally just a phase!" or "When are you going to tell your parents you're straight?" Children are asked to "ally" themselves with gay students to "keep them safe."[215] Safe from what, a wholesome childhood? Who will save Australia's minors from the malicious lunatics running their schools?

CHURCH ON FIRE

Ironically, with the gay movement so antithetical to the Roman Catholic Church, the institution has still been a veritable incubator for pederasts in recent decades. You could say, "homosexuality corrupts, and absolute homosexuality corrupts absolutely." Neither old age, frailty nor vows of chastity slowed down pederast Peter Ball, 83, of the UK. Bishop Ball was convicted of playing nude games and such with 18 vulnerable teenagers and young men, while impersonating his twin brother.[216] You couldn't make this up.

Defenders of gay organizations point to the many crimes of the Catholic Church as if they were a valid defense for their own. The deep gap between Church teachings and behaviour of a number of clergy is appalling, but there are significant differences. The Church doesn't push sex as their primary purpose. Missions of priests and pastors is first spiritual, and they provide many other services. Most are serious about their call and are not abusers. When anti-family organizations enable pederasty, they are fulfilling their purpose; although they won't generally admit it to your face, or in court.

It's possible that if priests were allowed to marry, they wouldn't be doing these monstrous things to children. But pedophiles are often married, and it hasn't stopped them yet. Homosexuals claim they don't easily change their orientation either (or cannot), in spite of church teaching that homosexual acts may land you in hell. Even the Vatican is warring gay terrorism. A survey by WND.com on church sex-scandals, revealed a consistent media cover up of the orientation of child abusers. It's all hush-hush.[217] Entire seminaries been closed because of this plague of gayness, for fear of breeding future attacks of pederasty.

Homosexuals are doing to general culture, what they've already started with the Church. Most of these crimes can be laid at the feet of gay-friendly bishops and Church leaders, who not only refuse to defend their flock, but persecute those who do. Father Michael Rodriguez is one of their victims. From his El Paso Diocese, he preached against the city's promotion of gay marriage, in 2011. Rodriquez met resistance from more than the usual suspects. He was prepared for hate from atheists, liberals, and radical homosexuals; but there were significant and strange rumblings from his own house. His archbishop, Armando Ochoa, filed a lawsuit to shut him up.

Father Justin Wylie of South Africa was a well-respected attaché, defending family values at the UN in New York. Suddenly he was removed and sent back to South Africa in 2014, in an obvious demotion. Holy Innocents, the New York church he had pastored, was pressured by Cardinal Dolan's Archdiocese to close. They planned to merge Wylie's conservative congregation with St. Francis Xavier Church, which adulates all things fabulously gay.[218] Complaints kept Holy Innocents open, but this was a rare victory for the church against homosexual hardball.

BLOODY PINK JOURNALISM

Media pushes pederasty by omitting news that reflects poorly on homosexuals. They've played interference for decades, by burying incriminating information and diddling with numbers. Links between criminals, politicians and prominent LGBT groups are routinely glossed over in our news. Only a few years after arrests and revelations of the baby-raping Stonewall executives, *The Independent* was quoting them as *experts* on gay matters.[219] They presented these violent, child raping organizations as victims – honest and deserving of sympathy! Possibly they were extorted or paid to do this, considering how many influential homosexuals have benefitted.

Dr. Gasper reveals how media coverage for child sex scandals was gay-scrubbed – such as pro-bono media work for an international pedophile ring calling itself "The Shadows Brotherhood." British police discovered 45 suspects making and distributing thousands of child porn videos of a "horrific nature."[220] Yet the press carefully avoided mentioning the sex of the children. News reports used the neutral word "pedophile", although boys were abused by men in most cases. Media also failed to mention that the "Campaign for Homosexual Equality" (CHE), organized this crime ring. One convicted pedophile, "Cooke", claimed that CHE was "the most vile organisation ever thought of."[221] Thanks to the BBC, its character is also never heard of.

When the world's most revered, state-supported news agency is sympathetic to pederasts, it's no accident Britain crawls with them. Over decades, BBC played defense for all UK pederasts with their inexplicable lack of curiosity and coverage. Not so shocking was the cover-up of their own employees. Entertainment celebrity and pedophile about town, Jimmy Savile, was accused of 450 sex attacks. Savile was an equal opportunity rapist, attacking all sexes and ages. He learned to control media and those who accused him – something the LGBT clan assiduously studies. Even allegations in BBC 's own interviews were edited out. Thus, Savile was rewarded with a long, illustrious career as a child molester and serial rapist.

Major British papers such as *The Guardian* made token efforts to cover child sex-crimes, back in the day. But when 15-year old Aaron Leafe killed himself in a care home after years of abuse from a gay employee, no one heard a peep. Perpetrator Anwar Ismail's trial in 2014 was covered only by *The Mirror*, proving tabloids the more dependable source of news in the UK. Prosecutor Mary Prior said the troubled teenager left a note saying he could not get over what had happened to him. Deference to strident LGBT demands is digging graves for youth like Aaron.

America's major networks are just as culpable. Gay lobbies so terrorize our timid journalists and editors that they shed all professional objectivity and standards. Gay media watchdog, GLAAD, inflicts punishment for those who have their own ideas. Obediently, they fail to report that gay activists campaigning to lower, or abolish the age of consent are often caught sodomizing children. Most of these perpetrators are men, and their victims often little boys – quelle surprise!

GAY.GOV

Less than 20 years ago, British officials at least feigned concern over pedophilia, but they barely make the effort now. Too offensive to some gay dilettante. Investigative reporter Nick Davies did a series of shocking exposés of entrenched pederasty in the late 1990s. Davies plumbed the scope and numbers of victims, as well as the powerful men who were into raping little boys, or covering up for them. Who knew this was an old, British tradition? Gasper summarized Davies' case that "sex abuse is organized, collusive and endemic, happening on a 'vast scale'."[222]

Feeling a little heat, leaders sluggishly reacted to public outcry in 2000. The *Waterhouse Report* was an investigation of 650 children who were assaulted in a small area of Wales between 1974-1994. Perps were adult males, such as Peter Howarth and Stephen Norris, who sexually assaulted and "buggered many boys persistently" over a ten-year period.[223] The Welsh Gay Horror Show brought chairman of the inquiry, Sir Ronald Waterhouse, to a few conclusions:

1. Sexual abuse by men led boys into homosexual experimentation, caused depression, injuries, and suicides.
2. Hundreds of boys were "significantly corrupted and their sexuality confused." [224]

Yet in 2009, UK government was still blacklisting *Christian* care-homes accused of turning away prospective gay employees.[225] Brits excel at inquiries, but resist protecting their children – at least the poor and orphaned ones. Did this attitude transfer to their old colony Down Under?

Revelations from Australia's campaign to promote the wholesome goodness of gay families are coming to the surface like bodies after a shipping disaster. Why is pederasty blossoming there? Perhaps because Victoria Premier, Daniel Andrews, is a such a great friend to pedophiles. Andrews backs, funds, rationalizes, and stumps for gay marriage and adoptions, from his bully pulpit. His government plans to outlaw provisions for counselling anyone, of any age, who desires to change their unwanted homosexual attraction. Keeping them confused is absolutely necessary for pederasty to flourish.

America's hands are no cleaner. Federal agencies at this point won't reveal sexual orientation of criminal child abusers. This covers for the gay community, while they feign mass victimization. Our children are doubting their sexuality and are emotionally battered. These small abuse victims have neither a voice, heroes, nor justice. Those coming to their aid are often denounced as homophobes, and thanks to "hate speech" laws, their complaints go unheeded. If Charles Dickens had grown up in our boy's homes, his tales would read like hard-core kiddie porn. Liberal, pro-gay politics are worse than Fagin, Bill Sikes, and all Victorian villains tied together.

SOCIAL SERVICES OR CHILD SEX SERVICES?

Boggling reports of mass buggery in America are often connected to negligent police or government agencies. It appears far worse in the UK, where Social Services and the Ministries over them often *are* the abusers. Lord Waterhouse charged officials with deliberate elevation and catering to pedophiles, after months of his investigations. [226] This means pedophiles and supporters truly are running the country; and it's not only right-wingers who observed this.

Social service offices are becoming hubs for pedophilia. They have access to vulnerable children with no families to protect them. Gay boy-lovers seek out these forlorn kids for the same reason woman-haters look for prostitutes; no one cares, or notices when they go missing. Working together, these men promote and refer each other according to court records. Keith Laverack raped boys with abandon at group homes in Britain, and was still sent to represent interests of children in court. Fortunately, he was caught. A 2011 audit found more than 1,000 California licensed care-facilities that matched addresses of convicted sex offenders. This included elderly and adult facilities, but most worked with children, such as day care, and foster parents. Alarmingly, the Los Angeles County Board of Supervisors not only resisted subpoenas against them, but brought in extra lawyers to *block* the inquiry. [227]

Weak complaints won't stop these men, as the tragic fate of Aaron Leafe shows. From 12 to 15, he was repeatedly raped by a gay, care-home employee. In spite of the boy's complaints, doors flew open to embrace his rapist; he was even allowed to follow Aaron to new homes. After begging police to "make it stop" (they didn't) the hopeless kid hung himself. Homosexuals have turned many British orphanages and care homes into child brothels, and encountered little resistance.

America is shadowing the UK in this dark movement. As New World sophisticates embrace all things continental, they take their children with them. They are not going into a good night. Our youth homes in Ohio, Georgia, Illinois, and South Carolina have notoriously high rates of sexual abuse. In Ohio's Cuyahoga Hills Youth Correctional Facility, 30% of youth reported either sexual misconduct or abuse. Yet only two cases were substantiated by authorities in Ohio, in 2012. Are all the others spinning tales?[228] Prosecution is further played down if abusers are gay. No one wants to take on these predators, their lawyers, or our cowardly officials.

Recently, the US uncovered at least one monster-sex offender who was intimately connected with child services, in Long Island. New York City's Administration for Children's Services and a contract nonprofit, SCO Family of Services, placed 106 vulnerable boys with Cesar Gonzales-Mugaburu, until his arrest in 2016. He was billed as a stellar foster and adoptive father, despite complaints from neighbors and his "boys" for almost 22 years. They included eight boys Gonzales-Mugaburu was allowed to adopt as well. Authorities carelessly waived multiple complaints from a concerned school counselor.[229]

How this happened stumped everyone, including *The New York Times* and *New York Daily News*. They noted the many complaints, the children's fears, and sundry testimonies. They found that Suffolk County ordered SCO Family of Services to cease sending Gonzales-Mugaburu children in 2001, yet they continued another 15 years. Reporters failed to come to the obvious conclusion; someone, or many people, were intentionally supplying a pederast with little boys. They disregarded orders from authorities, kept secrets illegally, and turned a blind eye and cold shoulder to children begging for help.[230] You can't do this unintentionally more than 106 times.

Suffolk County DA, Thomas J. Spota, couldn't fathom why the system failed so spectacularly. If he glanced at the "SCO Family of Services" website he may have a clue, because (as of 2016) they busily promoted the LGBT agenda. More human offerings for the Rainbow God. More damning are the denials and blame shifting on other social services. SCO insisted they informed New York city and state family services of each abuse allegation.[231] They were legion. If even a portion of this is true, family officials and courts there are unspeakably corrupt, unconcerned, or part of a pederast ring themselves. One or more of these organizations is responsible for a multitude of child rapes. So why is Gonzales-Mugaburu the only one in prison?

Pederasts shouldn't work with children, any more than arsonists should run a fireworks factory. These 106 New York boys were horrifically betrayed, by their social workers, judges, police, and media.

RAPE AS RECRUITMENT POLICY

Most homosexuals were abused or seduced in childhood, according to research and their own stories.[232] Dr. Judith Reisman, who was tapped by the Reagan DOJ to study such things, claims that in organization and rigor, "recruitment techniques of homosexuals rival the Marine Corps." But rather than deal with the abuse in their childhood, gay censors deny what it takes to spread homosexuality. Rape. Pederasty. Abuse. Shame. Lies. Manipulation. Then one morning, a gold-plated, tidal wave of denial settles over the land. It's a great day to be a pederast.

Former Californian Assemblyman Steve Baldwin sent the gay-friendliest state into fits, by quoting a study where 86% of convicted pedophiles swore they were gay or liked little boys best.[233] What happens to the kids they molest? A poll of 647 men at a gay pride in 2008 revealed that childhood sexual abuse of boys is associated with male prostitution, sexual violence, drug use, HIV-positive status, and unprotected anal sex.[234] What kid says "I want to be a dying, beat-up male prostitute when I grow up?" Only a broken and confused one, who was systematically lied to by adults. Men and women like this are not born, they are made.

Lord Waterhouse described the self-loathing inflicted by pederasts on children, in his epic report: "The lives of these already disturbed children were grossly poisoned by authority figure[s]... their self-respect and ability to look forward to the future have been shattered."[235] More significant is his observation that because of victims' guilt and humiliation, many "were led to question their own sexual orientation." [236] Homosexuality becomes penance for another man's sins. Only haters could do this to children, and only lunatics will allow them the honors, authority, and carte blanche to carry on.

Even the US Department of Veteran's Affairs admits a connection between emotional anguish and man-boy sexual assault. Claiming at least 10% of men are assaulted when young, they note this can bring on depression, post-traumatic stress disorder (PTSD) and other emotional problems. From a VA webpage: "Those who sexually assault males usually choose young men and male adolescents (the average age is 17 years old) as their victims and are more likely to assault many victims" compared to those who abuse girls.[237] As gay men age, most also tend to seek younger partners.

But pederasts aren't alone, it takes a village to make kids gay. Our governments are ready and willing. Dr. Joycelyn Elders, Surgeon General to the Clinton administration, wrote a foreword to Judith Levine's book, *Not Harmful to Minors: The Perils of Protecting Kids from Sex.* Levine claimed that in some cases, "quite young people [doublespeak for "children"] can have a positive experience with an adult."[238] The book makes a case for greatly lowering age of consent. Almost the entire US Democratic Party has functioned as a pederast booster club by continually voting such people into office. Straight pedophiles don't get breaks like that. They'd be wise to go gay, where even the government is their pimp.

Pederastic coupling (man-boy) is the most common of all gay relationships throughout human history. According to their porn and literature, it's still a preference. Easing access to children is one of the primary effects of the gay *anti-hate speech* movement, and a motivation as well. Out of the 30 pedophile organizations Wikipedia listed as campaigning to legalize adult-child sex, 28 were founded and run by gay men.[239]

Radical gay extremists are attempting to reclassify pedophilia in the medical world, decriminalize it in the legal world, and force the rest of us to hand over the kids. We are being conditioned to accept grievous assaults on the innocent, even to support it. Perhaps our Great Leaders didn't intend to, but refusal to condemn anything touching homosexuality offers a cover to people like John Wayne Gacy, Jimmy Savile, Jeffrey Dahmer ,and Peter Truong.

Infamous baby rapist, Truong, compared himself favorably to other sex-offenders in the hole with him. "I'm locked up with a lot of predators [who did] bad things to children, and that's not me," Truong insisted in 2014. It's understandable someone this deranged would think this, but Truong's attorneys and doctors were even worse, as they (presumably) were sane. Psychiatrist Dr. Robert Halon seemed to accept Truong's explanation that he assaulted children because it made them "happy" and his partner Mark Newton "likes it."[240] Astonishingly, Halon claimed Truong was *not* a pedophile. Who is then, Dr. Halon?

PEDERASTY, THE SERIAL-KILLER CONNECTION

Gay pederasts can reproduce – little pederasts, and killers. In an age of gay dominance, few dare mention it; but killers will tell you themselves, if you ask them. Direct from their mouths in several studies and databases: 69% of serial killers were "gay" if defined as "people who were self-described homosexuals or people who had engaged in homosexual behavior immediately prior to, during, or after committing their murders."[241]

Of the entire population of murderers (one or more victims), gays of some variation rated 43% of all murders. Keeping in mind that LGBTQs are 3.7% of the population, homosexuals are dozens of times more likely to kill, and kill often, than a straight person. (If sharing this infuriates someone, suggest they burn a few books on statistics. It may help them relax).

Carl Panzram (1891-1930) was considered one of the most sadistic killers ever known. Gang raped by a group of hobos as a teen, rage and humiliation led him to declare war on the world – at least the male half. Denying he was homosexual, it was still his sole sexual expression (gayness wasn't exactly fashionable then). Panzram left a bloody trail across the world, with 1000 boys and young men savagely raped, according to his own calculations. By his count, he also killed 21 young men and boys, of which he was quite proud.

Luis Garavito from Colombia is possibly the most prolific living serial killer (discounting mad doctors and nurses). He claimed to have been raped by a man himself as a child. Authorities suspect Garavito of killing over *400 victims* in revenge before his 1999 arrest. Gaining the trust of vulnerable boys living on the street, he raped and murdered them. Every pederast is violent to some degree, because predatory, statutory rape is their lifestyle. Murder is only optional.

In Pakistan, Javed Iqbal paid young men and teens to help him hunt down 100 little boys, mostly beggars or runaways. They sodomized and tortured these children, took photographs and dissolved their bodies in acid before hunting for more. Many of these boys could have been spared if Iqbal had been imprisoned for previous arrests for sodomy (since 1985), but they don't seem to mind it there.[242] Pakistan's authorities were so uninterested in solving these disappearances, that Iqbal had to preemptively confess before they moved at all.

Home grown, gay lunatic Jeffrey Dahmer tortured, dismembered, and ate 17 men and boys between 1978 to 1991. Most of his victims were African American, Asian, or other minorities. Dahmer was one of the first men to do such a thing in America, certainly the first on this scale. He inspired many copycats since then. Canadian bisexual porn star, Luka Manotta was arrested in 2012 for torturing and killer his lover Jun Lin. With murder so commonplace in North America, it took Manotta's switch to suffocating kittens to bring the full wrath and attention of the Canadian public on him.

Adam Lanza, who mowed down his mother, six teachers and 20 children, had a secret the big networks won't touch. While they blamed weapons and his mother (also a victim) for his 2012 massacre, there was just one other little thing; detectives found his computers were full gay kiddie-porn. Yep. They found a film about man/boy love, messages about "homosexual fantasies", a defense of pedophiles, and video games of shooting children. Why did media refrain from mentioning this, and who are they protecting?

Our newest fad of transgendering is not without its share of killers as well. In 2013, "Donna Perry", 61, was arrested for the 1990 deaths of three prostitutes in Spokane, Washington. Authorities didn't yet realize that "Donna" had been born Douglas Perry, and had a nasty habit of murdering women. Not a very convincing female, he may have transitioned merely to deflect suspicion – in fact he says as much. "I'm not going to admit I killed anybody, I didn't. Donna has killed nobody," Douglas told police.[243] Obviously he's counting on that old gay magic to nullify his past life in court. This could happen, in spite of his victims' panties found stashed away as murder trophies in his current closet. Apparently "Donna" hasn't cleaned house in 23 years.

Women are working hard at catching up, although they haven't racked up the body count yet. The first lesbian couple to legally marry in Verdun, France, celebrated with violence and cruelty.

In 2015, the sweethearts lured a mentally challenged younger woman into their flat, where they tortured and raped her for several weeks. Likely she would have died, if she hadn't escaped by climbing down a balcony. The girl was made a sex-slave, cut with knives, genitally militated and forced into bestiality – among other things. Media outside France remained silent, or reported vaguely. They obscured involvement of the women, their sexual orientation, and that it took place in their home.[244]

There are dozens of men and women like Iqbal, Lanza, Magnotta, and Dahmer. A majority of the killers above admit to either a seething hatred of their parents, or that they were molested as a child – or both. Yet, part of the crusade against conservatives is to block this information from the public, and to outlaw counseling for their victims. If that wasn't true, gay leaders would hold open civil discussions about it. Instead, they plot to criminalize such speech, and block the possibilty.

Panzram and Garavito are poster boys for pederasty. They illustrate both the cause and effects of unrestrained and unpunished pedophilia. Five-year old rape victims can't explain why they hurt, and it may take them 20 years for them to seek counseling. Pedophiles (gay and straight) count on that being past the statute of limitations in many places.

LEST WE FORGET WOMEN....

Lesbian gym teachers may be an old joke, but a rash of female teachers are molesting their charges. Most victims are female, but you won't hear much about that. These girls are definitely coming out, even if they end up in jail for their extracurricular activities. Homosexual normalization campaigns keep them going. Worse, ACLU, NAMBLA and the UN support "child rights" laws which effectively block parents from protecting their offspring. This keeps child molesters at schools happy, zippy, and gay.

One of the most remarkable findings on alternative families is how truly dysfunctional and damaging lesbian families are for children. A large study on effects of family structure found that 31% of children in lesbian households had been forced into sex against their will – which was higher than even foster or step-families. Children raised by lesbians also ended up in foster care more often, indicating household instability. These numbers came from adult children of homosexuals.[304]

Damning statistics like these should motivate gay parents to reconsider their lifestyle if they care for their kids. But thanks to gay.gov and docile media, homosexuals evade the scrutiny that others encounter— even after criminal charges are made against them. Pedophiles Truong and Newton made emotional pleas to friends in Australia after their arrests, claiming they were being "discriminated against" because of orientation. Their story was picked up by media who couldn't recognize child abuse if they were filming it live. Detective Sergeant Ian Wells said Truong and Newton were master manipulators, using gay marriage as a cover.[246] What else is gay academia, gay government, and gay media masking?

A study from the U of C San Francisco, (where every third staff member appears to be homosexual) insisted gay families are the very best.[247] Not that they would be personally motivated, or affected by the results. According to them, children of lesbians were happier, healthier, better-adjusted, better natured, and did all their homework. This totally contradicts findings by disinterested researchers. Who has a dog in this fight, and who will we believe? Research is now a warzone of clashing ideologies. Most troops have defected to Camp Rainbow, because that's where the money and jobs seem to be.

Robert Oscar Lopez was raised by lesbians and lived to tell. He describes what was missing in his childhood - the types of things gay-mediated researchers will never ask or acknowledge: "I just grew up in a house so unusual that I was destined to exist as a social outcast. As a result, I had very few recognizable social cues to offer potential male or female friends, since I was neither confident nor sensitive to others."[248] Lopez notes that no-one, *especially gay activists,* wanted him to speak honestly about his gay childhood.[249]

RUSSIA SAYS NYET!

Russian President Vladimir Putin openly resists homosexual incursions in their culture, but Western media fail to mention the reason – age. Restrictions in Russia are aimed at keeping children innocent of pedophilia, and especially "homosexual propaganda." This includes detailed, sometimes illustrated, non-age appropriate information about homosexuality, which no child ever asked for. *"Daddy, will you please read me the story about the magic box of sex toys again?"*

Religiously motivated pedophilia is also a problem across the world, especially with the rise of militant Islam. Perhaps criticism seems unfair, considering abuse at the hands of Catholic priests recently. But while a serious problem, child rape is not an inherent part of Judeo-Christianity. The Bible teaches against all forms of immorality. Jesus had hard things to say about child abusers of any type, as well as their fiery fate.

ISLAM-THEY ALWAYS LIKED THE BOYS BEST

Islam though, is a horse of a different orientation. *Everything* in Islam is about sex, and it is far from opposed to homosexuality. Man-boy sex is an Islamic subset, although they don't like to discuss it. Mohammed wrote about his cross-dressing habit in the Hadith: *"The inspiration did not descend on me while I was in the coverings (lihaf) of any of you (women) except Aisha."* Hadith #3941.[250] Apparently, "The Prophet" only received divine revelation while squeezing into his tiny child bride's clothing.

Mohammed also ran with transvestite-groupies, documented in the Hadith. His "mukhannathun" were translated as hermaphrodites, eunuchs, or effeminate men. In Persian (Islamic) literature from the 9th to 20th century, homoeroticism was the main topic of much love poetry.[251] Today, ISIS sexual torture of women and girls is well known, but witnesses claim gay rape and consensual male-male sex is common behind the terror tents as well. If this only involved consenting adults, it would be no problem – but they want little girls and boys. Lots of them, as they tend to wear them out fast.

The underlying subculture of homoeroticism and woman-hating in the Islamic world bears poisonous fruit. Early in 2016, a group of Pakistani Muslims hunting children in a Christian area, gang raped and strangled a 7-year-old boy. They belonged to wealthy families, and so far, haven't suffered a thing. But this wasn't a fluke. In a 2014 poll of Pakistani men, one-third claimed they saw nothing wrong with raping little boys.[252] Is this our future also, when power and sexual pleasure of men is god?

Now our soldiers must host Islamic pederasts or face discipline. Behold the dreary tale of Sgt. 1st Class Charles Martland and another soldier, who beat a serial child-rapist under their command in Afghanistan. This creature had chained a boy to his bed and repeatedly molested him, (between courses of US training, and on a US base). When his mother complained to Americans, she was also assaulted by her child's rapist. This disturbed Sgt. Martland, whose reactions were entirely humane and chivalrous. He paid a visit to this beast that he will likely remember. Martland was punished for this, and fought the Obama administration for five years to keep his job.

Is it a coincidence this happened in our new hyper-homosexualized army? Officials won't admit they function under pressure to decriminalize pedophilia and rape, but what else can explain this fine Green Beret's humiliation? Meanwhile, the Afghan boy-slaver is still alive, and probably knows where the kid and his mother live. As I wrote this, actor Harvey Keitel came to Martland's defense, asking "what the hell they would've done" if it had been their child? That's just the point; the militant gay vanguard have no children (not with each other), and their attention is elsewhere.

PEDERASTS 10- KIDS 0

Like all effective revolutions, this one has its icons and slogans. NAMBLA's old "sex before eight or else it's too late" jingle was too brutally honest. They changed it up, and employed the trusty victim meme, with a touch of guilt. Now we will be hearing about "sexual ageism" to remove prohibitions on consent, as well as "child rights" (to be molested).

As part of the non-heteronormative (gay) era, children are losers on every front. Enlisted to prove the wondrous normalcy of homosexuality, they are tools for sexual pleasure and stage props for faux-family photos. Just don't ask how they got there, or where their biological parents are. Thank politicians like former Labour Cabinet member Patricia Hewitt (UK Leftist) for all they have done to empower pederasty over the years. In 1976, she put out press releases for the "National Council for Civil Liberties" asking that age of consent be dropped to *ten*. Hewitt's group was working with the "Paedophile Information Exchange" who lobbied for *no* age of consent laws, or baby raping.[253] May they be accursed.

Contrary to gay spin, trafficked and molested boys are generally not gay, at least not in the beginning. Women almost never rent boys for sex, so they encounter homosexual demands only. Steven Pricopio counsels victims of human trafficking, and explained their vulnerability: "It's not an issue of sexual orientation" he told Jerome Elam.[254] Often these boys are trapped by threats of violence against their family. Eventually it becomes their identity, just as any habitual behavior or job becomes a source of identity to us all.

Militants insist male prostitutes freely chose homosexuality, and were never victims – much like plantation owners swore their slaves loved the plantation.[255] Because it's still taboo in America to speak of sexual violence against boys and young men, they rarely call for help. In a 2011 interview with an agent from Homeland Security on human trafficking, male victims weren't once mentioned.[256] Even worse, fascistic laws forbid or restrict counseling these youth, who may want to escape the gay lifestyle entirely. Offering help is considered "homophobic" unless they are tiny, perhaps under six. Even that is changing. Counseling in some states is limited to learning how to manage abuse, or to deal with trauma and shame. People who make these restrictive laws are despicable.

Many are working tirelessly to make child abuse easier, even if they label it as extensions of gay rights. The money helps too. Judith Reisman noted that homosexuality and transgenderism are is the only recognized sex cults receiving tax dollars and direct access to school children." [113] And in the end, it's all about the kids. Destroy their sense of identity early enough, and a child is putty in their hands. Or whatever else they want.

12

TRANSVESTITES & THE MADNESS OF CROWDS

Trailing demolition of the family is a plague of mass sexual turbulence. Thank you, LGBTQ people; it couldn't have been done without you. Bullying and school shootings aren't enough to torment our little ones, they desperately need your sexed-up insecurities as well. "God screwed up kid but we can fix it, with a knife and counselors." Sayonara childhood! You were only a pixel in the great blank-slate of Gaydom. Now you will be officially taught as much as gender instability comes to a school near you.

BOYS WILL BE GIRLS

Inhabiting a world of the impossible and magical, children naively trust their elders. Only little ones, who believe in Santa Claus and the Tooth Fairy, will accept that a man can instantly change to a woman, and back again – at will. (Precisely why LGBT evangelism is mandated at the youngest age possible).

Children live in fantasy, and need adults to grow them *beyond* magical thinking. Sadly, some of these little ones have no one fitting that description. Making it worse, "trans" and "gay" children are trotted across stages as if they were little poodles at a dog show. When they grow up and are (statistically likely to be) alcoholics, druggies, or suicidal, they can thank media for globally "outing" them at seven. Because they may never have the option of a normal life again.

Trans Children's Crusades are a part of a dark interactive saga. Led by Pied Pipers in dresses, they have weapons beneath their skirts. In the old fairy tale, the adult townspeople were naïve fools who cared, but still lost their children. Our 21st century version is sordid in comparison. Adults now flatter and *pay* their pipers. Strewing roses along the way, parents let strangers talk dirty to their children, and emotionally abuse and use them. They'll likely survive, but without their innocence, and forever changed.

Nowhere is child seduction via Fairy Tale more blatant than the benighted "Genderbread Person" created by Sam Killerman. It's a graphic, sexual induction tool-kit: simple line-drawings with lie upon lie about "gender fluidity." [257] Adults have the option to walk when presented this type of with self-serving drivel, but young students don't. "Genderbread Person" burdens tiny ones with the eternal quandary of never knowing who they are. They must determine "Gender Identity", "Gender Expression", "Sexual Orientation" and last and very much least —"Biological Sex."[258] "Genderbread Person" is a change agent, indoctrinating children for later adult use. [259]

Some lunatics allow LGBT agitprop experts to access desperately ill and vulnerable kids. Children's facilities are among what "*The Advocate*" hailed as "The Most LGBT-Friendly Hospitals in the Nation," receiving awards for "LGBT patient-centered" care.[260] And what did they do to earn this? Offer an optional sex-change with an appendix operation? The possibilities are endless . . .

Washington State plans to teach children in grades K-12 that "there are many ways to express gender." They may also show them. Most 6-year-olds know whether they are a boy or girl, but "gender" is a complex concept, because *it doesn't exist*. Gender is a cultural construct, while sex is a physical state of being, like blood pressure. Superintendent of Instruction, Randy Dorn, admits as much but assumes the right to impose this anyway. "Gender identity" is still being divined by sex swamis and crystal balls in our legislatures at this moment.

Washington State mandates that by 12 years, students will "understand the range of gender roles, identity, and expression across cultures."[261] "Understanding" roles and expression of transvestitism and homosexuality requires intimate knowledge of cross-dressing, fetishes, sex toys, sex acts, and fantasy roles of adults – or gay porn. This will benefit no student. Ever. Involving minors in these acts are also *crimes,* so why aren't proponents, curriculum writers, governors, and legislators who create this stuffed into tiny cells somewhere? "Self-identity" courses for kiddies are sexual conditioning, with teachers and staff forced to assist future predators. Britain, with their advanced pederocracy, has schools asking *four-year-olds* to choose one or more genders — like a game of Twenty Questions. [262]

Truly children are the target of legislative and media noise about gender. Quelle coincidence that the instant gay marriage was dictated by the Supremes, hordes of tiny tots publicly announced their unhappiness with their sexual identities. Not only that, but these little ones somehow knew to hire attorneys, defy elders, and mastered the art of press conferences! Case in point is a six-year-old from Katy, Texas who decided she would segue into being a boy; and had her teacher fired for not properly addressing Her Majesty. You can bet your Carmen Miranda hat that parents directed this horror show.[263]

Proving the deeply delusional state of these tiny "transvestites" (some as young as four) is easy; just listen to their demands. ABC News featured an 11-year-old trans "girl" (boy) who demanded "I want boobs." [264] Hey, his parents and teachers do anything he likes, why not be Cleopatra? Get him a yacht and a team of slaves while you're at it. Another boy of 12 announced "I want to be the mother of my own children." Adults clapped and cheered as this child deceived and humiliated himself, and which, through the everlasting life of electronics, will never be entirely forgotten.

There are always those who take advantage of the innocent, trusting nature of children; but only the worst cultures champion and support it. Australian kids face posters with moronic ditties like this; "If you're questioning the gender of someone in the washroom, don't." Is the KGB in every school now? "Don't think." "Don't question." "Don't speak." "Do as we tell you." How many parents marched their children into public washrooms to check out the local color before leaving them alone? No more, mama. A spectacular disregard for child safety pervades all things *gay,* and you are expected to follow their lead.

In America, proxies doing this work are aided by the ACLU. This band of attorneys initiate authoritarian programs in schools, without the knowledge or approval of concerned families. Their euphemistically named *"Schools In Transition: A Guide for Supporting Transgender Students in K-12"* is barely concealed legal extortion. Patronizingly, they inform administrators that they *will be supporting* whatever the hell the trans kid wants, and "in the manner in which they wish." [265] All facilities, time, funds, and attention *will be* afforded the pressing matter of sexual identity; because inordinate concern over the sex life of confused pre-adolescents is what Western education is currently all about.

Keep in mind that the ACLU is second only to the IRS in inducing compliance through fear of lawsuit. Who knew that having a pile of money and political clout qualifies you as experts on sexual identity, psychology and virtually everything? The ACLU is the Big Bad Wolf and a true bully in real life.

But never fear, new materials may ease transition of your child's identity, values, and mental health. *The Gender Fairy,* by Australian writer Jo Hirst, has this delightful quote on its publisher's page. *"Only you know whether you are a boy or a girl. No one can tell you."* [266] Well, well. Children ages four and up will take "joyful steps" toward their "authentic selves" in this covert sex-manual. Roz Ward (who conceived LGBTQ promotional gimmick "Safe Schools") collaborated with Hirst on this kiddie mind-warp.

Hirst, Ward, and activist politicians all battle intensely *against* natural sexual fluidity here. Research and human experience, show that at least 75% of sexually confused children and teens won't stay that way *if left to themselves.* Older kids often change their mind, if they are allowed to ("whoops we tossed it Georgy – sorry!").

From a place of innocence and vulnerability, cadres of gay sex specialists push kids into their camp, before they mature and wise up. This is the sole purpose of teaching "transgenderism" and homosexuality to children. Ward's "Safe Schools" urges children to make hasty declarations by "coming out" publicly at young ages. [267] Socially bound by their peers, students are pressured by constant reminders of their choice. This is also the sinister reason for the plethora of special favors and undue attention to "gay" kids, which appeals to emotionally starved and immature children. Recruitment by self-interested adults make "Safe Schools" treacherous and dangerous.

SEX NAZIS: KAGEN, GINSBURG, HOLDER, LYNCH, OBAMA & DER BLASIO

Straight adults are drafted into this as well, since someone has to the pay taxes. America was held captive to Obama's visions for gay life, delivered after his "divine" revelations on the subject. With far less than 1% of the population transgendered, they have been disproportionately present in Executive offices. Apparently, Obama's god was evolving on this subject, right along with the POTUS himself. Claiming God as an advisor on kinky sex was a brilliant power move, and some actually believed him

Using transvestites as political proxies for leftists is another coup. Perfect, because gender fluidity is impossible to *legally define* — and this is by their own admission. Courts are using the term to bully people anyway. One common LGBT demand is room to "expand" in various dimensions of their legal identities. Nothing is beautiful, natural, or free about transgenderism. It's a political movement with 24/7 demagoguery and a hemorrhage of lawmaking.

New York City Mayor, Bill De Blasio, took gay cronyism to new lows in 2015. Releasing "gender identity and expression protections" he hamstrung companies, gagged expression, and left citizens violated and threatened. Company dress codes were tossed in favor of trans-fashion emergencies. Lowly heterosexuals must alter vocabulary at the whim of random, self-described transsexuals. With at least 31 different gender identities to deal with, there should be hundreds of pronouns — do the math. [268] Restrooms and changing areas open with the magic words "I'm transitioning, here's my lawyer." Same incantation works for private homes in Trannytown. NY.

Nero used a fiddle to show his contempt for the people – but de Blasio makes ordinary speech risky and expensive in New York City (NYC) for everyone. If bureaucrats rule that you have spoken forbidden words as "the result of willful, wanton, or malicious conduct" (they are all psychics, so they know) it may cost up to $250,000 per "violation." As every opportunist in NYC feigns gender confusion, they add another appeal to greed with this promise: "There is no limit to the amount of compensatory damages the Commission may award to a victim of discrimination." [269] Will there be charges for blasphemy too?

Der Blasio's bigotry is tolerated because a new class of victims just invented themselves. He was their political mid-wife in NYC for reasons only he knows, or perhaps his wife. A former lesbian, Chirlane McCray broke the most sacred dictum of gay doctrine: "Thou shalt not return to the straight way." Their 19-year marriage is proof that homosexuals *can* leave the lifestyle, and permanently. Are the Kink Kaiser's draconian rulings penance for his wife's "sins" or just another instance of gay-directed hate, which the left finds useful?

Treading carefully, Australian writer Michael Cook explained that because transgender people are often "marginalised and vulnerable" it's easy for them to "conflate theoretical dissent with violent animosity." [270] Intelligent people aren't confused this easily, but a surprising number of people are not intelligent. See the strident condemnation against feminist Germaine Greer that read: *"Greer has demonstrated time and time again her misogynistic views towards trans women, including continually misgendering trans women and denying the existence of transphobia altogether."* [271] Consider that Greer is a woman, and "trans women" are silly-looking men with issues; any misogynistic views are coming from her denouncers. And the dreaded charge of "denying the existence transphobia"? Neither the word nor concept existed until a few years back. Who comes up with this garbage? Are they paid actors?

Proof of the big, bloody axe the "trans" community grinds, is their successful purge of ideological opponents from the highest courts and positions. Judge Roy Moore, a respected conservative and household name, was suspended in 2016 from his position as Chief Justice of the Alabama Supreme Court on the testimony of a transvestite and other gay activists. On what planet is someone called "Ambrosia Starling" given more consideration than a Supreme Court Judge? Planet Alabama. Moore stirred the ire of the sequined gods by questioning the authority of the US Supreme Court over the states in marriage issues (particularly extra-Constitutional rulings). He further infuriated sex-coup stars by noting that Justices Kagen and Ginsburg were actively promoting gay marriage *while adjudicating the gay marriage case.*[272] For ordinary mortals this is unethical, but this SCOTUS isn't concerned with that. Leftists are using woes of the almost entirely fictional "trans" community as a ruse to accomplish their goals. The miniscule population of "trans people" are almost all on television or being interviewed at any one time.

Trannys are so clearly pets of the state in the West, that criminals are falling all over themselves to adopt the identity when needed. Dutch dentist, Jacobus van Nierop, (called "the dentist of horror" in France for torturing and mutilating his patients) tried the rainbow pass in 2014. He claimed to be suffering from "psychological problems and gender identity issues" as a defense, but they didn't buy it. Go gay – it's the new Twinkie Defense.

PLANET LUNATIC -A TRANNY BY ANY OTHER NAME

Medically or legally, no one really understands what gender fluidity or transgendering actually *is*. There are no technical definitions, only an endless continuum of possibilities. Meaningless designations are manufactured ex-nihilo, and most never existed in reality. Below are actual examples, spoken by real persons of indeterminate sexuality, taken from gay sites or sources. They will likely change in a month.

" I'm genderqueer"
"Non binary-genderfluid/genderqueer"
"Some days I have other identities…evolving"
"I feel really trans today"
"Super femmy but still non-binary."
"Isn't there a "cis-trans" designation?"

Cis-gender" is what you are born with, or when your gender identity and chromosomes actually match. Gay theory equates this natural state to just another option, and reduces sexual reality to vocabulary and accessories.[335] Exciting possibilities in the sexual centrifuge include:

Bi-gender	*Agender*
Pangender	*Two-spirited*
Gender gifted	*Third sex*
Genderless	*Gender-neutral*
Intersex	*Androgynous*
Genderqueer	*Genderbender…etc.*

Another LGBT fabrication is the term TERFs (or Trans-Exclusionary Radical Feminists). These are otherwise acceptable leftwing women, even lesbians, who won't accept "trans women" as authentic females; because we all know they are not. Trans activists insist we all live outside our "binary" (or natural) identity, and claim that forcing someone to accept their birth sex is discriminatory and cruel.

In 2012, the APA removed the entry "Gender Identity Disorder" (which includes transgenders) from the Diagnostic and Statistical Manual of Mental Disorders (DSM-V). They replaced it with PC term "Gender Dysphoria" or distress over "incongruence between one's experienced/expressed gender and assigned gender." This is very big deal. Overnight, transsexuals lost their long-recognized diagnosis of mental illness, and became people merely unhappy with their sex. Making their body and inherent sexuality the *problem,* the medical profession is now enlisted to *fix* it for them. New APA classifications are only reactions to political pressure, and are utterly irrelevant at this point.

Lawyers and cash are absolutely vital for this to happen, especially in their kiddie crusades. This alone proves there is *nothing* natural about transitioning. Without modern medicine and legal duress, it could never happen. But our biggest home-grown bully, the ACLU, is there to help. ACLU darkly warns that failure to affirm a student's new identity leads to "debilitating psychological distress" (anxiety, depression, school phobia) and impairs children's ability to learn.[273] No proof is offered for their hysterical sex theories. The ACLU's *"Schools in Transition"* strong-arms K-12 schools into compliance with their sex-change program. Not officially—they are merely intimidating and blustering legal goons; but they are very good at it.

Cognitive Dissonance is also foundational to accepting gender fluidity. Transgendering can't hold up to logic, so expect to see that flushed in schools soon. Students must simultaneously believe any adult assertion and reject their own experience, feelings, body, and senses for this farce to work. Someone who can justify maiming themselves and enlisting a small army to back them up is not mentally sound. Below are only a few contradictory gay claims:

Premise 1: Classic LGBTQ line "I was just born this way" (or no choice involved). Used for decades, less popular lately.

Premise 2: "Gender is a choice." Closer to reality and impossible for trannies and other prolifically fluid persons to deny, unless they next claim it is a new form of evolution, or they were recently reincarnated. Wait for it. . .

Premise 3: "Flat denial of physical reality." (Binding breasts, hormones, mutilation- all in accordance with efforts to keep the fantasy afloat.) Denial brings money, books, attention; and the public seems willing to join in mass delusion.

Premise 4: "I was born this way but there's been a big mistake." Generic blame for God, chromosomes, parents, the universe, karma or something.

Premise 5: "There is no such construct as determined gender" or academic obfuscation and word games. Gaining momentum.

Exactly how crazy are we willing to get for this? If Marleen believes she has 77 million personalities, and is in fact an entire nation, can she send representatives to the UN? Must we give her a flag? Under current transgender "rules" Marleen is whatever the hell she thinks she is. If she changes her mind tomorrow, she may be an Irish Setter and demand a good home and owner. Perhaps with you. It's gay magic, and the rest of the world will just have to deal with it – a perfect symbiosis of selfishness and sociopathy.

Transitioning means anything is possible and nothing is fixed, natural, or as it appears. When transgendering is accepted as the norm, sanity will transition along with gonads and pronouns. "If Caitlynn can do it so can we" said the crazy cat lady in Norway, who now defies anyone to claim her as a homo sapien. Famous race-shifter Rachel Dolezal deceived everyone with her similar delusion. People mutilate themselves in bloody orgies in operating rooms, attempting to be Martians or trolls. But transgendering is the magic wand at the bottom of Pandora's Box that started it all.

There are holdouts to gay huckstering though. In 2015, former psychiatrist-in-chief for Johns Hopkins Hospital, Dr.. Paul McHugh, said transgenderism is a still a "mental disorder" regardless of current fads. He insisted it merited treatment, and denied the "biological possibility" of sex changes. McHugh charged sex reassignment surgeons with collaborating and promoting "mental disorders" and compared transsexuals to deluded anorexics. [274]

US transvestites polled in 2012 claimed 41% to 55% of them attempted suicide, compared to *only 1.6%* of the general population.[275] Swedish researchers found the suicide rate for surgically altered adults is 20 times the general population. [276] Sweden has long championed the lifestyle, so they can't blame "bullies" for this. Surgically altered persons are truly the most victimized of all in this ghastly charade.

World Magazine featured the tumultuous life of sex-change pioneer Walter Heyer. Transitioning in 1983, he assumed a knife could recreate him as "Laura." That's what his driver's license said, but his life was hellish. He lost jobs, family, and friends. Walter's son wished he "had cancer" instead, so he could tell people what was wrong with his father. A cute nose job couldn't fix this. Walter's original counselor, who approved the sex-change, apologized for his torment: "I had seen too many cases of post-surgical regret. . . I assure you that I share, as best I can, some of your pain that this mistake has caused you."[277] Eventually, a Christian couple took him in and sent him for counselling. Laura reverted back to "Walter" and is remarried – to a woman.

LGBTQ answers for these private tragedies are to beef up mandatory acceptance, although both Sweden and Walter Heyer proved it won't work. Gay advocates flatly reject these findings, as if that makes them fantasy. Escaping the lifestyle is anathema to LGBT forces, and they've effectively blocked help or counsel in many regions. Depression, misery, and suicide of their peers should be laid at *their* feet. But the surreal world of transgendering has only just begun. Welcome to the Gay World of Oddities and Wonders where each day's enormity is only surpassed by the next.

UHOS: UNIDENTIFIED HUMAN OBJECTS:

Testosterone-pumped women sporting beards can still have babies, yet insist they are men. Wasting space in the *Jewish Telegraphic Agency* in 2016, "Rafi" pretentiously droned on about educating hospital staff. As a "transgender man" (biological woman) she will be called "Abba" (father) by the baby.[278] God help that kid – it may be as mad as its mother. Rafi's demands force employees to join her altered states of reality, where men have a uterus. Whining that she was "misgendered" implies we should live in fear and trembling of incorrectly guessing the tranny's *deliberately obscured* sex. She misgenders herself.

Mutilation and trans-tinkering are fine in a wax museum, but this is real life with real consequences. Transsexuals who follow through with surgery are trapping themselves in an irreversible and unsustainable state. Later, many despair over their mangled bodies. This is why so many transsexuals are suicidal, not because someone snickered at them in the subway (which is the current LGBTQ appeal to stupidity). Will this stop before all anatomical terms are deemed homophobic?

Grotesqueries we must accept without question include a 52-year-old grandfather, dressed and behaving as a six-year old girl. Far from being in a psych ward, Stefonknee (formerly known as Paul Wolscht) is yukking it up with his dollies. Media take his fabrications at face-value, reverentially using the pronoun "she" when referring to this 6'2" male with braids and giant Mary Janes. Wolscht revealed he met his future adoptive daddy and mummy on a fetish site and quickly had sex with "daddy" at a swinger's club. Well isn't that sweet? The fawning, polyamorous couple brought Wolscht into their home, where he plays with their grandchildren. Since "Stefonknee" proudly claims to fluidly move between his "male and female identities" the children may be in for some creepy surprises.

Media interviews played up Wolscht's homelessness and depression before he walked into his current goldmine. "Stefonknee" may be smirking and simpering now, but he still isn't done hurting his real family, whom he was no longer supporting. In a 2015 Facebook tirade, he accused his ex-wife of theft and fraud at her workplace; which he helpfully named, along with whining over meany police and priests. You can't even mock this. Not because it's not funny (it is, in its own eerie, bathetic way). But who can keep up with the mutation of the day in Trans Universe?

NOT YOUR FATHER'S TRANSVESTITE

Chosen Identity ones claim they have never been happier. If trannies were born under a rainbow somewhere, sans human contact, no one would care. But most are part of a family and community. This escapes notice, because the gay creed is essentially "it's all about me." The real trans-tragedy is that sexual identity is far more than skin deep. The Self-Eviscerated often have family bonds, and they manage to keep them only because of pre-existing, traditional family dynamics. Children and spouses often remain loyal to the transitioners who left them in such a bizarre and degrading manner.

What girl is overjoyed when her father lops his penis and starts borrowing her sweaters? Cynically, the press views lack of public railing as proof children "accept" their parent's decisions. Kids may also "accept" if pops has cancer, or is beheaded by ISIS. It doesn't follow his progeny are thrilled with it, only that it's something they can't change. Even serial killers are visited by their families in prison; does this prove they were great parents and role models?

Bruce/Caitlyn Jenner's life alone is a textbook case of the sorrows and complications of "transitioning". Even with the world's media championing him, and offering millions in free PR, the anguish and embarrassment to his family can't be muffled. Multiply that by the thousands, as the Trans-Effect spreads. Father's Day 2015 brought confusion to the Jenner household as his daughters had to decide what to do on their previously special time with father. A "necktie or roses?" a headline mused.[279]

Jenner's mother is another casualty on the road to neurotic, self-fulfillment fantasies. Originally she admitted to struggling with Jenner's public eclipse, especially his demand the world call him "Caitlynn." I'd struggle too. Why should a woman, who carried him nine months in her testosterone-bathed womb, be forced to play these sick-mind games with him 65 years later?

TRANNIES GONE FERAL

Connoisseurs of gender bending commit grotesque crimes against their own bodies, so it comes as no shock that some are aggressive and violent to others. "Pussy" a cross-dressing, Russian rocker cut off his girlfriend's *head,* then used it to perform a sex act in 2015. Apparently, she deserved it for complaining about him using her lipstick.[280]

Popular media is loaded with complaints over undue amounts of violence against transvestites, but those claims are exaggerated or false. FBI numbers in 2014 for *all* "hate crimes" are infinitesimal compared to general offenses. Out of 1,165,383 violent US crimes (and millions of lesser ones) only 6,418 "hate crimes" are recorded.[281] Of these, 60% consist of minor vandalism, such as graffiti – and many of those are self-inflicted for sympathy.[282] Most "hate crimes" are acts of anti-Semitism, committed against Jews of any sexual persuasion.

Also, a percentage of transvestites work in the underworld of prostitution, where sex-workers are at high risk of assault and even murder. Men who choose to appear as weak and vulnerable women will be forced to share the same hazards valid women face in our violent culture. This has nothing to do with homophobia, and predators won't ask questions before they strike. Trans "women" may want to stop and think this over.

Genderbending is poisoning culture one lopped penis and injection at a time. Imagine the effect on films if this attack of stupidity continues. *The Godfather VII,* starring Ellen DeGeneres with a cigar, baggy suit and huge shoulder pads? Will Disney have Cinderella marrying her wicked step-sisters? Is she really a "he" who finally gets to dress up, go to the ball and have at the Prince? Disney is already headed that direction.

A new book also appears to have reached the bottom of that abyss: *"Promised Land"*, where a prince and farm boy end up kissing (fully illustrated) and start "their own family." [283] A prince can always commandeer some peasant woman's babies; nothing is new there. Parents may need to explain the Right of Kings, or other oppressive forms of government it takes to make this "happy ending" possible. But wherever this trend goes, be sure it will terrify the children and poison all art it touches.

Our tots are potential child sacrifices for the cause of gender equality. Doctors from the American College of Pediatricians (ACPeds) cautioned parents about disastrous emotional and physical effects of playing with their child's sexuality identity: "Conditioning children [that] impersonation of the opposite sex is normal and healthful is child abuse."[284] ACPeds also spelled out dangers of a lifetime of the carcinogenic and "toxic cross-sex hormones" required, and warned against unnecessary surgical mutilation of healthy body parts.

The good doctors also took shots at the team approach to child abuse, warning against norming "gender discordance." They described hellish scenes of children being sent from schools to "gender clinics" and shot up on puberty-blocking drugs. Benioff Children's Hospital of UCSF is one of these grisly places (as 2016). Instead of Boris Karloff sawing away at an unfortunate victim, the gayest community in the US sends children to be sexually tinkered with by Dr. Stephen M. Rosenthal and staff.[285] C'est la vie gay.

Transmongering is a rejection of traditional markers of human identity, as well as virtually all cultural, psychological, and religious standards. Intelligent adults won't let their worldview be jerked around to complete the fantasies of mentally ill persons; however questioning transgendering can be dangerous. Lunatics station themselves at events shouting slogans like this: *"Trans-exclusionary views should have no place in feminism or society!"* Why? How about "cannibal-exclusionary" views, or "Neo-Nazi-exclusionary" views? Transgendering hasn't proved to be more ethical than either of these.

We brought this on ourselves by giving up freedoms incrementally – fawning over trannies with little coming out parties in homerooms or coffee rooms. We learn new languages and customs to suit individual psychoses. Dugouts and locker rooms are likely to be unsexed, de-sexed, and re-sexed — all to make one extremely disturbed child more comfortable. Gender fluidity is a state of fantasy replacing reality and genetics, and is fast becoming policy. Isn't this the birth of some great, congregational dementia coming down the road? Yet, with even with this mass psychosis, only about 1 in every 2,400 Americans have changed even their name from one sex to another, according to the 2010 census. No significant number of people on this planet will *ever* change their sexual identity, unless the state pre-emptively decides to do it for us. Is that coming next?

Yes, it will, if the abuse in our public schools isn't ended soon. Australia is a case study on a state forcing this on their children. After a decade of intense sexual indoctrination, 1000s of kiddies there are announcing their sexual fluidity. Consider that many of these children have lived their entire lives under an entrenched LGBT curriculum. It's all they know.

Transgendering is to child safety, what Pearl Harbor was to world peace. This is all about seizing rights, not creating them. It's a dry run by leftists to see if they can convince us to give up our bus seats, and then hijack the bus. Every week brings new demands for unmerited respect, undue attention, and unwarranted resources. Heterosexuals are cheated, and needs unmet by the LGBT movement. No longer are transvestites the frilly, sad men with big hats that one had the option to engage, ignore, or pity. Trannies have gone feral.

13

MEAN WEDDINGS & SCREWING THE SCOUTS

While our hard-left/militant-gay alliance works valiantly at shredding traditional values, they leave the world a far more dismal place. Almost every institution that helps create a sense of refuge, peace, or stability is a target of their wrath. It takes almost supernatural effort to not see the cliffs at the end of their path. Children are the biggest losers at every turn, sacrificed at PC shrines all along the way. LGBT women aren't faring too well either, although they seem too dull in their fervor to catch on. Organizers of this death march have several things in common, but one is a will to dominate. There is a reason so many in the gay community are into sadomasochism. We just handed veto power to a small group of (mostly men) who see the rest of the world as submissive and cowering creatures. And judging by our votes and changing tastes in the West, perhaps we are. We have yet to see.

MISOGYNY ISN'T DEAD-IT JUST HAS A NEW ACRONYM

LGBTQ may start with an "L" but lesbians are rarely the stars of their shows. Gay spokesmen are just that, almost always *men*. Males hold press conferences and generally serve in higher political and corporate offices. They lead the parades. Other gay militancy work (such as harassment and death threats to conservatives) is almost entirely male domain as well.

Lesbians thrive in classrooms, and as nurses, and social workers, where women have been tolerated for centuries. Nothing new there. Our 21st century freak show known as transgenderism, is all about the boys. Girls who walk like Schwarzenegger just aren't that riveting, or they'd be getting their share of press.

Even gay attack organization "Human Rights Campaign" (HRC) was recently outed as sexist and discriminatory to its *own female staff.* Big whoop surprise. An internal diversity report complained that HRC allows only "gay, white, male employees" in their leadership positions. An (apparently female) worker claimed she feels "excluded every day." [287] There was no word on how trans "men" (women) fared, or if HRC bias follows genetics or political correctness in their bigotry.

TILL GENDER-CHANGE SURGERY DO US PART

Wives are expected to stand by their man, even if he decides he is a woman. Rejected in every possible way – wedding vows are broken, children abandoned; and the entire family takes a back seat to "transitioning." It's always about the *man* and his sexual fantasies. Fabulous dresses, hair styles, and dating problems.

How often do you hear about woman pounding on doors to the men's rooms? Paparazzi dedicated to them? Won't happen. Gender change is not "fluid" – it tends to solidify around male desire. No "Y" chromosome? You're out of luck honey. Even feted and ubiquitous "Caitlyn "is a man, and we all know it. Except him, apparently. Any place homosexuality is widely accepted and practiced is a bad place for women, even for lesbians. Pre-Roman to now, the fairer sex was discounted by gay men, who see girls as a mere necessity to reseed the race.

Men were gods in most of the world before Christians mucked everything up for them. Nowhere was this more evident than in the lives of homosexual men. But only for the *aggressors.* Slaves, and boys they managed to mount, were treated with great disdain. Nero killed his wife, then castrated a boy who caught his eye, dressed him as a woman and forced the hapless kid to "marry" him. Such are the sordid ancestors of gay marriage and transsexuality.

WOMEN NO LONGER EXIST... LEGALLY

Recall that Bruce/Caitlyn Jenner was an Olympic star in *men's* track. Facts like these will never disappear, unless the government next decrees space/time is "transitioning" and no longer exists. Jenner's charade is inspiring a raft of males who have no sense of decency or sportsmanship, but want a title at any cost. That cost is you honey, if you are a female competitor. Young women can look forward to a future of being trounced by big, ugly, faux girls on tracks, fields, ice, pools, and courts. More than pride and trophies are at stake; they will lose *women's* sport scholarships, professions, cash prizes, and sponsorships to *men*. Thank your government and LGBTQ leaders for this injustice, which will only get worse, unless you do something to end it now.

Alaskan "trans" girl, Nattaphon Wangyot, (born male, looks male) naturally beat all females in 200m track events, and the girls are steamed. Having been indoctrinated to cover abuse with platitudes about gay life, even their disgust is prefaced by careful apology though. One girl, who missed a spot because of Wangyot's ruse, claimed the win wasn't fair; yet the poor kid felt obligated to first congratulate the cheater! "I'm glad that this person is comfortable with who they are and they're able to be happy" she said in a CBS interview.[288] Is she really? Why should athletes be forced to concern themselves with Wangyot's "happiness" at the theft of their own? CBS had nothing helpful to say — as usual. This will be far more prevalent as sub-optimal men discover the newest way to cheat and exclude women. Chalk one up for the patriarchy!

Drastic changes loom over women if government doesn't bow out of translunacy. None are good. Allowing men to claim full legal identity as women endangers existence of women as a discrete class. Erika Bachiochi and Daniel Moody write about this at length, warning that "women" may no longer refer to natural, identifiable beings, but merely abstract entities, changeable by redefinition. What "rights" can be assured when the Constitution was written for individuals with bodies, rather than concepts or surgical alterations? Moody warns that if we are only made of language, our innate, physical state may no longer be legally admissible.[290] It sounds like the plot of a bad science fiction novel:

"Fiendish creatures devise plot to eliminate earth-females, using tools of mass cultural delusion."

Women recently evaporated at the Federal level, and jolly leftists cheering them on are too dull to see it. In 2016, the DOJ's Vanita Gupta insisted that people who feign being their opposite sex (if they wish hard enough and look upon a star) do in actuality become that. This is due to magical legal maneuvers known as the HB2 Law, where Gupta and Lorretta Lynch served as ad hoc Fairy Godmothers. "Transgender men are men — they live, work and study as men. Transgender women are women — they live, work and study as women," said Gupta. Only believe. Apparently the DOJ is now a devotional group with articles of faith and its own perverse doctrine of *trans*-substantiation. They have no savior though. Who will save America's women from people who have so deeply bought into their madness? Reducing womanhood to pronouns and shoes is degrading, and a legal landmine.

Ironically, one of gaydom's most powerful cheerleaders, Supreme Court Justice Ruth Ginsburg, supports the clan that may yet deny women many positions in the future. In 2012, she announced her hope for an all-female Supreme Court someday.[291] Yet trans narratives and imbeciles at the DOJ plainly announce there is no such thing as a literal "female". The gender can be claimed at any time, by any male. How will Ginsburg and her lesbian devotees deal with their Pyrrhic victory if seven future Justices have penises under their robes, yet force the rest of us to use "she" when speaking of them? Who won Ginsburg?

Denying women's biological abilities won't work for pregnancy and motherhood either, which will never be delegated to males. Elton John and his lover claimed otherwise, and were blasted by feminist Germaine Greer. While Elton calls Furnish his *husband*, he also listed him as the boys' *mother* on their birth certificate. Hhhmm. . . but that isn't likely to confuse their boys when they are older, because by then such terms may be illegal. Greer was one of the few public personalities to point out this madness. Even the UK press noted there seemed to be no details concerning "birth" on the poor, test-kit children's birth certificates. The feminist icon was disgusted by the state's willingness to name Furnish as a "mother" as if women had no part in making babies at all.

Reaction to Greer was swift and predictable. Gay threats. Gay hate. Gay invective – the usual. Why should the well-known mechanics of childbirth enrage those in the gay-dominance movement? John and his cohorts comprise a Gay Inquisition, denying conception, childbirth, nurture and nature, while remaking reality to better serve them. Elton's kids share the same invisible, surrogate mother. Greer, hardly a conservative, was close to capturing the sheer nastiness of their scheme. She noted the elephant that was not even allowed in the room – the vanished and demoted *mother* in the entire drama. "That will give you an idea of how the concept of motherhood has emptied out. It's gone. It's been deconstructed" Greer complained at Hays Literary Festival in 2015.[292]

CLUB PEN

Prisons are hothouses for trannies, as the favors and free stuff appeal to criminals. The majority of these are men. What better thing for a psychopathic women-slayer to do with his time, but come up with sordid narratives to his benefit? Such is Robert Kosilek. Imprisoned in 1993 for killing his wife in cold blood, he spent the next 20 years insisting he needed a sex change. One is as reasonable as the other. Unrepentant and self -pitying, "Michelle" (Robert) wept over his offending genitalia in 2006, but not for the mother of his children. "The greatest loss is the dying I do inside a little bit everyday" he claimed. Hasn't every trans wanna-be used that line?

Histrionics worked for a while. District Judge Mark Wolf ruled in 2012 that the state must pay for re-sexing little Michelle, so he can feel better about himself. (Sounder minds prevailed and overturned Wolf's decision in 2014).[293] Kosilek is far from the only case like this. Feds are hurting for cash after insisting we pay for their sex changes, hormones, electrolysis, hair dressers, counselors and so forth. What to do? Cash strapped IRS just informed American athletes that they will be taxed on their Olympic medals, forcing some to sell them. Soldiers are being asked to return re-enlistment bonuses. This may not be directly related to sex-reconstruction surgery, but we will all pay to satisfy LGBT demands.

WE WILL CONQUER YOU (TOILETS FIRST)

Butch types have been using the boy's room for years. No one much cared, because they were quietly minding their own business. Most Americans didn't complain about trannies in the ladies' room for the same reasons. Trans-women who were seriously into the part were camouflaged into the rest of us, and we weren't doing genital checks at the door. But this happy state of affairs wasn't enough for the sex-Nazis who decided to stage a showdown at toilets across America. Hence invitations to all males to make themselves at home in the ladies' room. This was a power move, and a way to force their balls into all of our courts.

In Toronto, a sexual-offender claiming to be "Jessica" assaulted several women at shelters in 2014. Toronto's "gender identity non-discrimination law" made it all possible for this man, who had previously raped disabled women and a *five-year-old girl,* to be welcomed into the gay fold. In spite of this and other highly publicized crimes by faux or real trannies, a 2016 article in the *Charlotte Observer* insisted there were no cases of sexual predators benefiting from transgender protection laws in the US.[294] Because children and homeless women are inconsequential in the LGBTQ family picture.

Only months into the Trans Potty Crusades, dozens of women and girls report being threatened by men in their restrooms. Seattle's fair sex were unnerved by having to undress next to a nude man, who made no claim or physical attempts to even resemble a woman. Here are a few other headlines:

Transgender Does What Many Feared Would Happen At Target Store (ID);
Man Disguised as Woman Recorded "Hours" of Mall Restroom Video (CA);
Man Dressed as Woman Arrested for Spying Into Mall Bathroom Stall, Police Say (DC);
Man Accused of Peeping in Women's Restroom Also Faces Child Porn Charges (PA);
University of Toronto Dumps Transgender Bathrooms After Peeping Incidents.

Do we really think criminals are so dense they won't walk through doors held wide open for them to conduct their business? This is so obvious that straight criminals are conjuring up their inner transvestite to aid them. A wily European fugitive fought extradition from Canada by claiming to have killed his wife, a plea of insanity – and claiming transsexuality. None were true, but these were used for his *defense.*

By now, Canadian men may assume that transgendering will get them off any crime.[295] The entire sex-flex thing is really just another kick in the teeth to women. It's an invasion of privacy, and mass show of disrespect. Massachusetts legislators have such contempt for females, that they refused to bar even male sex-offenders from the hallowed stalls. Freedom, comfort, identity, and safety of women are left in the balance. Like all things gay, the Transgender Bathroom Wars harm women and children disproportionately.

Thanks to the potty wars, North American women may yet live like their third-world sisters, where answering nature's call can cost them chastity, health, or their lives. This is a true war against women. If sex continues to be defined and legislated by courts and gay edict, will straight persons need permits to copulate in the future? It's not that far off, if we follow the current trajectory.

NOTHING SAYS GAY MARRIAGE LIKE HATE

Gay marriage is the invitation you can't refuse – like a deranged emperor marrying his cat, while the Senate is forced to throw gardenias. It's not too far from what is happening now. Pressure to celebrate gay marriage is applied like a tourniquet by a three-branched government of courts, media, and corporations. After the SCOTUS Gomorrahgate rulings, oppression hangs in the air. Non-celebrants of gay marriage are in danger of being shot — with hate-crime accusations.

Militant devotees of Sappho and Dionysus are so eager to suck conservative blood that they aren't letting their nuptials slow them even a bit. Dozens manage to find time in the midst of wedding plans to torment religious folk. Now *that* is true hate. Is this part of a new, Fascist-themed wedding trend? No American population has ever celebrated their wedding days with scourges, bitterness, and lawsuits; but this is a new era, with conservatives being hauled into courtrooms (in lieu of lions). If that sounds like the gates of Hell slamming against the church, it was only the SCOTUS playing with their gavels.

THE CUPCAKE WARS

Almost before the ink dried on Washington State's 2012 gay marriage referendum, attorneys lined up like taxis, hoping to pick up enraged homosexuals with a great deal of money and hostility. They didn't have to wait long. The moment gay weddings are enforced rather than *accepted*, an onslaught of harassment unleashes against the Church. It is seen as granting permission to do so. Conservative spokesmen such as Matt Barber warned this would happen, while gay marriage campaigners engaged in mass lies. "*We would never do that*" they insisted and mocked the political prophets.

Compare this fiasco to Alabama, circa 1959. African Americans sought reasonable, fair, and constitutionally mandated treatment. If Martin Luther King had sunk to the moral depravity of the molester's booster club, HRC, we would have burnt to the ground long ago. Or if King had taken the low road of gay Congressmen and Senators, laws would be twisted for personal pleasure and power. But early civil rights leaders were fair and reasonable, because they sought justice. Gay militants have no just cause at this point, and they know it.

Peevish homosexuals were trampling on a historic Christian camp in New Jersey, as far back as 2008. It was a Scrooge-like warning of future weddings to come. When a lesbian couple asked to celebrate their civil union there, they were politely refused, for obvious religious reasons. Fleeing to rights commissions, the vindictive women ensured nuptials may never be celebrated there again, although camp policies hadn't changed for decades. Because if lesbians aren't happy, no one can be happy.[296] It's beginning to be a pattern here.

After Washington State enacted gay marriage, Christian florist Barronelle Stutzman was charged as a criminal for declining to do flowers for a gay wedding. Flowers arrangements for weddings often require a physical presence, and it isn't comparable to simply selling objects. Details of these lawsuits are hidden by abetting media, because the truth often makes gay plaintiffs look like garbage.

In this case, Stutzman's client, Robert Ingersoll, was clearly an ungrateful sniveler. Far from being excluded, she claims he'd been her customer for nearly a *decade,* and she considered him a friend. Beyond that, Stutzman had previously served and employed homosexuals; so there was no "discrimination." The joyous little gay couple just made it up.

They couldn't have done it without help from the ACLU, Washington State Governor Jay Inslee, and AG Bob Ferguson. Apparently, they have nothing better to do than to harass Christian constituents. Aiding and abetting the debacle, Judge Alexander Ekstrom denied Stutzman even a court hearing by issuing a summary judgment against her. Washington's Gay Enforcers punished the florist for her faith, and destroyed her livelihood. Ironically, early gay petitions for equal rights centered on just that – fair work and rental situations. Now gay militants deny basic human rights to those outside their tribe – making our support for gay rights appear to have been a grave mistake.[297]

Tolerating quirks of homosexual marriage lowers standards for everyone, as a recent British ruling proved. Lord Justice Jackson and Lady Justice King were so concerned over the privacy of a gay celebrity couple, that they customized law just for them. Because the anonymous couple (with children) couldn't keep their todgers tamed, the Court of Appeals blocked media coverage.[298] This latitude isn't extended to straight parents who hold orgies around their progeny. They land in tabloids and are likely to lose their children, because they just aren't gay enough. Facts are, the majority of Brits have never supported gay marriage – they are merely being informed that they must.[299]

Continue this oppression and the sky's the limit. Petitions for group marriage are showing up. A man and his son thought it would be great to tie the knot; and we know how people *love* their dogs. Will some fall-guy florist be conscripted to do flowers for nuptials between a man and his chicken, should law so allow? AG Ferguson is apparently up for it, and the ACLU and Jay Inslee will have their backs. Or whatever chickens have.

SCREWING THE SCOUTS

Baser sorts of male sodomites have a yen for chaste meat, and nothing piques their appetite like a tasty Boy Scout. Why the Scouts? Probably the same attractions that straight molesters crave: youth, innocence, morality, wholesomeness, purity and health. Everything that isn't them. Like foppish old vampires, pedophiles trawl the world looking for sexual rejuvenation. In the case of extremely "active" gay men, there is also the guarantee that of all their partners, children and youth are most certain to be virginal and disease free. It's a theme that goes back to Aztecs and Druids; sacrifice the virgins to cover their own sins. But they might play around with them first.

Energy and enthusiasm of the Boy Scouts of America (BSA) seems to be a big hit, stirring gay lust. Less they deny this, only a few moments research on internet, libraries, or gay-porn magazines reveals that screwing Scouts is a classic gay fantasy. One website offers "Loads of Boy Scout Videos!!" while another screams "Hot BoyScouts F*#k" with explicit photos across the home page.[300] Most Scouts had no idea they served as pin-ups for pederasts, but the poor kids are far more likely to find out now. Let's not forget the "homoerotic" appeal that little boys in military-type uniforms hold over certain types of grown men. This is a subset of the Nazi obsession, and was a hot thing in Germany, as part of the "Bündisch" Youth Movement.[301]

Once upon a time, the Scouts (under pressure to show largesse and modernize) allowed one gay teen to become an Eagle Scout. Pascal Tessier showed his gratitude by campaigning against his patrons, after they fired a gay scout master – which had always been their policy. With the help of media heads grinding their axes against two million BSA families, Tessier demonized his fellows and patrons. The disgruntled Scout launched boycotts to deny the BSA means of support and meeting places.

Tessier was following in the footsteps of another petulant gay youth, James Dale, who sued the BSA in 1999. One piece in the Huffington Post was all it took to drive hundreds of businesses from supporting the Scouts – like rats off a ship.[302] It wasn't news that the BSA "discriminated" against open homosexuality, in the same sense that they "discriminate" against drowning. Cowed execs and board members didn't change their values overnight, they just submitted to bullies setting fires under them. Kiddie-pimps posing as corporate executives worked hand-in-hand to trash one of America's most beloved institutions.

CORPORATE PEDERASTY

Encountering rare corporations who didn't fall in a swoon at the mention of their divine gayness, they upped their antics. Intel, UPS, and Merck withstood the first onslaughts of gay venom, but eventually buckled. Instead, they joined forces with "Scouts for Equality" a gay anti-Scout group, which exists to substitute for the core values and mission of the BSA.

Amazon, and its founder Jeff Bezos, have withstood a flood of condemnation and bogus shock over their refusal to join the "Screw the Scouts" drive. As of 2015, Amazon still allowed Scouts to receive donations from their site, although they've dropped several conservative groups at the behest of the hate-titan, SPLC. The anti- Scouting crusade appeared to have more support than reality, thanks to media promotion of a few gay youth who turned on their teammates.

One petition against Amazon was trumpeted loudly as being signed by 125,000 people. Big deal. Millions have been supporting the BSA for years, and none of them had a dedicated staff of reporters assigned to it. All spotlights went to monster corporations, old money, and big media dedicated to getting gays out of the bathhouse and into the Boy Scouts.

Under fierce duress, the BSA began admitting openly gay scouts in 2014. "Open" means practicing, and in some kid's face. Because Scouting wasn't dead enough yet, BSA President Robert Gates gave yet more opportunities to pedophiles, by announcing a lift on their ban on openly gay (adult) leaders and employees, in 2015. You don't need a degree in prophecy to predict the demise of scouting as we knew it. Liberals wax ecstatic, and the kids are bolting as if it were a forest fire.

Was this an attack of mass stupidity? BSA battled pedophiles for years in efforts to keep their charges safe. Banning openly gay boys and men (and using background checks) was the most obvious way to do this. Even then, hundreds of boys were molested or raped by *homosexuals*, despite all efforts to protect them.

One of my sons was a scout as a teen and heard all about it at the time. Attorney for abused children, Tim Kosnoff, had a massive dossier on 1,892 abusers up to 2012.[304] Boy Scouts were forced to settle multiple lawsuits and paid out millions.

INNOCENCE IS A CRIME

Scouting was one of the last refuges for innocent, outdoor sport and character growth – but it didn't pass the gay sniff test. As with all creation, Scouting should exist to make adult homosexuals happy. Founders just didn't realize it when the BSA was established on Christian ideals in 1910. BSA also prohibited atheists and agnostics, but they haven't warred to force this private organization to its knees. Militant homosexuals and their retinue worked furiously to tear a cherished institution to ribbons, as part of a successful, nationwide bullying campaign.

But the drive to destroy all aspects of virtue and innocence in the lives of children didn't leave girls behind. Girl Scouts of the United States of America (GSUSA) wasn't content with character, camping, and cookies. Thanks to the burgeoning pedophiles who seem to be in leadership everywhere now, little girls must navigate adult sexuality, gender, and (special bonus!) abortion. Perhaps a *Girls' Guide to Transgendering in Emergencies*"? Not inconceivable considering the lopsided presence of gay leaders such as Timothy Higdon, their Chief of External Affairs.[305] New policies for GSUSA include norming transgendering in the troops. Not to scare the little girls, they came up with the ingenious plan to just not inform them of "transgender girls" (boys) as their bunk mates.

It doesn't take an oracle to see that the fallout of the new Scouts will be the *few Scouts* - or none; which may be the goal of the self-righteous harpies and pederasts that brought down one of the best things American kids ever had. No one knows the future of the tattered corpse of the BSA, but there is already less focus on morality, and much attention on social engineering.

Allowing James Dale and Pascal Tessier to continue scouting was a huge mistake. They quickly proved they were far from trustworthy or loyal. The old Boy Scout Pledge demands they also be "morally straight." Considering that the BSA has settled huge sums when boys were molested, despite their best efforts –what will happen now they've removed most protection? And in future years when you need that old-school Scout to help you cross the street or put out a forest fire? Good luck finding one.

14

GAY HATE AND THE ARTS

Homosexuals own the arts. Perhaps not the whole enchilada, but it's a perception – mostly their own. A New York panel discussion by gay artists some years back yielded this incredible boast: "Queer art practice and theory can be said to have powered art from the Renaissance onwards."[306] The rest of the world's artists just didn't know it yet.

Ironically, the creative world is possibly the least tolerant community in America at this point. We can thank creeping fascism and intolerance of faith for that. As a result, people who lived to satirize everything, suddenly have *no personal opinions* about homosexuality or other controversial topics. Nada. The liberal code of silence demands orthodoxy, and has its own list of "dirty words you can't say on television." Gaycensors are legion. They never sleep, or run out of cash, lobbyists, or lawyers.

Nothing is treated with as much reverence and awe as homosexuality in progressive, academic circles – and especially in the art world. It's like they discovered the Holy Grail and lost their sanity in the process. Musicians may be most pressed to kneel before our new gay gods, or feel their wrath. Many secular artists enthusiastically support the gay movement, which is their right; though most of them seem to have issues with the ones who don't. Absence of gay criticism in Hollywood isn't a sign of solidarity, but can be chalked up to the need to pay the rent. Like xenophobic villagers, they've developed an ingrown, protective code of behavior and speech, and they don't care much for cultural "foreigners."

Christians and conservatives are exotics in Hollywood and in the larger world of the arts. They may be tolerated, if they watch their mouth – but no promises, even then. Meanwhile, the glamouratti issue statements that sound like they've been whipped up by the same press secretary with a limited vocabulary. But would you admit you were cowed and controlled? Better to pretend life has always been this way, and stick to the script you've been handed.

MUSICIANS REFUSE TO BOW (A FEW ANYWAY)

Popular musician Lauren Hill found herself in the crosshairs of the Great Gay Arbitrators of Art over her 2013 song, "Neurotic Society."[307] Appears it was not sufficiently flattering, and they called out their press fairies (BET and Huffington Post this time). Hill's transgressions include using terms such as "girl men" and implying they may have issues. Say it isn't so! Because of Hill's take on our "godless" culture, she's been dissed at music awards and fiercely criticized in social media. Her continued popularity is galling to anti-Christian *haters,* who can't bring themselves to admit all creation is not singing their praise in six-part harmony.

To her credit, Hill refuses to back down, snivel, or apologize. Instead, she urged fans to consider the cost of allowing things to continue as they are. If there were more like her, the Art Police and gay harpies who goad them might crawl back to the obscurity they so richly deserve. Where Hill manages to find regular gigs due to sheer talent and an established fan-base, lesser known artists face crushing pressure to self-censor and conform.

Unwritten social regulations are rarely explicit, but most artists got the memo. Few slip past the swords of secularity standing at the gates. All forms of the arts do this to an extent: museums; music and film producers; concert halls; and some private galleries and festivals. The liberal agenda (including deference to homosexuality) must be observed, like some deranged court etiquette. Neither religion, tradition, nor cultural taboos get any respect from the platinum-plated derrieres waiting to be kissed. It's the cult that replaced that Old-Time Religion.

Some artists are feeling mutinous and balk at joining the order of gay acolytes. One of Jamaica's biggest dance hall music stars, "Sizzla" Kalonji, was banned for years, because he lost patience with the music-militia. After years of European and American lobbying, festival organizers now demand Jamaicans rewrite their lyrics, or join a blacklist. Kalonji responded with "I don't care who want vex, Jamaica no support no same sex. . ." revealing his thoughts on immoral, Western, white people. [308] Standing up to homosexuals really ticks them off, as Kalonji observed with his song on the subject, "Nah Apologize." Because of this, he was barred from entering the US and Canada.

Kalonji isn't the only musician to face a First World offensive on his culture. Island musicians were banned in 2008 from visiting 29 European nations, because they hadn't come up with enough gay tribute material. Fans of reggae and dance hall must know Jamaicans are hostile to public gay passions. It's their tradition and they sing about it; although it may be rough, or even hostile. But Sizzla is still vanilla milk compared to the average gay crusader. Considering some of the vilest people command Jamaicans how to live, this could conceivably cause resentment.

WHITE, GAY MEN ARBITRATE TASTE FOR THE WORLD?

No one enjoys being ordered about by arrogant outsiders, and gay spokesmen fairly ooze with condescension. Their hyperbolically titled campaign "Stop Murder Music" sounds like an edict from Catherine the Great during a serf uprising. Artists are denied publication, sponsorship, grants, and production because of iron fisted, pro-gay censorship. Resistors who defy them face their crimes and punishments read in public venues. Musicians feel the hate until acquiescence or professional death – whichever comes first. Homosexuals now decide who gets concerts and artistic sponsorship as well. This enforced submission to homosexual dominance is close to planetary, at least in the arts.

Scrappy Eminem, one of their original targets, meekly complied after the following was leveled at him: "These unrepentant homophobic performers are the moral equivalent of neo-Nazis and the Ku Klux Klan" spokesman Peter Tatchell theatrically charged. UK activist David Allison purred "In recent years he [Eminem] has become quite well-behaved."[309] Now the rapper joins the ranks of those who are rewarded with concerts and sponsorships. The organization patronizingly claimed that they hoped these singers were not motivated "merely to fill concert halls", but from a sincere commitment on their part. Yeah, that was it.

Astonished at gay politics calling the shots during the *50th Anniversary MLK Concert,* celebrated gospel artist Donnie McClurkin described an organized, gay hate-campaign. Clearly in a state of shock at the time, McClurkin described his last-minute 2013 banning, thanks to the bigotry of Mayor Vincent Gray and the DC Arts Commission.[383] Marveling how a black artist could be "uninvited to a *civil rights* event," McClurkin met the gaystapo that day.

McClurkin's real crime was testifying how God had delivered him from homosexuality, the only unforgivable sin in the gay community. You may not leave; and God isn't allowed to "deliver" you either. The singer spoke to an aide from Mayor Gray's office, who insisted it was all in McClurkin's best interest, so he wouldn't "suffer from the fall out" of it.[310] That sounds like a threat, and not a veiled one.

"BORN THAT WAY" BUT COERCION HELPS

Although gays are purportedly "born that way" the condition seems to be contagious in the entertainment community. Dozens of stars are suddenly discovering their inner Sodomite and hawking it to the world. With the attention homosexuals are getting, it's understandable that Red Carpet wannabes might consider sex-change a shrewd career move. It tends to cover for many sins as well.

When UK's "Boy George" was denied entry into the US, in 2008, media went into their usual auto-reactionary mode. Some implied it was over sexual orientation, although he was facing criminal charges back home. Specifically, George was charged with "assault and false imprisonment of a paid [male] sex partner" on their first encounter. Gay etiquette insists that assault and imprisonment be reserved for the second date.

Russia been a difficult gig for openly gay artists, particularly if they politicize their art. Since the Russian people are dead set against norming homosexuality, gay activists resorted to stealth, deceit, and humiliation to promote it. Danes hosting Eurovision in 2014 were embarrassed by the cruel reception that Russian entrants received from gay supporters in the audience. Expecting gay advocates to behave boorishly as usual in 2015, Eurovision deployed countermeasures: noise cancelling "anti-booing technology." Homosexual militancy is not totally without merit – it spurs science to find new ways to avoid it.

During the 2014, Olympic games in Sochi, the press was mesmerized by Russia's gay artists/activists, almost to the neglect of great athletes. Officials there invited the gay world to attend, asking only that they "leave the kids alone." Feigning shock and dismay, the gay community swore they would never approach a child. Yet only a few months earlier, two of Russia's leading gay activists, Nikolai Alexeyev and Yaroslav Yevtushenko, stood before a children's library with banners proclaiming, "Gays aren't made, they're born!" [311] Fined a measly amount ($115), the duo weren't thrown to Siberian wolves. Why did these men take their adult fight over sexuality to children? This is what the Russian government describes as "homosexual child propaganda" *because it is.* And Russians know a thing or two about propaganda.

Militant homosexuals often use art as just another recruitment tool. They scream foul play if questioned over artistic merit, or sincerity of their work – yet much of it is explicitly pornographic. "Gay art's about men fucking men," a prize-winning, gay novelist crudely acknowledged in 2007. Still, there is a vast divide between creators of gay porn and artists who happen to be homosexuals. Over 3000 years, gay writers, musicians, and painters created work that all humanity could relate to on some level. Tennessee Williams, Sergei Diaghilev, and David Hockney are among them. Some were outed as gay during their lives and others volunteered, yet their art wasn't myopically focused on genitals. There is a limited audience for close-up scrotums, even with a free press and vast state funding.

BIG-SCREEN HATE

Not all contemporary films and plays featuring gay protagonists center on sex. Some plots are built on war – against the church and its people. A 1990 film *Stop the Church* takes up the sword, with its clearly threatening title. But that's just the beginning. A true hate flick, it's crammed with disinformation and incitement against the Roman Catholic Church. Resorting to no less than Nazi-style blood-libel, it claims the Church "practices ritual sacrifice on the bodies of gay men, lesbians, women, and people of color."[313]

No one really believes this garbage, but blatant lies didn't stop an avalanche of awards and praise for the hit piece. Ann Arbor Film festival bestowed its "Best Commentary" award on *Stop the Church*. PBS attempted to pick it up, but met a backlash of disapproval. Television stations rescued it from deserved obscurity, and aired the ode to ACT UP's 1989 invasion of St. Patrick's Cathedral in New York. Producer/director Hilferty co-opted the arts to excoriate the Catholic Church, which he blamed for the death of his partner by AIDS. As an adult, Hilferty must know how this terrible illness is spread, and it isn't through saying the rosary.

Apparently, even liberal sophisticates have a limit to crude, poorly made, gay propaganda disguised as art films. Attendees of the 2016 Sundance Film Festival fled one in disgust. This was in spite a gay kiss, normally commanding awe in those circles. "*Swiss Army Man*" is like a metaphor for homosexual life: vulgar obsession with sex (in this case long discussions on masturbation); an apparently dead man who prominently farts; and an isolated island love nest. Apparently, there are depths even political correctness can't plunge people.[314]

Hollywood at this point is a giant, public-relations campaign for adultery, violence, homosexuality, and child sex. Art doesn't follow life there, as the popularity of conservative reality shows reveal. Once those cameras venture out of Oz and back to Kansas, there is no way to censor real families in America. This is globally understood. Bishops in Nigeria spoke against US-enforced gay marriage, claiming it threatens Africa because they are so influenced by American culture – particularly our films. Specifically, the bishops called it "a sad, unjust and lamentable situation based largely upon a distorted perception of natural law, the will of God and human nature."[315]

Stage mother to gay Hollywood is "GLAAD" or *Gay & Lesbian Alliance Against Defamation,* a promotional group created by, and for, media hirelings. Actors and singers are endlessly trotted onstage in grand galas, where they must make sycophantic speeches and paeans to homosexuality. It's a mutual suck-up society. Nominees are generally straight, and are forced into a public litmus test before photographers. If they accept the unsolicited honors, they are considered de facto supporters of every gay game in Hollywood. Denying it paints a pink bullseye on their backs.

Art itself is a victim of gay hate. Anything prefixed with the word "gay" is accepted, funded, and lauded without question. It may not have occurred to the geniuses running film studios and art museums that they could turn out a boatload of crap that way, while losing viewers and support. Art is sacrificed somewhere under the rainbow, and if that doesn't matter; the practical implications of a disgusted public should. For instance, Adam Sank (aiming for comedy) claimed that without the Stonewall Riots he wouldn't be able to stand as a gay man telling "dick jokes."[316] Imagine the loss to humanity.

OCCUPY ART

Gay fascists have issues when celebrated artists won't paint them in the colors they choose, and Frank Miller is one of their problems. Lionized as a writer, comic artist, screenwriter, novelist, and film director – he just didn't come up to gay code. Miller isn't particularly hostile, but all artists are expected to follow gay guidelines. Miller had plenty of his own social justice ideas, and he didn't need theirs. Out of hundreds of plots, characters, and storylines, Miller was found to have trespassed against Gay Orthodoxy once, in 1990. Specifically, his *"Give Me Liberty"* series has protagonist "Martha Washington" battle campy, flamboyantly gay Nazis (The Aryan Thrust) and their evil leader, (Colonel Crotch). Perhaps it was a premonition, but Miller's gay Nazis were attempting to destroy Washington, DC.

Homosexual thought monitors are just as vicious to their own, especially in the art department. When photographer/artist Lucian Wintrich "came out" as a Donald Trump supporter in 2016, he was summarily fired and demonized by his peers. Apparently, Trump wasn't promising as many fortune cookies as the competition on the left. It took advertising company "Anomaly" only five hours for their knees to jerk, as they dumped a previously acceptable employee. Wintrich claimed he was ordered to sever his ties with Anomaly immediately, and his email was deactivated to avoid contamination.

Doug TenNapel is a talented American graphic artist and designer, who weathered the wrath of art crusaders and lived to tell the tale. It wasn't pleasant. TenNapel was fiercely criticized over his – get this – "past dismissive views towards homosexuality" (an actual quote). [317] Not abusive, but *dismissive,* and *past.* Someone is keeping records. Lack of effusive appreciation for homosexuality nearly grounded TenNapel's projects, and even faint praise can poison a career. Apparently, everything spoken, published, painted, sung, or filmed by living artists is now carefully "gaycensored."

TenNapel was shamed for his family lifestyle, which he never brought up in his work. Yet gay code enforcers organized an extensive campaign against the heinous thought crimes he *may potentially* commit. Because Homophobia. Because petty little fascists who need to get a life. Blogger James Eldred insisted TenNapel's belief in traditional marriage constituted "sexist, racist… hateful bullshit" and drummed up a boycott of his games, art and associated films.[318]

One never knows what belligerence lurks in the heart of man, unless he properly exalts your sexual preference. TenNapel humbly explained his motivations (which were clearly not hateful) and otherwise mollified his persecutors. Apparently, it was enough and his punishment was light – thought probation.

15

NAZI LOVE

What do Hell's Angels, homosexuals and Skinheads have in common? It's not a joke – it's Nazi-themed leather bars. A big draw. Check random photos of any gay parade, and you'll find SS costumes and "prisoners" on dog leads and chains. Leather shops are generally in gay neighborhoods for a good reason, they can't get enough of that Nazi chic. San Francisco's "Leather Pride Week" is a fixture; and they never tire of variations of S&M (heavy on the "S"). Leather is symbolic of domination, pain, control, and ways der Führer has to make you obey.

I happened on the Nazi-adoration thing quite by accident on the Fourth of July, 1996. Passing by an elegant estate in my neighborhood, I noticed a noisy party replete with barbecue, beer, music and...Hitler Youth? Neighborhood buzz was that the owners were gay, but no one much cared. Staring in disbelief, I watched the all-male crowd celebrate the birth of our nation. Various military ranks lounged about, and a sprinkling of "officers" with jackboots, riding crops, and dashing peaked caps. Most of the Nazi-fetishers were dressed as Aryan country boys, with lederhosen and pert little shorts. What a jolly bunch!

If I had read *The Pink Swastika,* I may have known this Deutsch boy playground scene wasn't so rare. Scott Lively and Kevin Abram's book reveals the enduring gay affair with Nazism.[399] Much of Lively-Adam's material was from concentration camp survivors or other first-hand testimony. But that didn't stop gay militants from viciously attacking them, as well as many of his sources – even the dead ones. Because conservatives are persistently branded "Nazis" by gays and by leftists, we can't afford to ignore overwhelming evidence that Nazi ranks were (and are) heavily populated by homosexuals. Particularly their leaders.

NAZIS – GAY BOY'S CLUB

Gay Nazis were notorious even before WWII, and it's taken a global effort to deny this. Germany was the most gay-friendly nation on earth, from the late 1880s to beyond the Third Reich. They published the first gay journal, *Der Eigene* (The Special) from 1896 to 1932. Something like Grindr existed for hook-ups. Even Kaiser Wilhelm's cabinet was stocked to the gills with homosexuals. Headlines shrieked of the "Harden–Eulenburg affair" in 1907, revealing liaisons between a prince and general, and a man dying in a woman's ballet tutu. Sex-change operations pioneered in Germany, and nascent gay theory budded in its colleges. The Fatherland was a gay, gay world.

Considering Nazi luncheons were gay affairs, their occasional purges against homosexuality were likely motivated to remove rivals. Ernst Röehm, Supreme leader of Nazi militia (SA) was one of those victims. "Röehm made no attempt to hide his homosexual activities" claimed a 1941, Office of Strategic Services (OSS) document.[320] OSS wasn't hazarding a guess, as the bureau was an early version of both the CIA and U.S. Special Operations Command. Authored by psychoanalyst Walter Langer, he noted that Röehm had publicly flaunted his sexual inclinations since 1919. His arrest and death in 1934 was part of a larger purge of the SS.

Running the Sex Research Institute in Nazi-era Berlin, Ludwig Lenz claimed "not ten percent of the men who, in 1933, took the fate of Germany into their hands, were sexually normal."[321] By "normal" he meant straight, among other things. Lenz should know, since he pioneered the first sex-transplant surgery there.

Magnus Hirschfeld, founder of the Institute, had made the concept of "the third sex" a household term in Germany by the 1930s. He also wrote the first academic book on transvestites, *Die Transvestiten*" in 1910. Oh, those Nazis were light years ahead of us puritanical, old Yanks, preoccupied with saving Europe.

Lively and Abrams are hardly the only writers to assert widespread Nazi homosexuality. William Shirer's definitive *Rise and Fall of the Third Reich* asserts "Many of its [Nazi] top leaders, beginning with its chief, Röehm, were notorious homosexual perverts." A Pulitzer prize-winning American journalist in 1941 claimed that virtually all ranking Storm Troopers were homosexuals.[322]

Correspondent H.R. Knickerbocker observed Nazis in the flesh, and insisted "unless a Storm Troop officer were homosexual, he had no chance of advancement." [323] Below are just some of the Nazi Party's verified gay leaders, or what Goebbels called the "Munich Clique":

> *Herman Goering*: Gestapo head, founded Luftwaffe – a transvestite, who often wore lipstick and painted nails (you can see it in his photos). Second in command under Hitler.
>
> *Rudolf Hoess*: Deputy Fuhrer of the Nazi Party – generally known as "Fraulein Anna." Third in command under Hitler
>
> *Gerhard Rossbach:* (The Blond Beast): "Sadistic murderer….and notorious homosexual." [324]
>
> *Ernst Röehm*: Head of Storm Troopers, openly homosexual since 1919. Executed in 1934.
>
> *Ludwig Tiene*: Kapo at Auschwitz, still ranks as world's "most prolific mass murderer" who strangled, crushed and gnawed up to 100 young men and boys to death daily, while raping them. [325]
>
> *Lt Edmund Heines:* Munich SA leader – a homosexual, convicted murderer, and procurer of boys for Röehm.
>
> *Max Bielas:* Worked at Treblinka and kept a "harem of little Jewish boys" there.[326]

Emile Maurice: Hitler's male secretary was gay or bi-sexual.

Reinhard Heydrich: Designer of Kristallnacht pogrom and death camps- was homosexual and considered likely successor of Hitler.

Baldur von Schirach: Leader of Hitler Youth – bi-sexual
Walthur Funk: Minister of Economics – a "notorious homosexual."[327]

Hans Frank: Nazi Minister of Justice – a homosexual.

Lieutenant-General Albert Foerster: Led genocide in Poland –possibly one of Hitler's lovers.

Walter Buch: Early gay SA leader – President of the Nazi Party Supreme Court.

Wolf-Heinrich Graf von Helldorff: Gay Berlin police chief and plunderer of Jewish property.

Deniers of the extent of the lifestyle claim that married Nazis, with children, were solid proof of their heterosexuality. Yet, gay activists now insist that life before sex-change is meaningless, as they applaud men who are leaving wives and children to embrace their new identities.

Only Heinrich Himmler, head of the Gestapo, was energetically "anti-gay." In a 1937 speech, he complained that in Germany, two to four million men were "officially registered" in gay clubs.[328] Since there were only 34 million males in the entire nation (and many children or elderly) that's big chunk o' gayness. Consider this was the gene pool for der Fuhrer's troops and the SS.

Himmler wasn't the only one who considered the Nazi Party an induction center for homosexuality. Henry Gerber, founder of America's earliest known gay rights group, admitted as much to papers after the sacking of Hirschfeld's Sex Institute in Berlin: "Thus we get a glimpse of the insanity of the whole [Nazi] movement: A Jewish doctor working for the interests of homosexuals is persecuted by a heterosexual mob, led by homosexuals." [329]

Public face of the SS was almost Puritanical, yet pederasty and sexual violence constantly plagued them. In just a few months, in 1943, 22 gay-related convictions were recorded in their internal SS court records.[330] Citations were for activities like assaults or public sex acts, not merely gay preference. Anecdotal evidence of violent, homosexual crimes is preserved in a secretly made film of SS men whipping, raping, and murdering beautiful boys and young men. This is asserted by gay historian Frank Rector in *"The Nazi Extermination of Homosexuals"*, and said to be still floating around Europe somewhere.[331]

Persecution of feminine men was real, while alpha males were free to practice their vices. Many virile types were released from camps to enlist, especially at the war's end. Auschwitz Commandant Rudolf Hoess was a hyper-masculine, gay man who despised effeminacy, or what he called "genuine homosexuals." He detested what he described as their "soft and girlish affectations and fastidiousness, their sickly sweet manner of speech, and their altogether too affectionate deportment." [332] One camp survivor recalled that "guards lashed out with special fury against those with "effeminate traits." [333] Nazis stood for strength and virility. Feminine men were publicly unacceptable, although they were privately useful. At any rate, Nazis weren't in need of bodies for sexual release. They had millions of men, women, and children at hand in death camps.

Finally, the big shark himself. Everyone disagrees on how "gay" der Führer was, but almost no one seriously believes he was entirely straight. Contemporaries such as Carl Jung declared "Hitler's unconscious seems to be female." In 2000, German historian, Lothar Machtan, released a bombshell of a book on the gayness of Hitler. Witnesses claimed Hitler was not only homosexual, but murdered people to keep it quiet. Police records appear to back this up.[334] A fellow soldier from WWI claimed Hitler slept every night with "his young whore, Schmidl." [335] Consider also that Hitler was a protégé of flamingly gay Röehm, who raised him up from nothing, and in the midst of other gay men. He had Röehm shot eventually; but that's old Adolph, never much for loyalty.

Most likely, Hitler was bi-sexual. The OSS psychological assessment in 1941 concluded that Hitler was "troubled and abnormal sexually, possibly homosexual." [336] Although Adolph had recorded relations with at least four women in his life, they all attempted suicide, and two finished the job. Documents from Nazi doctors revealed Hitler "did not sleep in girlfriend Eva Braun's bedroom, and was doped up with multiple drugs, including female hormones." [337] Evidence of Hitler's sexual orientation is circumstantial – but there is a mountain of it. He intentionally surrounded himself with gay men from his youth and his greatest hero was Frederick the Great, a well-known homosexual. Hitler's personal bodyguards were described as "almost always 100 percent homosexuals" [338] Didn't Adolph notice?

WOMEN - GOOD FOR SOMETHING

Banned from prestigious professions and terminated from universities, women were almost invisible in Nazi Party activities and records. Their misogyny may not have been entirely due to aversion to women in the bedroom, but it must have been an influence. Igra, a witness to the Reich, believed so. "German homosexualism is a manifestation of primitive savagery, of physical lust for which the female is too refined an object of gratification" he claimed.[339]

Lesbians are largely absent from Nazi accounts as well. Still, the lurid lives of two lesbians, Sonia Boukassi and bi-gendered Violette Morris, were exceptions. Both worked at interrogating and torturing suspected French Resistance members. Violette was notorious for her bloody rituals, and was so hated that Resistance fighters ambushed her car in 1944. Irma Grese was a cruel camp kapo, and one of the rare women executed by Allies. Olga Lengyel survived Auschwitz-Birkenau, and wrote about Irma's frequent "homosexual relationships with inmates", whom she then had burnt alive.[340] Irma's other hobbies were making human lampshades (liberators found three in her hut), and beating or shooting women to death. To be fair, Irma was bi-sexual, carrying on with Josef Mengele and others.

Even if transgender pioneer Lenz exaggerated and most Nazis weren't gay – they have other charms in common. The Führer's brigades conspicuously modeled Rome, including Roman art, architecture, glorification of war, and almost a worship of masculinity. Swedish homosexuals march in togas in gay parades today. It's all about "Mein Kopulation" without much consideration of Kinder, Küche or Kirche. It's Nazi love.

SUFFER THE CHILDREN

For Nazi leaders, children were creatures to enlist, work, rape, or murder if it pleased them. But this should have been evident long before the war – about the time Germans were forced to pull grown men off their sons, in their version of the Boy Scouts. "Der Wandervögel" (German scouting) hosted everything from nudists to Christian hiking clubs in the early 1900s. But the combination of strength, nature, and sleek youth proved an irresistible draw – Nazis went where the boys were.

In 1911, letters came to parents of all Wandervögel boys insisting that gay scouts would soon be at their doors, with their mentors. First run of what happened in America, 2015. Ludwig Lewisohn described their corrupting influence in *The Nation,* in 1933. He charged the Wandervögel as the source "from which thousands of storm-troopers came...the entire movement is in fact and by certain aspects of its avowed ideology drenched through with homoerotic feeling and practice."[341] From that seed sprouted Baldur von Schirach, leading Hitler Youth from 1931 to 1940. By 1939, it was impossible for German 10-year-olds to avoid conscription into the (by then) "homoerotic" organization.

America's Wandervogel holds court in our public schools. Homosexuals in the Nazi movement were just better armed. The Nationalist Socialist German Worker's Party (Nazism) is our only modern example of what began as a gay, Fascist state. They may have denied it, and even changed policies as time went on, but Nazis are what unrestrained, hostile, and fully militarized homosexuality looks like. It's in your history books— but you may buy an older one to find it.

NAZI PRIDE, OR BETTER THAN DU

Ernst Röehm zealously preached gay supremacy, which is the sexual equivalent of racism. He believed homosexuals composed an elite "race", which should be central in the Nazi movement. Calling themselves the "Community of the Special" or "Der Eigene" in pre-war Germany, they were male supremacists and pederasts. The flaming Röehm sought to create a society where "homosexuality would be regarded as a human behaviour pattern of high repute."[342]

Eye-witness Louis Snyder commented on Röehm's arrogance in 1933: "He flaunted his homosexuality in public and insisted his cronies do the same. He believed straight people weren't as adept at bullying and aggression as homosexuals, so homosexuality was given a high premium in the SA."[343] Röehm lauded his boys for carousing, window smashing, and even killing "for the hell of it." [342] His OSS psychological assessment noted that "homosexuals, too, frequently regard themselves as a special form of creation, or as chosen ones whose destiny it is to initiate a new order."[344] A "Gay Aryan Resistance" statement from the 1980s follows almost word for word the Nazi mantra that white, gay, men are "nature's elite" who possess a singular "genius." This appeals to weak, damaged people, just as it did 70 years ago. How else could an uneducated, resentful sociopath galvanize a nation? Hitler plied them with a toxic mixture of self-pity and pride.

In America, Canada, Europe, and Australia we are bullied less overtly, but also forced to hold homosexuality in high repute. Christian bakers today are feeling the heavy boots of Röehm's seed. Just as Nazis burnt the Reichstag to hasten their coup, we have cultural attacks on all fronts. It's 1938 all over again.

ONLY THE ACCENTS HAVE CHANGED

Allies wiped out their government, (Wehrmacht), but by the 1960s they were reincarnated as Neo-Nazis. These "skinheads" emulate Nazism, Jew-hating and all. Racism is the most common quality attributed to Neo-Nazis, but it's by far their only trait. Routinely omitted is the sexual orientation of their leaders, which is almost never straight.

The world's most notorious Nazi in the 1970s, was Martin Webster, organizer of the National Front (NF) in Britain. He was also a practicing homosexual. In the 1990s, the NF was run by Nicky Crane, a committed gay-Nazi who admitted "Adolf Hitler was my God." Using Nazi salutes and slogans, Crane was considered an extreme right-winger – while secretly making hardcore gay porn. Another gay neo-Nazi, Peter Marriner, worked with Webster. Marriner was also an MI5 plant from the 1970s to 1991, proving that British intelligence assumed a homosexual man was the most likely to gain a Nazi's heart.[345] Years later, the BBC interviewed

Marriner under the code-name "Steve" and he claimed he had gained a great deal of information via gay pillow-talk. [346]

Everyone gaped in 1977, as America's Nazi Party marched through a Jewish neighborhood in Chicago. Frank Collin led the parade, in Nazi regalia. Officials attempted to block them, but the American Civil Liberties Union (ACLU) argued for their rights. Years later it came out that Collin had a peculiar taste for little boys between 10 to 14, and had been arrested for taking "indecent liberties" in 1979.[347] Which may account for why the ACLU (generally loathe to touch "right-wingers") came to the rescue of this particular Nazi.

Nazi love encircles the planet. In France, neo-Nazis never even attempted to conceal their sexual appetites. Their magazine, *Gaie France* was freely sold at newsstands. Michel Caignet, a "confessed and crusading paedophile" organized the movement in the 1970s, but made the mistake of handing copies of *Gaie France* to his comrades. They were not all amused. Even the secular *Réseau Voltaire* warned in 1997 of alarming links between AIDS charities, Neo-Nazis, and the pedophile community in France.[348]

Not surprisingly, Berlin is a major Nazi hub. Michael Kühnen gained power and notoriety as the leading Nazi of his era there. He robbed banks, worked with Holocaust deniers, planned mayhem, and was in and out of prison. Alas, his life was cut short when he died of AIDS in 1991. Kühnen will never build his "Anti-Zionist Legion" in Iraq, or establish a global, gay Fourth Reich, with Hitler on their postage stamps. He was considered an intellectual, and left the world his theories on homosexual fascism, such as this: "Fascism is based on the love of comrades . . . having sex with your comrades strengthens this bond." [349]

Although these facts were once freely shared, it's difficult and dangerous to even speak of now. Unless you are gay, like Johann Hari. In a tell-all for the Huffington Post, Hari stirs up almost as much scum as *The Pink Swastika.* He points out gay, leathered-up, neo-Nazi lads around the world. Working his way from Dutch far-right leader Pim Fortuyn, to Britain's Martin Webster, Hari sniffed out homosexuals wherever contemporary Nazis tread. The truth, Hari claimed, is that gay men were central not only in Nazism, but in every major fascist movement, past and present.[350] There you have it – a true confession.

Hari's revelations were previously exposed by many other writers. But while Scott Lively faced charges of "crimes against humanity" for saying *exactly the same thing*, Hari is paid a nice sum and saunters off into the sunset. Few even debated the bombshells Hari dropped, proving that others know it to be true.

WHY 'OUT' THE NAZIS?

Children of the millennium hear much about Nazi murders of homosexuals, but never the rest of the story. Samuel Igra was a Jewish historian who escaped Germany in 1939. He documented what he called the "poisoned stream" of homosexuality running through Nazism.[351] Because authors like Igra are so credible, their writing is a grave threat to gay supremacists, even now. Machtan in *"The Hidden Hitler"* also stresses the impossibility of ever understanding Nazism without taking this into consideration; specifically, that Hitler acted against blatant homosexuality to counter rumors of his own.

In the spirit of gayscrubbing history, one Wikipedia entry on "Hitler's sexuality" blithely claims there is "no evidence that [Hitler] engaged in homosexual behavior" and rejects any sexual perversions ascribed to der Führer.[352] Adolph? He was always such nice boy! History is close to extinction, because so much of it is off limits now. Quotes, figures, and documents – much is buried under a landslide of politically correct enforcement. Headlines from a 2004 newspaper show how far and how fast we've fallen. In "Gay-Dolpf Hitler. . ." the writers ask if fear of being "outted" moved Hitler to throw thousands of gay men into concentration camps.[353] Media is as likely to run such a column in 2017 as they can dead-lift a Panzer tank.

After more than 90 years, the gay community still denies its starring roles in the Nazi Party. They use reactionary laws to squelch speech, and information embargos to evade history. Gay influence at college is their major garrison. Targeted books and sources are dropped from courses, or given very critical reviews; which eventually effects public libraries, and the ability to find them. It isn't necessary to burn books – just complain, threaten, and sue until they vanish. Gay activist Pater Tatchell insisted we gut the world's libraries because they don't back up his constructs, starting with the most reputable history of Nazism, William Shirer's *"The Rise and Fall of the Third Reich."* Tatchell accused Shirer of portraying homosexuals "as protagonists in the fascist state" and remaining silent about "gay victims of Nazism." [354] Shirer was there, and Tatchell was not. Tatchell has something to gain and to hide. Shirer is dead.

Cyberspace is tougher to troll. But using social media and financial pressure, significant amounts of information can be blocked from the public. Sites created for web safety and malware jam or "warn" people from information. Obscurity swallows most articles and research that shine a little too harshly on Gay/Nazi phenomena. We live in a time of such gay muscle-flexing that criticism is successfully blocked. It is the devout wish of militant, gay bigots to make this a global practice.

As witnesses and victims of Nazism die off, denial is ramping up of both the Holocaust, and Nazi perversion. The specter of neo-Nazism in our time is far more potent with a public ignorant of the forces which nurtured it in the first place. And the rehash is this: there were possibly as many homosexuals in the Nazi Party as were persecuted – just different sorts, duking it out.

16

STUCK ON THE HATE CHANNEL

Soldiers in this war make vicious losers and bitter winners. Militants have about run as far as they can with the "inequality" and "victim" thing, since no one really believes it anymore. Gay agitators must constantly manufacture anger against conservatives to stay relevant and in the public eye.

Hate incubators like Chicago's "Sidetrack the Video Bar" regularly featured hate-gigs, where fuming gay progressives fantasized about all the people they hate, and what they would like to do to them. Especially detested is Sarah Palin. A visitor described videos of Palin being "gunned down, beaten up, bloodied, or otherwise savaged." They found it hilarious, and also rejoiced with progressives over Andrew Breitbart's death. You know those little jokesters – they were just bullied too much. Sidetrackers were mild compared to a demented crowd of homosexuals who mobbed and sexually assaulted a group of San Francisco Christians in 2008. It was so intense that police escorted them out, fearing for their lives. [355] Bashing street preachers is beginning to be a rather common gay activity.

Homosexual assaults of this type are censored gratis by media, so you're unlikely to have heard a thing. Meanwhile, we are becoming more selfish, fearful, violent, unkind, and uncooperative than ever – thanks to guerilla warfare on decent people. And that is precisely *why* they are despised. "Decency" as defined by 4000 years of Judeo-Christian ethics is offensive to crusading gay zealots, and other hate groups.

THERE'S NO MORE KANSAS, HONEY

Nothing brings out the baseballs bats faster than mentioning an *ex-gay.* According to homosexual doctrine, there is no such person. They may not exist. Escaped gays are viciously attacked by media and sometimes in person. They are the most feared and hated people in the pink universe – and that's saying a lot. Wayne Besen, executive director of Truth Wins Out wrote a book denying ex-gays the right to even choose their own sexual orientation. Can you be more arrogant? One news network meekly queried "Do gay people have the right to be ex-gay?" Who are they asking for permission?

A website called "Ex-Gay Watch" reveals the obsession gay fundamentalists have over ex-gays. Websites extolling traditional values and especially *ex-gay ministries,* are often off-line. "Page not found." Links don't work from Google and other info-control bastions. Searching for them by name often leads to sites railing *against* them. More than anyone else, those who escaped homosexual identity threaten the web of lies gay militancy has so carefully woven. Ex-gays are constantly watched, and their every word analyzed. Although they "don't exist", information about their movements, speaking schedules, supporters, employment, income, and family life are revealed to the world. Basic stalking procedures.

How many homosexuals led straight lives (even with marriage and children) to only "discover" their orientation much later in life? We all know someone like that, but are forbidden under gay gag-rules to bring it up in polite conversation. Changing from straight to gay *proves* that homosexuality is not innate, in itself. Many homosexuals experienced this in their own lives, but won't deal with it. Gay militants will attempt to criminalize any mention of their gender/sex changes, either to homosexuality, or back out of it. Queer narratives are endangered by it.

There is no difference between the reactions of gay militia groups to an ex-gay than if he had left a cartel. They'll hunt him down, slander him and never stop. Gay crusaders are in a huff over the term "gay mafia" but they've firmly joined this family of cultists, street gangs, and sociopathic lovers. You may not leave homosexuality without paying dearly, along those who assist you. Hypocritical gay activists are heavily pro-choice though when they're inveigling children to join them.

Wayne Besen and other "human rights" activists are doing their best to shut conservatives down for good. One of their most detested organizations is "American's for Truth About Homosexuality" (AFTAH) and spokesmen Peter LaBarbera and Matt Barber. Recipients of constant threats, they reveal the ugly side of gay extremists and their enormous arsenal of hate. For ratting out the gay underworld, AFTAH is now designated a "hate group" by *true* hate-mongers, in America's Orwellian inversion of reality.

Virtually every attempt to define or protect traditional marriage drew fury from gay activists. Gatherers seeking to put measures on ballots are vandalized, as well as their advertisers. Some were under gunfire in Oregon. Contributors are "exposed" as if they have committed great crimes, and put at risk by revealing personal information. Operating openly, gay oligarchs make no effort to cover their own identity. Why? It's obvious: those they label "haters" are not the type they expect will harm them in return.

SERFS FOR THE GLORIOUS PLENIPOTENTIAL EMPIRE OF HOMOSEXUALS & THEIR FOLLOWINGS, REALMS, HOLDINGS AND COLONIES

Where would the Boy Lovers be without their straight drudges? Case in point: Iowa's 2015 "Governor's Conference on LGBTQ Youth", was a giant hatefest for teens. It was intended to address bullying and issues important to the gay and lesbian community, but — stuff happens. In this case, drag queen Coco Peru sang to teens about how bullies should be "poisoned."[356] Gaystapo groups billed Peru as a comedian, because they find it so funny.

Other hilarious gags were how to literally "eat each other's shit" (with flavored oils) and how to slash tires on cars belonging to traditional pro-family types; possibly those of many parents. Any lamenting these gay revival meetings are labelled "bullies", and their complaints ignored.

More trouble in Iowa. Within 24 hours of receiving letters from the Obama administration on federally mandated policy for "transgendered" students, Iowa's Fairfield High School experienced a series of vandalism and unpleasant incidents in bathrooms and locker rooms. Taking cues from older bigots, LGBT students passed out black armbands – but those choosing not to wear them were taunted as "rednecks" and "haters." Disobeying a pompous, 16-year-old bully now qualifies kids as "haters" in Gaysville.

In April 2015, Loyola Marymount University allowed student services to hold an LGBTQ Awareness Week. Later, a 15-year employee was suspended and investigated for possible "hate crimes." Her violations? Telling her students that there are only two genders, "male and female." Universities are now so glutted with mindless stoolies that they persecute their own instructors. Los Angeles sent police to investigate this heinous thought-crime, and a campus Bias Incident Response Team was sent to monitor for non-received speech. It's gay terrorism, but Loyola is complicit in its own destruction.

Students now demand heads of their instructors on a platter. This isn't many steps from the genocidal treatment of elders in China's Cultural Revolution. Teachers have always been honored in every place, unless that culture was near to being annihilated.

Why won't we admit the obvious? Promoting homosexuality over other lifestyles was a colossal mistake. Gay militancy is a hostile presence that erodes the rights of others in direct proportion to the power it gains. Holdouts to gay fascism (in schools especially) are reeling under unjust and abusive treatment every day. This is not widely reported. But surely everyone over the age of 12 has experienced the checking of speech, and awareness that they are only allowed "approved" opinions in public. We are now more cowardly and less honest as a nation thanks to the exaltation of true hate.

TEN THINGS TO HATE ABOUT MEAN & MILITANT HOMOSEXUALITY

This may seem excessive to gay power brokers and their leftist SWAT teams. So be it. Militants threw the first sucker punch and continued to bash, while no one interfered with their lives. Americans have long proved they are willing to coexist with homosexuals, but peace isn't the goal of these fanatics. At this point, politely asking for generic human rights is interpreted as "hating." Prepare for it, since this psychological ploy is their greatest weapon. They assume you will never catch on, and will live in terror of being insulted. Your role is to curl up in a fetal position and apologize, leave, or die.

The right to "hate" or make moral declarations about right and wrong, is a remnant of our once vibrant and healthy freedom of conscience. Only leftists or designated victims are allowed this honor at this point. These are the unjust laws of an occupation, and of a sexual caste system. But if you *hate* oppression, deceit, and conscription of children on the magnitude of a war, then consider learning to hate it as your grandparents did – reasonably and justly. Let us count the ways:

HATE "HOMOPHOBIA"

"Homophobia" is the gay community's baby. They conceived it, nurtured it, named it, and thrust it into the public. Now the construct of "homophobia" is working as a political litmus test. Deniers of the fictional illness stand accused of "mental disorders" which could end with forced allegiance to homosexual doctrine. No one benefits by keeping this insipid narrative alive.

Without "homophobia" gay Brownshirts such as Dan Savage couldn't publicly threaten to rape Christian politician Rick Santorum (with lewd details), and to defame him for years. Charges of "homophobia" banished paparazzi magnet Paris Hilton since 2012. Hilton was secretly recorded by a cabbie, speaking to a friend about gay websites that supported random sex with strangers. She allegedly was disgusted and said something about gay guys being "the horniest people in the world." [357] That was a well-researched and scientific fact. But reality wasn't enough to protect Hilton from homophobia at work, forcing both low and high to flee honesty – and to fear cabbies.

Gay theory (father of homophobia) is an incubator of anti-Christian bias, and a source of injustice, confusion and child abuse. Promoting *Gayland über alles* has left millions of gutless creatures, as "homophobia" makes cowards of us all. Traders in this phony philosophy must be strenuously opposed. Stop living in fear of homosexual threats and tantrums, because "homophobia" has cursed us long enough. Stop using terminology created to entrap you and strip your civil rights. You will be instantly freed of the pernicious grip of "homophobia."

HATE DISEASE & DEATH

Homosexuality is unhealthy for the general population, yet it's even more dangerous to mention it. HIV/AIDS was spread into the world primarily by sexual excesses of homosexuals, and they now hasten the spread of other venereal diseases, such as meningitis, syphilis, and HPV. At one time, San Francisco press reported that about 10% of their homicides resulted from gay, sadomasochistic abuse alone.[358] But in a bazillion anti-AIDS campaigns, have homosexuals ever owned up to their major role in this? We appear to be virtually invisible to a self-absorbed group, who is becoming legally immune to requests of reasonable restraint.

A 1997 study in the *International Journal of Epidemiology* found that gay men sliced an average 8 to 21 years off their lives. For their concern, researchers were heaped with abuse. Eventually, the scientists emerged with little white flags. They were forced to dilute their findings in government gayocracy, as well as "repair" their papers.[359] Heterosexuals also spread disease and death, but gay blogs show a critical difference – with many *supporting* sexual pathology. Former wrestler Michael Johnson knew he harbored HIV in 2013, yet continued having unprotected sex until arrested many hook-ups later. One supporter in a gay publication claimed it was barbaric to punish Johnson, because those laws are "severely outdated", irrational and criminal. *Whaaat*?

In 1995, Dr. Judith Reisman authored *"Why no Arrests of Thou-*

sands of Men Who Give AIDS to Boys?" Considered the leading expert on such things in the 80s and 90s, she is not inconsequential. For that reason, Reisman was pilloried before her work forced too many plague-bearing child molesters off the streets. Although she was working in their best interest, no one wanted to know about that old science and medical stuff – which is so *boring*.

HATE LIES & SLANDER

Offensive, anti-family crusades are built on embedded falsehoods. First, that homosexuality is genetic, contrary to all research. Scientists just haven't brought themselves to fudge statistics that much. Tragically, many gay men and women were introduced to their lifestyle through rape or molestation at young ages. It's the big secret that the current batch of molesters desperately want silenced, so they can work unhindered.

The unpleasant task of exposing this has fallen to organizations such as the American Family Association (AFA). In retaliation, the Human Rights Campaign (HRC) posted gruesome photos of a Kenyan mugger who had been burnt alive by a mob.[360,361] They accused members of MassResistance and the AFA of causing the death of this "gay" "Ugandan" "martyr." Not one word was true. Like hags at a Salem witch-trial, the HRC just makes things up. Even their name is a lie, as only something like Boko Haram is less interested in human rights than the HRC.

Lies are also the chief method of gay recruitment in public schools. Violent deaths and tragically brief lives are divined for "gay" kids, if someone questions their sexual orientation. This is presented as the worst fate a gay teen can meet – yet questioning the gender and orientation of *every straight student* is routinely scheduled at our schools. That's what this Hokey Pokey is all about. Truly, radical homosexualists and their corporate lawyers have made lying into an elaborate art form. One which is lovingly embellished by leftists and their media retinue. So much gay hatred . . . so little time.

HATE SEXUAL TERRORISM

British authorities occasionally admit their boy-raping epidemic is on an industrial scale, while feigning concern.[362] Attorney Gavin Boby notes that the UK government needs to aggressively prosecute it as a national security threat, on the grounds that its "viciousness and genocidal motivation" will likely provoke violent vigilantism.

Homo-Fascists put on a show of violence and contempt in Germany as well, in 2016. Sons of the Führer attacked about 1000 people who peacefully protested the German government's intensely pro-gay education being forced on their children. Gay thugs pelted the group with eggs, tore up their Bibles, and even threw human excrement at them.[363] From a population with a high incidence of AIDS, that was attempted murder. German police wrung their hands and eventually disbanded the parents, but didn't touch their neo-storm troopers.

Even as gay extremists deny they are sexually interested in children, they feverishly work across the world on lowering the age of consent. Why is that? Julia Gasper warns that once the "concept of a child's legal consent is accepted" molested children must always prove they didn't consent.[364] Tough for a six-year old, but the UN and our universities are working on it.

Child molesting isn't the only fruit of gay dominance, just the worst. California lights the shining path the rest of the way to oblivion. In 2017, California officially became a 163,695.57 sq. mile AIDs incubator and safe haven for rapists and pederasts. This is no exaggeration. California Gov. Jerry Brown signed a bill lowering the crime of intentionally exposing sex partners to HIV, from a felony (very bad!) to a misdemeanor (no big deal). Victims can be any age.

While he was diligently servicing gay men, Brown also decreed HIV positive persons (the majority are gay men) could donate blood and conceal their health status. Why not? They could be offended or inconvenienced! You, or your friends, or loved ones, can just go home and die. In California, the innocent have no protection, while malicious persons attempting murder are promised legal immunity. Hospital patients will be gambling with their lives as well.

Children elsewhere are no safer. In 2017, a Maryland school coach, Carlos Deangelo Bell, was arrested after molesting at least 42 boys (ages 11-17) while *knowing* he was HIV positive. Thank the bigots who lobbied for this rank health terrorism, fueled by sexual fanaticism.

Citizens of the entire United States now walk in fear of failing gay dogma, and Hollywood is particularly septic. Drake Bell (a Nickelodeon star) didn't make it past the Gay Taliban fire wall. He stood accused of making a "transphobic tweet" about Bruce Jenner, whom he refused to call "Caitlynn" as ordered. Although Bell explained he was honoring Jenner's athletic record by calling him "Bruce", he had to temporarily disappear from the deranged Pink Shirts roving Cyberland.

Gay zealots are a type of sexual fundamentalists – utterly devoted to their cause, and committed to do anything necessary to further it. One of their godfathers, California Gov. Jerry Brown, now terrorizes an entire state by proxy.

HATE HUMORLESS ELITISM & IMPERIALISM

Gay militancy is to comedy, what Henry VIII was to his wives. Censorship and peevishness are merely a few of its toxic effects. Will humor survive them?

CNN host Anderson Cooper seems to struggle with laughing at himself. From a 2015 Saturday Night Live (SNL) impersonation by Jon Rudnitsky, the newscaster was left gravely offended. Complaining that the only thing Rudnitsky appeared to know about him was that he "was gay" Cooper seemed amazed. Yet he gladly provides the entire world details of his sexual preference, unsolicited. Impersonators, impersonate, Mr. Cooper. Some of us are offended by pretentious celebrities, but will they shamefully trot off stage? Not likely. Cooper's thin-skinned posturing over homosexuality is stereotypical. Media heads in his position have the biggest, bulliest pulpits to stifle all mocking of their Eminences, and they use them daily. Anyway, SNL is far nastier to conservatives any day.

Gay elitism also hosts its own caste-system, as well-off men from North America and Europe call the shots for a gay agenda. Typical colonialists, they invade first, establish a beachhead, and begin shouting orders like Great White Sahibs. African bishops accused homosexuals of "cultural imperialism" in 2013.[365] Under pressure to change traditional attitudes toward homosexuality,

Kenyan President Uhuru Kenyatta nixed US plans for gay expansionism. All types of American aid dried up after this interchange. While leftists rage about corporations "exploiting" Africa, some of the most powerful and destructive special-interest groups are gay organizations and gay diplomats.

From Los Angeles to Berlin, gay hegemony now dictates how natives are to have sex in Ugunda and Nigeria. When Christian missionaries did something like this a century ago, it was considered terribly oppressive – and a major complaint of liberal educators. Not all Europe is on board with gay revisionism either. Robert Lopez met French homosexuals who resent same-sex marriage as an American construct "forced onto them by powerful, well-funded lobbyists."[366] Why so silent now, haters of colonialism?

Comments on an old gay message board from the 1980s noted the abundance of these privileged men: "Their wealth and their sex insulate them, and since they are protected, they don't feel any need to care about anyone else" a member complained.[367] A decade later, "The City Nightclub" opened in Portland, Oregon, claiming to assist street youth.[368] Witnesses reported a string of chauffeured, wealthy men picking up homeless boys and helping themselves – in exchange for cash. Investigations splashed across the front pages at the time are impossible to find in any archives. Just as in Britain, the issue was buried, and is now dismissed as utter fantasy.

Poverty stricken men are still being abused and degraded. In 2017, gay websites pimped out "Hot Homeless Gay Studs" and "Filthy Homeless Men Desparate for a C*** to Please."[369] Apparently, there are enough well-heeled homosexuals who feel they can make the rest of the world their prostitutes and political hacks.

HATE SEXUAL NARCISSISM & SOCIOPATHY

It's the orientation that never stops congratulating itself. There was a reason homosexuality was considered an illness over all those centuries. Sociopathy in militant gay leadership is endemic. Convinced their opposition has little value, they don't offer the respect they demand for themselves. According to high priests of homosexuality, conservatives have no right to have opinions, to freely speak, or much else. They make statements that we should be imprisoned, tortured – or at least run out of business.

Shutting down Betty and Dick Odgaard's bed and breakfast in Iowa left fascists across the world jubilant. The Odgaards were conscientious objectors against forced enlistment in gay marriage. Now that their "Gortz Haus Gallery" doesn't exist, Their Worships still can't be married there, proving the entire thing was an underhanded ruse. Journalists and officials are often too dull to comprehend this though. Gaystapo bullies accomplish these anti-rights coups through intimidation and power. They've used one to obtain the other quite successfully.

Later, the Odgaards put up billboards with a simple graphic implying marriage is between one man and one women. There was no reference to homosexuality. Gay website *"The Advocate"* interpreted this as follows: "Iowa Couple Plans 1,000 Antigay Billboards." [370] Because all creation is about homosexuality, even if it isn't. Gay hate-groups interpret all things in relation to themselves, and the enmity the rest of creation has for them; such as natural conception of children.

Early in the dim dawning of civilization, Narcissus appeared. Myths attempted to explain mysteries of human behavior, and one was the origin of these tragically self-absorbed persons. Why were they like this; what would their end be? It's telling that in Ovid's tale, the pretty boy never even peeked at girls. Narcissus embarked on his first and only love affair in his short life —with himself. He withered to nothingness. Freud believed homosexuality was a type of narcissism, an infantile mental state. Until recently, many psychiatrists and psychologists also believed and practiced it.

Artists are often accused of being enamored with themselves as well, but the gay sector focuses on their vaginas and penises and such, almost exclusively. Phallus Rex. Art duo Douglas Gordon and Tobias Rehberger managed to project gay sex acts all over the place in Ibiza, Spain, in 2015. Their centerpiece was a video of men sodomizing each other, but they were modest – and showed only the lower halves of their bodies. This was projected on the front of a museum. How else will children ever be introduced to gay porn? [372]

Facts are, much of the gay community is self-interested and

self-promoting. If they had left us alone, we never would have discovered this. As it is, we've all been drafted into their queer global orgy and assigned walk-on roles. We don't have to accept this script; and could we ask gay exhibitionists to please keep it in their pants?

17

QUESTION HOMOSEXUALITY

We thought we'd been asked to a celebration, and came full of Christian love and liberal tolerance. We tried accommodation, diversity, and kumbaya. We even allowed intrusions into our work and our children's lives – as long as it was voluntary. And therein lies the rub; there is no choice about homosexuality now, it is decreed.

LGBT extremism and traditional American values can't coexist because of gay aggression. Instead, our goodwill is turned against us, like someone coming to tea with machetes. Children become persona non-grata when gay bigots are in positions of power, as recently proved by the *Boy Scout Putsch.* This is splendid for leaders who believe we are all part of their personal play box. Now, some of them are claiming the unenlightened masses who reject sodomy for themselves and their families should have no rights at all. Earlier we met Marian, who revealed the true goal of gay militancy: *"Please understand that the destination of the LGBT rights movement is consolidated state powers and a virtual end of the First Amendment."*

Tyrants count on apathy, and Hitler was absolutely giddy about it. *"What good fortune for governments that the people do not think"* he said, as he devoured Europe. Many people realized Nazism would end badly – yet few tried to stop it. Now resurrected fascism in service of homosexuality is becoming so odious in Europe that conservatives are organizing underground, like WWII resistors. America is under that state of siege and denial at the same time, which is how many nations have lost their liberties. W. B. Yeats' description of European passivity after WWI could describe many of us now: *"The best lack all conviction, while the worst are full of passionate intensity."* [373]

Why are Western nations allowing gay fundamentalists to deconstruct the world's human rights, after we fought so hard for them? This is counter-evolutionary and moronic. Canada is a decade ahead of us, legalizing gay marriage in 2005, and reaping its great rewards. Canadian conservatives live with commissars monitoring their speech — exactly as the People's Republic of China. It's a well-known principle that tyrants tend to be boorishly alike, regardless of sexual orientation, or longitude.

Many expected the Gay Fight Club would move on if it was well fed and patronized. But it just gained weight and belligerence. Since the Supreme Court tossed them the keys with a little wink, Christian organizations may be inundated with faux "job seekers" who actively oppose their mission and hate their God. Gay militants will continue to order others about, while liberals fall at their feet swearing fealty and loyalty. Both are equally culpable for the siege of hate they've unleashed over America.

Assuming we're not hit with Armageddon first, gay thugs will wax nastier and louder. It's become a habit, and it's probably amusing. Malicious gay couples will stalk and generally make life miserable for people who have never said an unkind word to them. Leftists haters don't care much about truth, mercy, faith, kindness, forgiveness, honesty, accuracy, history, families, justice, safety, or fairness. They use these words to confuse and shame their enemies, but not from deep concern. This is apparent in their words and deeds.

Earnest people have hard time wrapping their minds around that degree of deception. We all want to love our neighbor and believe the best of them. Because of this, stunned conservatives are often paralyzed by false charges of "hate." Since targets are largely Christians (who aren't comfortable hating), radicals use this to maximum advantage. Bewildered victims generally do nothing but grovel and hope their accusers will go away. But passively allowing evil to flourish only encourages more harm.

Why would Americans champion people who watch "boy shit videos"? Who insist on conscripting entire nations into a class of servile voyeurs, by force, and starting with tots? Yet, narcissists convince themselves that because you are forced to endure their dreary, self-congratulatory admiration, it must all be true. "We are the ones we have been waiting for!" as their patron claimed. Strident gay extremists are possibly some of the nastiest people on the planet – hating loudly, boldly, and proudly. As free persons, we have every right to battle their aggression, and their hate. This isn't a call to arms, but to defense of speech and sanity. In 2017, it's illegal to even say this in parts of Europe, and is barely permissible in America now.

You have rights — use them! Speaking the truth is your chief weapon. Question the narratives, statistics, world-view, curriculum, and especially the legislation of gay militants anywhere. Feel free to tell others if you do not enjoy gay sex, or hearing about theirs. Object forcefully to indoctrination disguised as education, and to government-imposed diversity training. You are more than an object of cultural experimentation for special interest groups. Refuse to use hostile political slogans, or to be branded by them. Do not politely ignore this aggression. There is nothing noble about meeting injustice and child abuse with good manners.

Gay doesn't appear to be particularly good for anyone, but you have a right to be gay if you choose. It's legal. Most Americans don't care where you put your schlong either, but please keep it out of our lives and our children's faces. Even metaphorically. You are free to surgically mutilate yourself, play dress-up, or put your family through hell if that's your wish. The rest of the world doesn't have to applaud you, or pay for it though. Compulsory celebration of sex acts is sadistic.

For gay extremists; you may want to rethink what you are supporting or silently condoning at this point. Oppressors never fared well in the long run. Regardless your hatred of conservatives, you won't like the face of this monster once you've summoned him up. Moloch will devour you too at the end – but this will be up to you.

Decent gay men and women might also consider what the end of aggressive and militaristic homosexuality could be in our near future. Human rights are only possible when all of us are allowed to keep them. There is no other option, and history proves this. If government abuse in the name of gay rights doesn't end, America will likely die an unnatural death at some point. Since extremists ignited this uncivil war in your name, will you continue to support them? Or will you speak up for a fair and reasonable coexistence with your neighbors?

America has been a prototype of freedom and a womb for diversity, unlike any place on earth. Together we cohabited for centuries, and overcame many differences. We survived deep divisions, yet found ways to mutually honor and respect each other. Our history has been a beautiful experiment in tolerance and justice, and we exported this to the world. Don't let this die! We can still live in peace again, but it will take courage, determination, and a willingness to change. Let's do this together – because there really is no other choice.

REFERENCES & NOTES

1. Towle, Andy. "Frank Kameny Gay Rights Items Join 'Treasures of American History'". Towel Road. Sept.10, 2007. Retrieved Mar. 20, 2016 from http://www.towleroad.com/2007/09/frank-kameny-ga/

2. Buckley, William. "On Experiencing Gore Vidal." *Esquire Magazine*. August, 1969. p. 132.

3. PBS Series American Experience. "Why Did the Mafia Own the Bar?" Retrieved Feb. 13, 2017 from http://www.pbs.org/wgbh/americanexperience/features/general-article/stonewall-mafia/

4. Kurtzleben, Danielle. "Gay Couples More Educated, Higher-Income Than Heterosexual Couples. *US News*. March 1, 2013. http://www.usnews.com/news/articles/2013/03/01/gay-couples-more-educated-higher-income-than-heterosexual-couples

5. Johnson, Ramon. "Gay Population Statistics in the United States." Gaylife.About. Updated December 04, 2016. http://gaylife.about.com/od/comingout/a/population.htm.

6. Chen, Joyce. "Hillary Clinton, Ellen DeGeneres Write Sweet Responses to Gay Teen. . ." *US Magazine*. July 5, 2015 http://www.usmagazine.com/celebrity-news/news/hillary-clinton-ellen-degeneres-write-sweet-responses-to-gay-teen-201557

7. Singh, Lea. "$104 million lawsuit against Christian activist threatens to chill free speech in Canada." MercatorNet. August 23, 2016. http://www.mercatornet.com/mobile/view/103-million-lawsuit-against-christian-activist-threatens-to-chill-free-spee

8. Baklinski.Pete. "Pro-family leaders attacked by arson after German play depicts them being mutilated on stage". Lifesite News. Nov, 20, 2015. https://www.lifesitenews.com/news/pro-family-leaders-attacked-by-arson-after-german-play-depicts-them-being-m

9. Newton, Mark. "States resisting same-sex marriages." Online FortyNiner-CSULB. MARCH 15, 1999. http://web.csulb.edu/~d49er/spring99/v6n88-samesex.html

10. Eisenberg, Daniel. "Homosexuality". *Encyclopedia of Medieval Iberia*, (New York: Routledge, 2003), 398–399. http://users.ipfw.edu/JEHLE/deisenbe/Enc_of_Medieval_Iberia/homosexuality.pdf

11. "Catholic Archbishop in Australia faces fines, punishment over marriage pamphlet". MassResistance. Dec. 5, 2015. http://www.massresistance.org/docs/gen2/15d/Australia-bishop-letter/index.html

12. Duffy, Nick "Peer urges government to 'disestablish' Church of England over anti-gay vote". Jan. 20, 2016. http://www.pinknews.co.uk/2016/01/20/peer-urges-government-to-disestablish-church-of-england-over-anti-gay-vote/

13. DeParle. Jason. "111 Held in St. Patrick's AIDS Protest". *The New York Times.* Dec. 11, 1989. Retrieved on Mar. 14, 2016 from http://www.nytimes.com/1989/12/11/nyregion/111-held-in-st-patrick-s-aids-protest.html

14. Moon, Ruth . "Gordon College Studies Same-Sex Behavior Ban Amid Accreditation Questions". Christianity Today-online. 10/2/2014. http://www.christianitytoday.com/gleanings/2014/october/gordon-college-studies-same-sex-behavior-ban-accreditation.html.

15. Cassandra, Adam. "Gender identity policy adopted for Nebraska school sports despite bishops' objections". LifeSite News-online. Jan 15, 2016 https://www.lifesitenews.com/news/gender-identity-policy-adopted-for-nebraska-school-sports-despite-bishops-o

16. Hallowell, Billy. "Bakery Found Guilty of Discrimination and Forced to Pay Damages. . ." The Blaze-online. May 29, 2015. Retrieved Nov. 21, 2015 from. http://www.theblaze.com/stories/2015/05/29/bakery-found-guilty-of-discrimination-and-forced-to-pay-damages-to-a-gay-activist-for-injury-to-feelings-is-fighting-back/

17. Evans, Glenn. "Same-sex couple denied cake by Longview bakery". *Longview-News Journal*. Feb, 24, 2016. http://www.news-journal.com/news/2016/feb/24/same-sex-couple-cake-refusal-dehumanized-us/

18. Donohue, Bill. “Dan Savage Savages Pope”. StandardNewswire.com. http://www.standardnewswire.com/news/608968056.html

19. Browning, Bil. “Why You Shouldn’t Donate to the Salvation Army Bell Ringers.” The Bilerico Project-online. Nov, 21, 2011. http://www.bilerico.com/2011/11/why_you_shouldnt_donate_to_the_salvation_army_bell.php?utm_source=front_page&utm_medium=best_of_box&utm_campaign=Best_Of

20. Braverman, Faith. “Millionaire gay couple is suing to force a church to hold their wedding”. thelibertarianrepublic.com. March 18, 2014 http://thelibertarianrepublic.com/millionaire-gay-couple-suing-force-church-hold-wedding/

21. Ellis-Petersen, Hannah. “China bans depictions of gay people on television”. *The Guardian*-online. Mar. 4, 2016. https://www.theguardian.com/tv-and-radio/2016/mar/04/china-bans-gay-people-television-clampdown-xi-jinping-censorship

22. Gibbon, Edward. *The Decline and Fall of the Roman Empire*. (first published 1776-1788), Vol 1, ch.II, footnote 31.

23. Rosin, Hanna. “Chickenhawk.” *The New Republic*. May 8, 1995. https://archive.org/stream/Chickenhawk_942/Chickenhawk_The_New_Republic_MAY_8_1995__djvu.tx

24. Eberstadt, Mary. “How Pedophilia Lost Its Cool.” FirstThings. The Institute on Religion and Public Life. December 2009. http://www.firstthings.com/article/2009/12/how-pedophilia-lost-its-cool

25. “How schools are pushing transgenderism to children”. MassResistance- online. June 6, 2014. http://www.massresistance.org/docs/gen2/14b/GLSEN-Conference-040514/transgender-agenda/index.html

26. “Homosexuality and Child Sexual Abuse”. FRC.org. July 2, 2002. http://www.frc.org/get.cfm?i=IS02E3

27. Starnes, Todd. “Teens Shocked by Graphic Content at Anti Bullying Conference”. Town Hall- online. https://townhall.com/columnists/toddstarnes/2015/04/17/teens-shocked-by-graphic-content-at-antibullying-conference-n1986750

28. Skinner, Victor. “Parents outraged after middle schoolers attend LGBTQ sex conference”. EAG News-online. July 24, 2015. http://eagnews.org/parents-outraged-after-middle-schoolers-attend-lgbtq-sex-conference/

29. Cook, Michael. “Gross? Parents might think so”. MercatorNet. Dec 4 2015. http://www.mercatornet.com/conjugality/view/gross-parents-might-think-so/17294

30. Cook, Michael. “Behind Australia’s safe schools campaign”. Mercator Net. Dec 2 2015 http://www.mercatornet.com/articles/view/behind-australias-safe-school-campaign/17276

31. Romero, A. and Abril, P. 2009-08-08 “Introducing affective-sexual diversity in Early Childhood Education:” American Sociological Association (paper) San Francisco, CA Online <PDF>. 2014-11-29 http://citation.allacademic.com/meta/p306683_index.html

32. “Policies on Lesbian, Gay, Bisexual, Transgender & Queer (LGBTQ) Issues”. American Medical Association. n.d. http://www.ama-assn.org/ama/pub/about-ama/our-people/member-groups-sections/glbt-advisory-committee/ama-policy-regarding-sexual-orientation.page?

33. Fenn, Peter. “Rick Perry’s Fringe Views on Gay Marriage and Gay Rights”. *US News*. Sept. 13, 2011 http://www.usnews.com/opinion/blogs/peter-fenn/2011/09/13/rick-perrys-fringe-views-on-gay-marriage-and-gay-rights.

34. Honan, Edith. “Factbox: List of states that legalized gay marriage”. Reuters. Jun 26, 2013 http://www.reuters.com/article/us-usa-court-gaymarriage-states-idUSBRE95P07A20130626

35. VD. “It really doesn’t get better”. Vox Populi-online. Jan. 19, 2012. https://voxday.blogspot.com/2012/01/it-really-doesnt-get-better.html

36. McCain, Robert Stacy. “Neutral Objective Incompetence”. The Other McCain-online. July 2, 2013. http://theothermccain.com/2013/07/02/neutral-objective-incompetence-how-ginger-gorham-aided-pedophile-network/

37. “Institutions, Reports, and Documents About Intolerance and Discrimination Against Christians”. Observatory on Intolerance and Discrimination against Christians-online. http://www.intoleranceagainstchristians.eu/reports-and-documents.html

38. Lopez, Robert Oscar. "The Global Fight for Children's Rights: Europe". The Public Discourse webpage. Oct 29, 2013. http://www.thepublicdiscourse.com/2013/10/11101

39. ibid.

40. Koukl, Greg."Intolerant Tolerance-The Myth of Moral Neutrality". Salvo Magazine-online. Autumn 2008.http://www.salvomag.com/new/articles/salvo6/6koukl.php

41. Unruh, Bob. "Military punishing officer who halted lesbian 'make-out' session". WND.com. 11/13/2014 http://www.wnd.com/2014/11/military-punishing-officer-who-halted-lesbian-make-out/#CeeuiEjtx9QRxg0p.99 `

42. Haynes, Deborah. "Soldiers accused of gang rape in 'routine' bullying". The Times UK-online. Dec. 20, 2014 http://www.thetimes.co.uk/tto/news/uk/defence/article4302991.ece

43. ibid.

44. "Chicago Liberals Want Conservative Books Banned". Fox News. July 11, 2011. http://nation.foxnews.com/book-banning/2011/07/11/chicago-liberals-want-conservative-books-banned

45. Bourne, Lisa. "Professor will flunk students who refer to students as 'male' or 'female'". LifeSite News-online. Aug 31, 2015. https://www.lifesitenews.com/news/professor-will-flunk-students-who-refer-to-students-as-male-or-female

46. ibid.

47. Douglas, Donald. "Elton John's Homosexual Husband Named as 'Mother' on Couple's Children's Birth Certificates." American Power blog. May 30, 2015. http://americanpowerblog.blogspot.com/2015/05/elton-johns-homosexual-husband-named-as.html

48. Wagner, Adam J. "A Queer Poet in a Queer Time: John Milton and Homosexuality". Presentation at Cedarville University. Apr. 3, 2015. http://digitalcommons.cedarville.edu/research_scholarship_symposium/2015/podium_presentations/23/

49. Boyd, Brian. *Vladimir Nabokov: The Russian Years*. p.72. Princeton University Press. 1993

50. Nabokov, Vladimir. *Bend Sinister*. (Introduction) Time Books, New York (1964) http://nabokovandko.narod.ru/Texts/Bend_Sinister.html

51. Stinson, Marvin. "DOJ employees force Christians to verbally affirm homosexuality". Free Republic-online. 10/9/2015. http://www.freerepublic.com/focus/f-news/3346751/posts

52. ibid.

53. Gasper, Julia PhD. *The Myth of the Homocaust*. (n.d.). https://archive.org/stream/TheMythOfTheHomocaustJuliaGasper/The_Myth_of_the_Homocaust_Julia_Gasper#page/n1/mode/2up

54. "Persecution of Homosexuals". US Holocaust Memorial Museum.(n.d.) http://www.ushmm.org/learn/students/learning-materials-and-resources/homosexuals-victims-of-the-nazi-era/persecution-of-homosexuals

55. "US State Department backs gay envoy, raps Dominican cardinal." Catholic Culture. Dec. 22, 2015. http://www.catholicculture.org/news/headlines/index.cfm?storyid=27017

56. Advancing the Human Rights of Lesbian, Gay, Bisexual and Transgender Persons Worldwide. US State Department. Retrieved May 7, 2016, http://www.state.gov/r/pa/pl/2013/211478.htm

57. Wong, Edward. "U.S. Diplomat's Same-Sex Marriage Causes Stir in China". The New York Times-online. May 3, 2016. http://www.nytimes.com/2016/05/04/world/asia/us-diplomats-same-sex-marriage-causes-stir-in-china.html?_r=0

58. Lopez, Oscar (See #38)

59. "Meeting with young people on the Caracciolo seafront." Libreria Editrice Vaticana-online. 21 March, 2015. http://w2.vatican.va/content/francesco/en/speeches/2015/march/documents/papa-francesco_20150321_napoli-pompei-giovani.html

60. "The martyrs of 3 June 1886: "The day anti-gay hate came to Uganda". Gay Star News. June 3, 2014. http://www.gaystarnews.com/article/martyrs-3-june-1886-day-anti-gay-hate-came-uganda030614/

61. Iaccino, Ludovica. "Ugandan King Proves that Homosexuality is African". Jan.30, 2014. IB Times-UK online. http://www.ibtimes.co.uk/gay-ugandan-king-proves-that-homosexuality-african-1434416

62. "Anita Bryant Pie in the Face"Anita Bryant- pie in face." Youtube video posted by ws945. https://www.youtube.com/watch?v=dS91gT3XT_A- Accessed on 12-3-2016.

63. ibid.

64. ibid.

65. "Initiative, Referendum and Recall: 1988-1995". Oregon Bluebook online. http://bluebook.state.or.us/

state/elections/elections21.htm
66. Wentz, Patty. "He's Back". Willamette Week. Feb 11, 1998. Accessed July 30, 2016 from: https://web.archive.org/web/20010629081504/http://www.positiveatheism.org/writ/lonmabon.htm.
67. "Patty Wentz". Strategies 360 website. https://www.strategies360.com/team/patty-wentz/
68. Wise, Talia. "Gutsy theater owners take a stand against new Disney movie, then this happens!" Breaking Christian News-online. Mar 6, 2017. http://www.breakingchristiannews.com/articles/display_art.html?ID=20724
69. Schneider, Walter. Dads & Things at WordPress received "Badge of Recognition. Fathers for Life blog. April 14, 2013. http://blog.fathersforlife.org/2013/04/14/dads-things-at-wordpress-received-badge-of-recognition/
70. Schlesinger, Laura Dr. "Setting My Record Straight About Gays." Dr. Laura's blog. June 22, 2010. http://www.drlaurablog.com/category/homosexuality/
71. "Dr. Laura Asks Gays for Forgiveness". ABC news-online. Oct 11- no year. http://abcnews.go.com/Entertainment/story?id=114735&page=1
72. Haverluck, Michael F. "Employee to Home Depot: Stop pushing homosexuality". OneNewsNow.com. Mar 22, 2015 https://www.onenewsnow.com/culture/2015/03/22/employee-to-home-depot-stop-pushing-homosexuality
73. Commentator in response to article in Brietbart.com.
74. Faust, Katy. "Children like me need a voice in gay marriage debate". USA Today. April 27, 2015 http://www.usatoday.com/story/opinion/2015/04/27/supreme-court-same-sex-parenthood-column/26452519/
75. Opposing Gay Marriage Doesn't Make You a Crypto-Racist. The Daily Beast.com. April 24, 2014. http://www.thedailybeast.com/articles/2014/04/24/opposing-gay-marriage-doesn-t-make-you-a-crypto-racist.html
76. ibid.
77. Wikipedia s. v. "Kaseem Reed". Last modified 25 March 2017. https://en.wikipedia.org/wiki/Kasim_Reed
78. Gasper, Julia PhD. *Homosexuality and Paedophilia: A Reference Guide* (introduction). Found in http://voice1nthecrowd.blogspot.com/2014/09/homosexuality-and-paedophilia-reference.html
79. Capuzza, Jamie & Ekstrand, Sandra R. "Protecting Transgender Workplace Rights". Profiles in Diversity Journal. (n.d.) http://www.diversityjournal.com/13976-protecting-transgender-workplace-rights/
80. "HIV & AIDS in the news: A guide for reporting in a new era of prevention & treatment". GLAAD.org website. (n.d.) https://www.glaad.org/publications/hiv-aids-news-guide-reporting-new-era-prevention-treatment. Accessed Sept. 14, 2016.
81. "Data, Analysis & Documentation: Federal Employment Reports". OPM.gov. (n.d.). https://www.opm.gov/policy-data-oversight/data-analysis-documentation/federal-employment-reports/historical-tables/total-government-employment-since-1962/
82. Scarborough, Rowan. "Combat troops to get gay sensitivity training".The Washington Times-online. Feb. 24, 2011. http://www.washingtontimes.com/news/2011/feb/24/combat-troops-to-get-gay-sensitivity-training/
83. Fischer, Bryan. "The mark of the beast is here". Oct 14, 2014. Renew America website. http://www.renewamerica.com/columns/fischer/141014
84. Capuzza, Jamie & Ekstrand, Sandra R. "Protecting Transgender Workplace Rights". Profiles in Diversity Journal. (n.d.) http://www.diversityjournal.com/13976-protecting-transgender-workplace-rights/
85. "Diversity Training on Gender Identity and Gender Expression". Human Rights Campaign website. (n.d.) http://www.hrc.org/resources/diversity-training-on-gender-identity-and-gender-expression. Accessed July 22, 2016.
86. "Southern Poverty Law Center's Teaching Tolerance Project". Family Research Council website. http://www.frc.org/issuebrief/southern-poverty-law-centers-teaching-tolerance-project
87. ibid.
88. Ruse, Austin. "Powerful Leftist Group Sues to Close Jewish Counseling Service for Gays". Breitbart. 29 May 2015http://www.breitbart.com/big-government/2015/05/29/powerful-leftist-group-sues-to-close-jewish-counseling-service-for-gays/
89. Gallagher, Maggie. Quoting Yancey, George & Williamson, David A. in The National Review-online. February 20, 2015. http://www.nationalreview.com/articles/414149/god-hatred-hollywood-and-

government-discrimination-maggie-gallagher

90. Gunn, Steve. "Suburban DC school district passes transgender bathroom policy amid outrage from parents". May 11, 2015. http://eagnews.org/suburban-dc-school-district-passes-transgender-bathroom-policy-amid-outrage-from-parents/

91. ibid.

92. Farley, Harry. "Vietnam: Christian lawyer beaten by police after human rights conference". Dec 9, 2015. Christianity Today. https://www.christiantoday.com/article/vietnam.christian.lawyer.assaulted.by.police.after.human.rights.conference/73067.htm

93. Lavers, Michael K. "Ted Osius says Vietnam ambassadorship 'dream come true'". Washington Blade website. Nov 20, 2014. http://www.washingtonblade.com/2014/11/20/exclusive-ted-osius-says-vietnam-ambassadorship-dream-come-true/

94. "Out Ambassadors: Global Trade Agreement Will Lift Up LGBT Lives". Letter from gay ambassadors printed in The Advocate. June 09 2015. http://www.advocate.com/commentary/2015/06/09/out-ambassadors-global-trade-agreement-will-lift-lgbt-lives

95. "White House Calls for Ban on LGBT 'Conversion Therapies'". VOA News. Apr 08, 2015. http://www.voanews.com/content/white-house-lgbt-conversion-therapies/2712282.html

96. Morgenson, Gretchen & Rosner, Joshua. "'I Really Have No Recollection'. . ." The Huffington Post. Jul 26, 2011 http://www.huffingtonpost.com/2011/05/26/gretchen-morgenson-reckless-endangerment_n_867158.html

97. ibid.

98. Frank, Barney. "My Life as a Gay Congressman". Mar 12, 2015. Politico.com. http://www.politico.com/magazine/story/2015/03/barney-frank-life-as-gay-congressman-116027

99. Leahy, Michael Patrick. "Barney Frank Confirms: No Congressional Oversight of Clinton Cash Uranium Deal". May 19, 2015. Brietbart.com. http://www.breitbart.com/big-government/2015/05/19/exclusive-barney-frank-confirms-no-congressional-oversight-of-clinton-cash-uranium-deal/

100. Jaffe, Alexandra."Obama backer, Democratic fundraiser Terry Bean charged in sexual abuse case". CNN News-online. November 23, 2014 http://www.cnn.com/2014/11/23/politics/terry-bean-sex-abuse-charges/

101. Griffin, Anna. "Mayor to respond to reports of sexual relationship with teen". The Oregonian online. Dec 17, 2009 http://www.oregonlive.com/news/index.ssf/2009/01/mayor_sam_adams_on_monday.html

102. "Corporate Partners". HRC.org. Page dated 2017. http://www.hrc.org/hrc-story/corporate-partners

103. "Family Research Council". (n.d.) SPLC website. https://www.splcenter.org/fighting-hate/extremist-files/group/family-research-council

104. Ham, Mary Katharine. "FRC shooter: I targeted them because SPLC list said they were 'anti-gay'". HotAir.com April 24, 2013. http://hotair.com/archives/2013/04/24/frc-shooter-i-targeted-them-because-splc-list-said-they-were-anti-gay/

105. Harrington, Elizabeth. "Feds Holding Summits for Lesbian Farmers. . ." Freebeacon.com. Aug 16, 2016. http://freebeacon.com/issues/feds-holding-summits-lesbian-farmers/

106. Comments made in Odinist.org. http://redicecreations.com/ul_img/33879poofs.png. Accessed June 25, 2016.

107. Kumar, Anugrah. "Hillary Clinton: 'Religious Beliefs ... Have to Be Changed' About Abortion". Christian Post. Apr 25, 2015. http://www.christianpost.com/news/hillary-clinton-religious-beliefs-have-to-be-changed-about-abortion-138179/

108. Davidson, Terry. "Ben Levin sentenced to three years for child porn". Toronto Sun. May 29, 2015. http://www.torontosun.com/2015/05/29/ben-levin-sentenced-to-three-years-for-child-porn

109. Court of Appeal for Ontario-documents between Khurrum Awan and Ezra Levant. Results released: December 22, 2016. http://www.ontariocourts.ca/decisions/2016/2016ONCA0970.htm

110. See # 38

111. "MassResistance hammers Education Committee. . .". MassResistance website. May 10, 2015. http://massresistance.org/docs/gen2/15b/School-surveys/hearing_050615.html.

112. O'Neil, Tyler. "Former Diplomat Warns: The LGBT Ideology is 'Inherently Totalitarian'". Sept 15, 2016. PJ Media. https://pjmedia.com/faith/2016/09/15/former-diplomat-the-lgbt-ideology-is-inherently-totalitarian/.

113. Reisman, Judith. "Where are the arrests of thousands of men who give AIDS to boys?" 1995 (revised

2006). http://www.drjudithreisman.com/archives/CALIF%20HEARING5.pdf

114. Meotti, Giulio. "Putin's Puritan Piety: The Ideological War against the West". Gatestone Institute website. Oct 9, 2016 https://www.gatestoneinstitute.org/9063/putin-piety-church

115. Nicolosi, Linda A. "Psychology losing Science Credibility, Say APA Insiders". NARTH website http://www.narth.com/docs/insiders.html

116. Nicolosi, Joseph. "APA Task Force Report -- a Mockery of Science". Joseph Nicolosi website. (n.d.) http://www.josephnicolosi.com/apa-task-force/

117. "American Psychological Association Task Force on Appropriate Therapeutic Responses to Sexual Orientation". American Psychological Association. 2009. http://www.apa.org/pi/lgbt/resources/therapeutic-response.pdf

118. Lytton, Charlotte. "Biological Same-Sex Parent Babies Could Be a Reality by 2017". The Daily Beast. Feb 2, 2015. http://www.thedailybeast.com/articles/2015/02/25/biological-same-sex-parent-babies-could-be-a-reality-by-2017.html

119. Irwig, M S.. "Testosterone therapy for transgender men". Lancet Diabetes Endocrinol. 2017 Apr;5(4):301-311. doi: 10.1016/S2213-8587(16)00036-X. Epub 2016 Apr 12.

120. Schumm, Walter R. "Why? We hanker after instant gratification." MercatorNet. Jun 6 2016 https://www.mercatornet.com/conjugality/view/why-we-hanker-after-instant-gratification/18172

121. See # 78

122. Eberstadt, Mary. "How Pedophilia Lost Its Cool." FirstThings, December 2009. https://www.firstthings.com/article/2009/12/how-pedophilia-lost-its-cool

123. ibid.

124. "History of Paidika". Boywiki.org. https://www.boywiki.org/en/Paidika:_The_Journal_of_Paedophilia Accessed Sept 2, 2015.

125. Rind B, Welter M. "Reactions to First Postpubertal Male Same-Sex Sexual Experience in the Kinsey Sample"Arch Sex Behav. 2016 Oct;45(7):1771-86. DOI: 10.1007/s10508-016-0719-1.

126. ibid.

127. Colapinto, John "The True Story of John/Joan". Rolling Stone: pp 54–9. Dec 11, 1997. https://web.archive.org/web/20000815095602/http://www.pfc.org.uk/news/1998/johnjoan.htm

128. Black, Alexandra. "Peadophile Peter Truong says he "misses his son'". Mar 10, 2014. The Sydney Morning Herald-online. http://www.smh.com.au/national/paedophile-peter-truong-says-he-misses-his-son-20140310-34i66.html#ixzz406mHU8PW

129. Batty, David. "Sex changes are not effective, say researchers". The Guardian-online. July 30, 2004. http://www.guardian.co.uk/society/2004/jul/30/health.mentalhealth

130. Dhejne, C., et al. "Long-Term Follow-Up of Transsexual Persons Undergoing Sex Reassignment Surgery." Feb 22, 2011. PLOS ONE- online. http://journals.plos.org/plosone/article?id=10.1371/journal.pone.0016885.

131. Gibson, B. & Catlin, A.J. "Care of the Child with the Desire to Change Gender – Part I".Pediatr Nurs. 2010;36(1):53-59. © 2010 Jannetti Publications, Inc. http://www.medscape.com/viewarticle/718619_13

132. "Aldactone Side Effects". Drugs.com. (n.d.) https://www.drugs.com/sfx/aldactone-side-effects.html

133. "DSM IV-Gender Identity Disorder". Mental health Today-online.(n.d.) http://www.mental-health-today.com/gender/dsm.htm

134. Liaugminas, Sheila. "Transitioning of children 'too risky' say Obama's own experts". MercatorNet.com. Aug 25, 2016. http://www.mercatornet.com/sheila_liaugminas/view/transitioning-of-children-too-risky-say-obamas-own-experts/18576

135. Gasper, Julia. See # 78

136. Tabirian, Alissa ."Child Trauma Expert: Pro-Pedophilia Groups Are 'Grooming' Public to Accept Adult-Child Sex". CNS News-online. Oct 16, 2013. http://www.cnsnews.com/news/article/alissa-tabirian/child-trauma-expert-pro-pedophilia-groups-are-grooming-public-accept

137. Gartrell, Nanette, Bos, Henny. "National longitudinal lesbian family study". 1986 to present. https://www.nllfs.org/about/

138. Heffernan, Dani. "The APA Removes "Gender Identity Disorder" From Updated Mental Health Guide". Dec 3, 2012. GLAAD.org. https://www.glaad.org/blog/apa-removes-gender-identity-disorder-updated-mental-health-guide

139. "2016–2017 Student Injury and Sickness Plan for The University of Chicago". 2016–2017". United

Healthcare Resources. (n.d.) https://wellness.uchicago.edu/sites/wellness.uchicago.edu/files/uploads/2016-451-1%20Summary%20Brochure %20072216.pdf.

140. Ford, Zack. "How The FDA's Revised Blood Ban Caters To Religious Anti-Gay Beliefs". ThinkProgress.org. https://thinkprogress.org/how-the-fdas-revised-blood-ban-caters-to-religious-anti-gay-beliefs-d5d75da588b0

141. Minor, Jack. "Doc faces boot for citing 'gay' health dangers". WND.com. June, 27, 2015. http://www.wnd.com/2015/06/doc-faces-boot-for-citing-gay-health-dangers/#rZDoBgE7M3OyLc0p.99

142. Camenker, Brian. "Dr. Church loses final appeal at hospital". Dec 17, 2015. http://www.massresistance.org/docs/gen2/15b/DrChurch-BIDMC/bod-appeal-lose.html

143. Regnerus, Mark. "How different are the adult children of parents who have same-sex relationships?"New Family Structures Study Social Science Research, Volume 41, Issue 4, July 2012, pp 752–770. https://utexas.influuent.utsystem.edu/en/publications/how-different-are-the-adult-children-of-parents-who-have-same-sex

144. McWhirter, Mattison. The Male Couple (1984). Quoted by Joseph Nicolosi in http://www.josephnicolosi.com/an-open-secret-the-truth-about/.

145. Dhanagom, Christine. "'Gold standard' study's striking findings: children of heterosexual parents happier, healthier". Lifesite News. Jun 11, 2012. https://www.lifesitenews.com/news/gold-standard-studys-striking-findings-children-of-heterosexual-parents-hap
146. ibid.

147. Lopez, Robert Oscar & Rice, Georgian. Audio file. KPDQ radio broadcast. July 20, 2015. https://soundcloud.com/georgenerice/07-20-15a

148. Erickson, John. "Gay Kids! Sue Your School for a Million Bucks!" Createspace. July, 2011. found in https://www.bookdepository.com/Gay-Kids-Sue-Your-School-for-Million-Bucks-Professor-Chair-Finance-John-Erickson/9781463711146

149. Regnerus, Mark. See # 143

150. http://ijr.com/2016/10/718321-a-magazine-for-0-2-year-olds-responds-to-reader-request-for-more-lgbt-pictures-and-parents-are

151. Savin-Williams, Ritch C. "The Dubious Assessment of Gay, Lesbian, and Bisexual Adolescents". Archives of Sexual Behavior. Apr 2014, 43, Issue 3, pp 413-422. Dec 24, 2013 http://link.springer.com/article/10.1007/s10508-013-0219-5

152. "Lexington, Mass., father of 6-year-old arrested". MassResistance"Oct 30, 2005. http://www.massresistance.org/docs/parker/main.html

153. Robinson, B.A, Vidal-Ortiz, S. "Displacing the Dominant ''Down Low''. Deviant Behavior. 34: 224–241, 2013.Taylor & Francis Group, LLCISSN: 0163-9625 print/1521-0456 online DOI: 10.1080/01639625.2012.726174

154. "The little boy who started a sex change aged eight -"Daily Mail UK -online. Sept 30, 2011. http://www.dailymail.co.uk/news/article-2043345/The-California-boy-11-undergoing-hormone-blocking-treatment.html

155. "New Danish Study of 6.5 Million: Health Benefits of Marriage are Unique to Male-Female Unions". National Organization for Marriage. JUNE 12, 2013. http://www.nomblog.com/35598/#sthash.tHajaqal.dpuf

156. ibid.

157. "Oregon gay history timeline". Gay & Lesbian History of the Northwest. (n.d.) http://www.glapn.org/6020timeline.html

158. "Australian man jailed for 40 years in US after trafficking adopted son". ABC.AU News-online. 29 Jun 2013 http://www.abc.net.au/news/2013-06-29/man-jailed-trafficking-adopted-son-paedophile-ring/4789730

159. Gorman, Ginger. "Two dads are better than one". ABC AU private archive. Accessed May 28, 2016. https://dl.dropboxusercontent.com/u/1701569/GingerGorman_ABC_TwoDadsAreBetterThanOne.pdf

160. ibid.

161. Gorman, Ginger. "A journalist's second thoughts". July 9, 2013. ABC.AU-online. http://www.abc.net.

au/news/2013-07-10/gorman-second-thoughts/4809582

162. ibid

163. Cook, Michael. "A toxic combination: paedophiles, baby farms, and same-sex marriage". July 1, 2013. MercatorNet.com. http://www.mercatornet.com/conjugality/view/12408

164. Newton, Mark. "States resisting same-sex marriages". Forty-Niner. Mar 15, 1999. http://web.csulb.edu/~d49er/spring99/v6n88-samesex.html

165. Michelle, Kara. "Family of the Year". Celebeat.com. Mar 6, 2015. http://www.celebeat.com/articles/19476/20150306/family-year-abc-casts-raising-hopes-martha-plimpton-new-role.htm

166. Orr, Asaf & Baum, Joel, lead authors. " "Schools in Transition-A Guide for Supporting Transgender Students in K-12 Schools". American Civil Liberties Union. https://www.aclu.org/report/schools-transition. Accessed Aug 31, 2016/

167. ibid.

168. Heller, Corinne. "Elton John Calls for Dolce & Gabbana Boycott. . .'" ENews-online. Mar 15, 2015. http://www.eonline.com/news/635824/elton-john-calls-for-dolce-gabbana-boycott-over-synthetic-children-comments-shame-on-you

169. Zahn, Drew. "Elton John boycott called act of 'Taliban'". WND.com. Mar 16, 2015. http://www.wnd.com/2015/03/elton-john-called-taliban-for-designer-boycott/#Yd3VqCG3B1VPA1Mq.99.

170. "Who's the daddy? ". Jan 17, 2013. http://www.dailymail.co.uk/tvshowbiz/article-2263764/Elton-Johns-partner-David-Furnish-named-baby-Elijahs-mother-AGAIN-newborns-birth-certificate.html#ixzz4divrCMva

171. Dubuisson, Martine. "Delphine Boël peut poursuivre sa recherche en paternité à l'égard d'Albert II". Le Soir-Be. Feb 3, 2016. http://www.lesoir.be/1110938/article/actualite/belgique/2016-02-03/delphine-boel-peut-poursuivre-sa-recherche-en-paternite-l-egard-d-albert-ii

172. US Supreme Court. "Brief of the Amicae Curiae Heather Barwick and Katy Faust in Support of Respondents". Nos. 14-556, 14-562, 14-571, and 14-574. David Boyle - Counsel of Record. Long Beach, CA. March 24, 2015.

173. Alexander, C.J. "Violence in Gay and Lesbian Relationships". Journal of Gay & Lesbian Social Services. Vol. 14 , Iss. 1,2002. http://www.tandfonline.com/doi/abs/10.1300/J041v14n01_06?src=recsys.

174. ibid.

175. Xiridou, M., Geskus, R., de Wit, J., et al. "The contribution of steady and casual partnerships to the incidence of HIV infection among homosexual men in Amsterdam". AIDS. 17(7):1029-1038, May 2, 2003. http://journals.lww.com/aidsonline/Fulltext/2003/05020/The_contribution_of_steady_and_casual_partnerships.12.aspx.

177. Besse, Gail. "Support for Adult Children of Homosexual Parents". The National Catholic Register. Oct 8-14, 2006 issue. http://www.theroadtoemmaus.org/RdLb/22SxSo/PnSx/HSx/AdltChlHsx.htm

178. Badash, David. "Dan Savage: Parents of Trans Teen Leelah Alcorn. . .". Thenewcivilrightsmovement.com. Jan 1, 2015. http://www.thenewcivilrightsmovement.com/davidbadash/dan_savage_parents_of_trans_teen_leelah_alcorn_threw_her_in_front_of_that_truck

179. Swift, Michael. "Gay Revolutionary." Reprinted from The Congressional Record of the United States Congress. May 23, 2012.http://www.jamaicaobserver.com/news/Full-text-of-the-gay-manifesto.

180. Bohon, Dave. "Pastor 'at Peace'". New American. Aug 17, 2012. https://www.thenewamerican.com/culture/family/item/12506-pastor-at-peace-after-conviction-in-lesbian-partners-custody-case

181. ibid.

182. Ring, Wilson. Pastor sentenced in Vt. lesbian custody case". CNS.news. Mar 4, 2013. http://www.cnsnews.com/news/article/pastor-sentenced-vt-lesbian-custody-case.

183. Roth, Mark. "Janet Jenkins Sues Christian Aid Ministries". AEF.net. Aug, 2012. http://www.eaf.net/mvp/2012/janet-jenkins-sues-christian-aid-ministries/

184. Roth, Mark. "Timo Miller Update". EAF.net. (n.d.) http://www.eaf.net/mvp/2011/timo-miller-update/

185. Eckholm, Erik. "New Charges in Virginia Kidnapping Over Custody". Oct. 8, 2014. The New York Times- online. http://www.nytimes.com/2014/10/09/us/new-charges-are-brought-in-same-sex-custody-case.html

186. Dougherty, Jon. "Report: Pedophilia more common among 'gays'". WND.com. Apr 29, 2002. http://www.wnd.com/2002/04/13722/

187. Elam, Jerome. "The story of one. Trafficked Boys. . ." Communities Digital News. Sep 20, 2014. http://www.commdiginews.com/life/trafficked-boys-vandalized-innocence-hidden-in-plain-sight-26356/.

188. Dailey, Timothy. Homosexuality and Child Sexual Abuse. 2002 for FRC. http://www.orthodoxytoday.org/articles/DaileyHomosexualAbuse.php254

189. ibid.

190. ibid.

191. Reisman, Judith. See # 113

192. Herek, Gregory/ "Facts About Homosexuality and Child Molestation". UC Davis http://facultysites.dss.ucdavis.edu/~gmherek/rainbow/html/facts_molestation.html. Last updated 2013.

193. See # 188

194. Angella Johnson, "The man who loves to love boys," Electronic Mail & Guardian, June 30, 1997. http://www.mg.co.za/mg

195. Dougherty, Jon. See # 186

196. Brown, Stephen. "Professors For Pedophilia" FrontPageMag.com. July 14, 2014. http://www.frontpagemag.com/fpm/236228/professors-pedophilia-stephen-brown.

197. Davies, Nick. "The sheer scale of child sexual abuse in Britain". The Guardian-online. April 1998. Accessed at http://www.nickdavies.net/1998/04/01/the-sheer-scale-of-child-sexual-abuse-in-britain

198. Taylor, Brian. Ed. "Perspectives on Paedophilia." Feb 26, 1981. London; Batsford Academic and Educational.

199. "MassResistance hammers Education Committee at public hearing on "student survey" bill". MassResistance website. May 10, 2015. http://massresistance.org/docs/gen2/15b/School-surveys/hearing_050615.html

200. See # 25

201. Reisman, Judith. See # 113

202. ibid.

203. Gasper, Julia. See # 78

204. ibid.

205. "Scotland Paedophile Ring". TheUKdatabase.org. Mar 31, 2012. https://theukdatabase.com/2012/03/31/scotland-paedophile-ring/

206. Gasper, Julia. See # 78

207. "Here is a list of 130 peadophile councillors or UK political party affiliated members" Timetostartcaring.com. (n.d.) http://timetostartcaring.com/here-is-a-list-of-100-paedophile-councillors-or-uk-political-party-affiliated-membersthey-are-among-the-people-who-help-run-our-country-they-are-in-no-particulour-order-this-list-does-not-contain-a/.

208. Campbell, Beatrix. "The scale of historical sexual abuse in the UK is a catastrophe.". The Guardian-online version. Sept 6, 2016. https://www.theguardian.com/commentisfree/2016/sep/12/child-sex-abuse-inquiry-uk-scale-catastrophe.

209. Removed.

210. Philipson, Alice & Holehouse, Matthew. "Rotherham sex abuse scandal. . ." The Telegraph. Aug 27, 2014 http://www.telegraph.co.uk/news/uknews/crime/11057953/Rotherham-sex-abuse-scandal-nobody-at-the-council-needs-to-resign-claims-deputy-leader.html.

211. "Rotherham abuse scandal: 'No misconduct' in first IPCC inquiries". BBC News site. http://www.bbc.com/news/uk-england-south-yorkshire-39208776

212. "Independent Inquiry into Child Sexual Exploitation in Rotherham" (1997 – 2013). Found Mar 8 2017. http://www.rotherham.gov.uk/downloads/file/1407/independent_inquiry_cse_in_rotherham

213. Unruh, Bob. "Magistrate axed for stand against same-sex duo adoption". WND.com Mar 12, 2016. http://www.wnd.com/2016/03/magistrate-axed-for-stand-against-same-sex-duo-adoption/.

214. Camber, Rebecca. "VIP child abuse whistleblowers were 'murdered'". Daily Mail-online. Dec 22, 2014.
http://www.dailymail.co.uk/news/article-2884471/VIP-child-abuse-whistleblowers-murdered-MP-says-men-poised-lift-lid-scandal.html#ixzz4dp4c4cxF

215. Cook, Michael. See # 30.

216. Linning, Stephanie. "Paedophile bishop 'duped congregations. . ." Daily Mail-online. Mar 21, 2016 http://www.dailymail.co.uk/news/article-3503093/Paedophile-bishop-duped-congregations-471 impersonating-identical-twin-brother-bishop.html#ixzz43ayV3LLe.

217. Dougherty, Jon. See # 186

218. "By His Draconian Treatment Of Father Justin Wylie. . ." Restore-DC-Catholicism. June 14, 2014. http://restore-dc-catholicism.blogspot.com/2014/06/by-his-draconian-treatment-of-father.html.

219. Dugan, Emily & Bloodworth, James. "Homophobia exacts a chilling price as hate crimes climb". The Independent.UK. Oct 22, 2011. http://www.independent.co.uk/news/uk/crime/homophobia-exacts-a-chilling-price-as-hate-crimes-climb-2374674.html

220. Gasper, Julia. See #78

221. Waterhouse, Ronald (Chariman). *Lost in care, report of the tribunal of inquiry into the abuse of children. . .* 7 para 52.72. HC Session 1999-00 20-. National Archives UK. Feb 16, 2000. Crown Copyright

222. Davies, Nick. See #197

223. Waterhouse, Ronald (Chairman). *Lost in Care: Report of the tribunal of inquiry into the abuse of children. . ."* Feb 16, 2000. Crown Copyright. http://webarchive.nationalarchives.gov.uk/20130124064403/http:/www.dh.gov.uk/prod_consum_dh/groups/dh_digitalassets/documents/digitalasset/dh_134777.pdf

224. ibid.

225. "Christian care home boycotted by council". The Christian Institute. Jan 21, 2009. http://www.eaf.net/mvp/2011/timo-miller-update/

226. Waterhouse, Ronald. See #223

227. "State says 1,000 care facilities match sex offender addresses". LA Times blog. Oct 27, 2011. http://www.eaf.net/mvp/2011/timo-miller-updat

228. Gillispie, Mark. "Ohio has one of highest rates of sexual abuse". Cleveland.com. June 6, 2013. http://www.cleveland.com/metro/index.ssf/2013/06/ohio_has_one_of_highest_rates.html.

229. Blau, Reuven."School social worker filed multiple complaints about alleged L.I. pedophile. . ." NY DailyNews.com. Mar, 28, 2016. http://www.nydailynews.com/new-york/social-worker-repeatedly-warned-school-pedophile-article-1.2580519.

230. "Foster Father charged with sexually abusing boys on Long Island". MSN.com. http://www.msn.com/en-us/news/crime/foster-father-charged-with-sexually-abusing-5-boys-on-long-island/ar-BBqDxvD?OCID=ansmsnnews11.

231. Stewart, Nikita & Goldstein, Joseph. "An 'Exemplary' Foster Father, a String of Suspicions and Sexual-Abuse Charges". *The New York Times*-online. Apr 1, 2016. http://www.nytimes.com/2016/04/02/nyregion/a-foster-father-on-long-island-a-string-of-suspicions-and-sexual-abuse-charges.html?_r=0.

232. Radosh, Daniel."Why Know?" *The New Yorker*. Dec 6, 2004. http://www.newyorker.com/magazine/2004/12/06/why-know.

233. Gasper, Julia. See # 78

234. Kalichman ,SC, Gore-Felton, C, Benotsch, E, et al."Trauma Symptoms, Sexual Behaviors, and Substance Abuse. . ." *Journal of Child Sexual Abuse*. Vol. 13, Iss. 1, 2004

235. Waterhouse, Ronald. See #223

236. Waterhouse, Ronald. See #223

237. "PTSD: Men and Sexual Trauma". US Dept. for Veterans Affairs. Update Apr 8, 2016. http://www.ptsd.va.gov/public/types/violence/men-sexual-trauma.asp jany 27 2016

238. McCain, Robert Stacy. "Endorsement of adult-child sex on rise". *The Washington Times*-online archive. Apr 19, 2002. http://www.come-and-hear.com/editor/ca-wt-04-19-02/

239. Gasper, Julia. See #78

240. Black, Alexandra. "Peadophile Peter Truong says he "misses his son'". Mar 10, 2014. *The Sydney Morning Herald*-online. http://www.smh.com.au/national/paedophile-peter-truong-says-he-misses-his-son-20140310-34i66.html#ixzz406mHU8PW

241. "Homosexuality among Serial Killers: Statistics" Quoting "Homosexual Rape and Murder of Children", published in *Journal of the Family Research Institute*, Vol. 18 No. 1, Feb 2003. http://www.adherents.com/misc/hsk.html#source

242. Popham, Peter. "Child killer sentenced to be throttled, cut up and immersed in an acid bath". *The Independent*. Mar 17, 2000. http://www.independent.co.uk/news/world/asia/child-killer-sentenced-to-be-throttled-cut-up-and-immersed-in-an-acid-bath-282448.html

243. James, Susan Donaldson. "Transgender Defense: 'Donna' Says 'Doug' Is the Spokane Serial Killer".

ABC News. Mar, 19, 2014. http://abcnews.go.com/Health/transgender-woman-male-persona-serial-killer/story?id=22959423.

244. "Six charged in France for holding woman as sex slave". AFP News. Mar 22, 2015. https://www.yahoo.com/news/six-charged-france-holding-woman-sex-slave-025650544.html?ref=gs.

245. Regnerus, Mark. See #143

246. Meldrum-Hanna, Cara & Masters, Deb. "Boy with henna tattoo". ABC.net.AU News. Mar 10, 2014. http://www.abc.net.au/news/2014-03-10/boy-with-henna-tattoo-network-exposed/5310812.

247. Gartrell, Nanette, Bos, Henny. See # 137.

248. Lopez, Robert Oscar. "Growing Up With Two Moms". Public Discourse. Aug 6, 2012. http://www.thepublicdiscourse.com/2012/08/6065/.

249. ibid.

250. Demetrious & Shamoun, Sam. "Cross Dressing and Islam". Answering Islam. http://www.answering-islam.org/Responses/Abualrub/mhd_cross_dressing1.htm

251. "Homosexuality iii. in Persian Literature." *Encyclopaedia Iranica*. Last update Mar 23, 2012. http://www.iranicaonline.org/articles/homosexuality-iii%20

252. Styles, Ruth. "The bus driver who has raped 12 little boys". *The Daily Mail*. Sept 5, 2014. http://www.dailymail.co.uk/femail/article-2739799/Why-millions-Pakistani-children-falling-prey-vicious-paedophiles.html

253. Seamark, Michael. "Explosive new evidence. . .". *Daily Mail*. Feb 27, 2014. http://www.dailymail.co.uk/news/article-2569570/Patricia-Hewitt-breaks-silence-groups-links-National-Council-Civil-Liberties-boss.html

254. Elam, Jerome."The story of one. . ." Communities Digital News. Sept 20, 2014. http://www.commdiginews.com/life/trafficked-boys-vandalized-innocence-hidden-in-plain-sight-26356/

255. ibid.

256. "Male victims of sex trafficking". Toy Soldier. May 17, 2011. https://toysoldier.wordpress.com/2012/10/25/male-victims-of-sex-trafficking/

257. Harvey, Linda. "The creepy cookie corrupting our children". WND.com. Mar 1, 2016. http://www.wnd.com/2016/03/the-creepy-cookie-corrupting-our-children/

258. ibid.

259. Killerman, Sam. "Breaking through the binary". Last update Dec 26, 2016. http://itspronouncedmetrosexual.com/2011/11/breaking-through-the-binary-gender-explained-using-continuums/

260. Wurtzel. Katie. "These Are The Most LGBT-Friendly Hospitals In the Nation". *The Advocate*. July 11, 2013. http://www.advocate.com/health/2013/07/11/these-are-most-lgbt-friendly-hospitals-nation.

261. Hassan, Peter. "Washington State To Teach Transgenderism To Kindergartners". Dailycaller. June 16, 2016. http://dailycaller.com/2016/06/01/washington-state-to-teach-transgenderism-to-kindergartners/

262. Hughes, Tammy. "Now children as young as FOUR are asked to choose what gender they are before they start school" *Daily Mail*. http://www.dailymail.co.uk/news/article-3548962/Now-children-young-FOUR-asked-choose-gender-start-school.html

263. Foxhall, Emily. "Katy-area teacher fired for refusing to address girl, 6, as transgender boy". National Black Robe Regiment. Nov 19, 2015. http://nationalblackroberegiment.com/attorneys-katy-area-teacher-fired-for-refusing-to-address-girl-6-as-transgender-boy/

264. "Transgender at 11". ABC News-video. (n.d.) http://abcnews.go.com/2020/video/transgender-11-boobs-18260885

265. Orr, Asaf & Baum, Joel. See #166

266. Hirst, Jo. 2015. *The Gender Fairy.* Australia Oban Road Publishing. http://www.worldcat.org/title/gender-fairy/oclc/926086558

267. "Liberal Pawns for Degeneracy". The burning platform. May 24, 2016. (photo) http://www.theburningplatform.com/2016/05/24/liberal-pawns-for-degeneracy/

268. "NYC Commission on Human Rights Announces Strong Protections. . .". New York City government office. December 21, 2015. Retrieved Sept. 14, 2016. http://www1.nyc.gov/office-of-the-mayor/news/961-15/nyc-commission-human-rights-strong-protections-city-s-transgender-gender

269. ibid.

270. Cook, Michael. "Transsexuals trash a feminist icon". Mercatornet. Oct 26, 2015. http://www.mercatornet.com/articles/view/transexuals-trash-a-feminist-icon/17070

271. ibid.

272. Unruh, Bob."Alabama Supreme Court Chief Justice suspended". WND.com May 6, 2016. http://www.wnd.com/2016/05/alabama-supreme-court-chief-justice-named-in-complaint/#!.

273. Orr, Asaf & Baum, Joel. See #166

274. Chapman, Michael W. "Johns Hopkins Psychiatrist: Transgender is 'Mental Disorder'" CNS News. June 2, 2015. http://www.cnsnews.com/news/article/michael-w-chapman/johns-hopkins-psychiatrist-transgender-mental-disorder-sex-change

275. "National Transgender Discrimination Survey". Sept 11, 2012. TransEquality.org http://www.transequality.org/issues/resources/national-transgender-discrimination-survey-executive-summary

276. Dhejne, C., et al. See # 130

277. Lee, Sophia. "Walt's Story". *World Magazine*. Apr 15, 2017. https://world.wng.org/2017/03/walt_s_story

278. Birkner, Gabrielle. "Jewish transgender man gives birth and embraces life as a single 'abba'". *Jewish Telegraphic Agency*. Jan 22, 2016. http://www.jta.org/2016/01/22/news-opinion/united-states/jewish-transgender-man-gives-birth-and-embraces-life-as-a-single-abba

279. Vituscka, James. "Necktie Or Flowers?" Radaronline.com. Jun3 4, 2015. http://radaronline.com/celebrity-news/caitlyn-jenner-kids-confused-fathers-day-plans-gifts/

280. Priya, Joshi. "Punk rocker declared insane after decapitating girlfriend". IB Times -online. Mar 11, 2016. http://www.ibtimes.co.uk/russia-punk-rocker-declared-insane-after-decapitating-girlfriend-performing-sex-act-her-head-1549036

281. US Government. "Crime in the U.S." FBI.gov. Sept, 2010. https://www2.fbi.gov/ucr/cius2009/index.html

282. ibid.

283. Reynolds, Adam & Harris, Chaz. *The Promised Land*. Feb. 14, 2017. https://www.amazon.com/Promised-Land-Adam-Reynolds-ebook/dp/B01NBYY3T2

284. "Gender Ideology Harms Children". American College of Pediatricians. Jan, 2017. http://www.acpeds.org/the-college-speaks/position-statements/gender-ideology-harms-children

285. "Pioneering UCSF Clinic Helps Transgender Youth Be Themselves". University of California San Francisco website. 2017. https://www.ucsf.edu/news/2015/11/284401/pioneering-ucsf-clinic-helps-transgender-youth-be-themselves, Accessed July 19. 2017.

286. Goldstein, Richard. "Sense or Sensibility: Them Boys" *Whitehotmagazine*. Summer, 2007, Issue #4. http://www.whitehotmagazine.com/index.php?action=articles&wh_article_id=711

287. Villarreal, Yezmin. "5 Most Disappointing Things We Learned About HRC's 'White Men's Club'". Advocate.com. June 4, 2015.http://www.advocate.com/human-rights-campaign-hrc/2015/06/04/5-most-disappointing-things-we-learned-about-hrcs-white-mens-cl

288. "Transgender Track Star Stirs Controversy. . . " CBS New York News online. July 8, 2016. http://newyork.cbslocal.com/2016/06/08/transgender-nattaphon-wangyot-alaska-track/289.

290. Bachiochi, Erika. "Rendering the Sexed Body Legally Invisible". *Public Discourse*. May 26, 2016. http://www.thepublicdiscourse.com/2016/05/17033/

291. Arter, Melanie. "Justice Ginsburg: We Need An All-Female Supreme Court". CNSNew.com. Nov 26, 2012. http://cnsnews.com/news/article/justice-ginsburg-we-need-all-female-supreme-court

292. Brown, Kathleen. "Famous Feminist Laments". CNS News online. June 3, 2015. http://www.cnsnews.com/news/article/kathleen-brown/famous-feminist-laments-concept-motherhood-emptied-out-its-gone.

293. Kosilek, Robert. "Should a Man Who Murdered His Wife Get a Free Sex Change Operation?" May 25, 2015. Jim Fisher True Crime. http://jimfishertruecrime.blogspot.com/2012/09/robert-kosilek-rewarding-man-who.html.

294. Doran, Will. Apr 6, 2016. Charlotte Observer. "PolitiFact NC: Virtually no cases of sexual predators benefiting. . ". http://www.charlotteobserver.com/news/politics-government/article70255967.html

295. Charlton, Corey. "'Dentist of horror' who enjoyed inflicting pain. . ." Daily Mail. Apr 26, 2016. http://www.dailymail.co.uk/news/article-3559321/Dentist-horror-enjoyed-inflicting-pain-left-mutilated-patients-flesh-hanging-mouths-broken-jaws-jailed-eight-years-France.html.

296. Spoto, MaryAnn. "State sides with lesbian couple in fight against Ocean Grove association". New Jersey.com. Dec 30, 2008. http://www.nj.com/news/index.ssf/2008/12/judge_rules_monmouth_church_gr.html.

297. Backholm, Joseph. "Judge Rules Against Arlene's Flowers". Family Policy Institute. Feb 19, 2015. http://www.fpiw.org/blog/2015/02/19/judge-rules-arlenes-flowers/.

298. Barret, David. "The return of the injunction". Telegraph.co UK. Mar 21, 2016. http://www.telegraph.co.uk/news/uknews/law-and-order/12200464/The-return-of-the-injunction-Entertainer-PJS-wins-legal-bid-over-extra-marital-threesome.htm.

299. Majority oppose same-sex marriage, Govt report says". The Christian Institute. Sept 27, 2011. http://www.eaf.net/mvp/2011/timo-miller-update/

300. Tube8-online. Offered in search engines on July 11, 2016. www.tube8.com/gay/porntags/scouts/

301. Mosse, George. *Nationalism and Sexuality*. 1985. University of Wisconsin Press.

302. Dale, James. "The Boy Scouts Deserve More Than a Copout". Huffington Post. 02/06/2013. http://www.huffingtonpost.com/jamesdale/boy-scouts_b_2634330.html

303. Moore, Art. "Look which companies dumping Boy Scouts". WND.com. Feb 4, 2013. http://www.wnd.com/2013/02/look-which-companies-dumping-boy-scouts/#c2eyLHvE0D34H2fG.99

304. "The Boy Scouts of America:Lawyers Fighting Against Scoutmaster Sexual Abuse". Tim Kosnoff website. (n.d.) http://www.kosnoff.com/boyscouts.php

305. "The Cookie Crumbles for Girl Scouts in St. Louis". *National Catholic Register*. Feb 26, 2016. http://www.ncregister.com/daily-news/the-cookie-crumbles-for-girl-scouts-in-st.-louis/#ixzz42Sd684I1

306. Goldstein, Richard. See #286

307. Sieczkowski, Cavan. "Lauryn Hill Anti Gay?" huffingtonpost.com. May 28, 2013 http://www.huffingtonpost.com/2013/05/28/lauryn-hill-anti-gay-neurotic-society-_n_3347982.html

308. Feder, J, Lester."Jamaican Dancehall Star Sizzla Banned From Music Festival For Anti-Gay Lyrics". BuzzFeedNews. Jan. 2, 2014. http://www.buzzfeed.com/lesterfeder/jamaican-dancehall-star-sizzla-banned-from-music-festival-fo#.ckQ48okkk

309. Canada, Danielle. "Eminem To Censor Lyrics For Britain Concert". HipHopwired.com Dec 27, 2009. http://hiphopwired.com/2009/12/27/eminem-to-censor-lyrics-for-britain-concert/

310. "Donnie McClurkin DROPPED by DC Mayor to Perform at Concert Because of Gay Stance" video by America Preachers. Aug 10, 2013. https://youtu.be/7IMcVsN6laE

311. "LGBT Activist Fined for Breaking 'Gay Propaganda' Law". *The Moscow Times*. Dec 4, 2013. https://themoscowtimes.com/news/lgbt-activist-fined-for-breaking-gay-propaganda-law-30181

312. Goldstein, Richard. See #286

313. Brown, Marco. "Gay-marriage debate generates hate on both sides". *The Daily Nebraskan*. Jan 25, 2006. http://www.dailynebraskan.com/marco-brown-gay-marriage-debate-generates-hate-on-both-sides/article_ae66b8cc-61af-56bd-9b95-72304616fb9d.html

314. Williams, Holly."'Swiss Army Man' Saw Revolted Viewers Walk Out" Jan 25, 2016. http://www.contactmusic.com/daniel-radcliffe/news/swiss-army-man-sundance-2016-premiere_5104862

315. Oyoyo, Igho. "Catholic Bishops Advise Buhari Against Legalising Gay Marriage". Leadership.ng. Jul 12, 2015. http://leadership.ng/news/446422/catholic-bishops-advise-buhari-against-legalising-gay-marriage

316. Adam Sank is coming out on Christmas Day. . ." The Laugh Button. Dec 17, 2015. http://thelaughbutton.com/features/adam-sank-is-coming-out-on-christmas-day-his-live-comedy-album-actually/.

317. Reyna, Leo. "Armikrog funding and its boycotters". Examiner. http://www.examiner.com/article/tennapel-on-armikrog-funding-and-its-boycotters. Accessed July 20, 2015.

318. Eldred, James. "On Doug TenNapel, Bigotry and supporting Hate". Mostly Retro. June 2, 2013http://mostly-retro.com/2013/06/02/on-doug-tennapel-bigotry-and-supporting-hate/

319. Lively, Scott & Adams, Kevin. *The Pink Swastika*. Founders Publishing Corporation, Keizer, Oregon. 1995

320. Langer, Walter. *A Psychological Analysis of Adolph Hitler, His Life and Legend.* Office of Strategic Services. 1943/1944. Washington, D.C. Republished in 1972, Basic Books. https://www.scribd.com/doc/14251744/A-Psychological-Analysis-of-Adolph-Hitler-His-Life-and-Legend-Walter-C-Langer

321. "History of Hirschfield Institute". Forschungsstelle zur Geschichte der Sexualwisse. (n.d.) http://

www.hirschfeld.in-berlin.de/

322. Heiden, Konrad. *A History of National Socialism*. 1935. Alfred A, Knopf, New York.

323. Knickerbocker, H.R. *Is Tomorrow Hitler's?* 1941. Reynal & Hitchcock, New York.

324. Waite, Robert G. L. *Hitler and Nazi Germany*. 1965. Holt, Rinehart and Winston, New York

325. Lively, Scott & Adams, Kevin. *The Pink Swastika*. 1995. Founders Publishing Corporation. Quoting Rector in The Nazi extermination of Homosexuals 1981, p.143

326. Shirer, William. *The Rise and Fall of the Third Reich*. 1960. Ballantine Publishing Group. pg. 120

327. Lively, Scott & Adams, Kevin. See #319.

328. Himmler, Heinrich. Speech about Homosexuality to SS Group Leaders on Feb 18, 1937.from http://der-stuermer.org/english/Heinrich%20Himmler%20speech%20-%2018.02.1937.pdf.

329. Lively, Scott & Adams, Kevin. *The Pink Swastika*. 2002. Veritas Aeterna Press. Fourth Edition

330. Giles, Geoffrey J. "The Denial of Homosexuality: Same-Sex Incidents in Himmler's SS and Police". *University of Florida Journal of the History of Sexuality* 11.1 and 2 (2002) 256-290. https://muse.jhu.edu/article/31248

331. Rector, Frank The Nazi extermination of Homosexuals. New York, Stein and Day. 1981

332. ibid.

333. ibid.

334. Machtan, Lothar. *The Hidden Hitler*. 2001. Basic Books.

335. ibid. p.68

336. Langer, Walter. See # 320

337. Bedard, Paul. "Nazi doctors: Hitler was gay, took female hormones". Washington Examiner. Jan 7, 2013. http://www.washingtonexaminer.com/nazi-doctors-hitler-was-gay-took-female-hormones/article/2517746

338. Igra, Samuel. *Germany's National Vice*. Quality Press Ltd. 1945.

339. ibid.

340. Lengyel, Olga. Five Chimneys. 1946 (1995 in English). Academy Chicago Publishers. p.186

341. Lewisohn, L."The New Kultur". *The Nation* (vol. 136, no. 3546, 21 June 1933) pp. 695-696. quoted in "Judaism versus Homosexuality: A Historical, Religious, and Psychological Review" Dr. Nathaniel Lehrman 13-Feb-2007 retrieved from http://www.defendthefamily.com/pfrc/archives.php?id=5497666 December 31, 2016

342. Snyder, Louis L. *Encyclopedia of the Third Reich*. P. 55. New York, Paragon House. 1989 Quoted in The Pink Swastika.

343. Napier, KB. Nazis/Marxists and Homosexuality Historical Evils". Christian Doctrine. Feb 3, 2015. http://www.christiandoctrine.com/christian-doctrine/history/1215-nazismarxists-and-homosexuality-historical-evils

344. Langer, Walter. See #320

345. Stormfront Nazi Forum. Nov. 4, 2001 https://www.stormfront.org/forum/t42248/

346. "The spy left out in the cold". *BBC News* online. Nov 3, 2002 http://news.bbc.co.uk/2/hi/programmes/true_spies/2381521.stm

347. Lively, Scott & Adams, Kevin. See #329

348. "Gaie France: un magazine néo-nazi en vente libre en kiosques". *Réseau Voltaire*. June 1, 1997 http://www.voltairenet.org/article7507.html

349. Lively, Scott. "Homosexuality and the Nazi Party The militant homosexual core of the National Socialist party". 1996. Source: Leadership University http://modernhistoryproject.org/mhp?Article=Pink Swastika.

350. Hari, Johann. "The Strange, Strange Story of the Gay Fascists". Huffington Post.com. May 25, 2011 http://www.huffingtonpost.com/johann-hari/the-strange-strange-story_b_136697.html

351. Igra, Samuel. See #338

352. "Sexuality of Adolf Hitler". Wikipedia.org. Last update Mar 7, 2017. https://en.wikipedia.org/wiki/Sexuality_of_Adolf_Hitler. Retrieved Dec 29 2016.

353. Stasi, Linda. "Gay-dolf Hitler; Fussy Fascist dragged out of closet". *New York Post*. Apr 20, 2004. http://nypost.com/2004/04/20/gay-dolf-hitler-fussy-fascist-dragged-out-of-closet/

354. Tatchell, Peter. "No place in history for gay victims of Nazism". *The Independent*. July 1, 1995. http://www.independent.co.uk/voices/no-place-in-history-for-gay-victims-of-nazism-1589502.html

355. "Chased out of the Castro District" Youtube. Nov 14, 2008. https://www.youtube.com/watch?time_continue=2&v=PrRxFoBSPng

356. Pfannenstiel, Brianne. "Bill would require parent permission for LGBTQ conference". The Des Moines Register. Mar 23, 2016http://www.desmoinesregister.com/story/news/politics/2016/03/23/bill-would-require-parent-permission-lgbtq-conference/82172738/

357. Swift, Nicky. "The real reason we don't hear about Paris Hilton anymore". NickySwift.com. (n.d.) http://www.nickiswift.com/26545/real-reason-dont-hear-paris-hilton-anymore/s/her-comments-about-the-lgbt-community-didnt-go-over-well/?utm_campaign=clip.

358. Reisman, Judith. See# 113

359. Hogg, R.S., Strathdee, S.A., Craib, K.J.P., et al. "Gay life expectancy revisited". *Int J Epidemiol* (2001) 30 (6): 1499. DOI: https://doi.org/10.1093/ije/30.6.1499

360. Lively, Scott. "Gays" Smear Pastor Lively and AFA with Horrific Murder Hoax". Scott Lively Ministries. May 6, 2014. http://www.scottlively.net/2014/05/06/gays-smear-pastor-lively-and-afa-with-horrific-murder-hoax/.

361. Aloo, Kevin. "Crime in Kibera". Kevin Aloo blogsite. May 23, 2013. https://kevinaloo.wordpress.com/2013/05/23/crime-in-kibera/

362. Soeren Kern. "British Girls Raped by Muslim Gangs on "Industrial Scale". Mar 17, 2015. Gatestone Institutute. https://www.gatestoneinstitute.org/5386/british-girls-raped-oxford

363. Thaddeus Baklinski. "Gay activists hurl feces at German parents protesting pro-gay school curriculum: report". Lifesite News. Mar 28, 2014. https://www.lifesitenews.com/news/gay-activists-hurl-feces-at-german-parents-protesting-pro-gay-school-curric

364. Gasper, Julia. See #78

365. Ruse, Austin. "Obama State Department offers funding to trans pressure groups overseas" C-Fam. June, 9, 2016. http://www.wnd.com/2015/07/state-forbids-pastors-calling-homosexuality-sinful

366. Lopez, Robert Oscar. See #38

367. Comments from The Gay White Racialist Network. Accessed in Apr 22, 2015 from http://boards.straightdope.com/sdmb/showthread.php?t=227901

368. Singer, Matthew. "The story of Portland's original all-ages gay nightclub". *Willamette Week*- online. Aug 26, 2014. http://www.wweek.com/portland/article-22975-in-the-city.html

369. Hot Homeless Gay Studs - Bearded Men Having Anal Sex ..." From www.pornmd.com/gay/homeless. Accessed Jan 2017.

370. Broverman, Neal. "Iowa Couple Plans 1,000 Anti-Gay Billboards". *Advocate*. July 31, 2015. http://www.advocate.com/religion/2015/07/31/iowa-couple-plans-1000-antigay-billboards.

371. Bryner, Jeanna. "Study: Homophobes May Be Hidden Homosexuals". Apr 9, 2012. http://www.livescience.com/19563-homophobia-hidden-homosexuals.html.

372. "After the party: Douglas and Tobias decamp to Ibiza". *The Art Newspaper*. July 28, 2015.

373. Yeats, W.B. "The Second Coming" from *Michael Robartes and the Dancer*. 1920. Cuala Press, Churchtown, Dundrum.

BITTER RAINBOWS

BITTER RAINBOWS

BITTER RAINBOWS: Pederasts, politics, and hate speech